Effective Leadership Development

C.H. Sharma

RANDOM PUBLICATIONS
NEW DELHI (INDIA)

Effective Leadership Development

ISBN 978-93-5111-921-0

Published in 2016 in India by

RANDOM PUBLICATIONS

Reprint, 2017

4376-A/4B, Gali Murari Lal, Ansari Road

New Delhi-110 002

Phone : +9111-43580356, 011-23289044, 011-43142548

e-mail: sales@randompublications.com,

info@randompublications.com, randomexports@gmail.com

Reprint 2021

Type Setting by : Friends Media, Delhi-110089

Digitally Printed at : Replika Press Pvt. Ltd.

Preface

Leadership is both a research area and a practical skill, regarding the ability of an individual or organization to "lead" or guide other individuals, teams, or entire organizations.

Leadership, although largely talked about, has been described as one of the least understood concepts across all cultures and civilizations. Over the years, many researchers have stressed the prevalence of this misunderstanding, stating that the existence of several flawed assumptions, or myths, concerning leadership often interferes with individuals' conception of what leadership is all about.

Successful leaders come in a wide variety of personal characteristics such as their ability to make speeches in public or to relate to people in groups or individually. We have all met successful leaders that we wondered what enabled them to be effective. Some are smooth and some are rough.

While most organizations recognize the importance of establishing a leadership development plan, those that take the necessary steps to create a formal process will benefit from a keen competitive advantage in the future marketplace.

Today, leadership development and succession planning remain top organizational challenges for most non-profits. Unfortunately, not enough has been done to evaluate what types of investment can have an impact on the development of non-profit leaders.

This book provides deep insight into various dimensions of issues relating to the subject.

– Author

Contents

1

Leadership

Leadership is both a research area and a practical skill, regarding the ability of an individual or organization to "lead" or guide other individuals, teams, or entire organizations. Controversial viewpoints are present in the literature, among Eastern and Western approaches to leadership, and also within the West, on US vs. European approaches. In US academic environments leadership is defined as "a process of social influence in which a person can enlist the aid and support of others in the accomplishment of a common task". Leadership seen from a European and non-academic perspective encompasses a view of a leader who can be moved both by communitarian goals but also by the search for personal power. As the European researcher Daniele Trevisani states:

"Leadership is a holistic spectrum that can arise from: (1) higher levels of physical power, need to display power and control others, force superiority, ability to generate fear, or group-member's need for a powerful group protector (Primal Leadership), (2) superior mental energies, superior motivational forces, perceivable in communication and behaviours, lack of fear, courage, determination (Psychoenergetic Leadership), (3) higher abilities in managing the overall picture (Macro-Leadership), (4) higher abilities in specialized tasks (Micro-Leadership), (5) higher ability in managing the execution of a task (Project Leadership), and (6) higher level of values, wisdom, and spirituality (Spiritual Leadership), where any Leader derives its Leadership from a unique mix of one or more of the former factors". Studies of leadership have produced theories involving traits, situational interaction, function, behaviour, power, vision andvalues, charisma, and intelligence, among others.

WHAT IS LEADERSHIP?

What an obvious question! Just what is leadership? But it is a necessary one. If you want to be a leader you first have to have your own favourite answer, or definition of leadership. Favourite answer? Is there not one standard definition of leadership? No single characteristic of leadership that is so obvious that we all recognise it? Sorry but, no, there is not. Indeed, there are many different leadership definitions, ranging from the dictionaries, through the text books to those dreamt up by the practitioners. As you will see, each attempt to define leadership emphasises different aspects of leadership, or different leadership characterisitics, and reflects the originator's leadership values.

SOME LEADERSHIP DEFINITIONS

Unfortunately, most dictionaries don't really help us. For example, one actually defines leadership as: "The ability to lead." Thankfully, Wikipedia is more helpful. It says that leadership is: "A process of social influence in which one person canenlist the aid and support of others in the accomplishment of a common task." Another answer to what is leadership, by Akhil Shahani, puts it more simply as: "The process by which a person influences others to accomplish an objective."

ELEMENTS OF LEADERSHIP

We find these interesting because they contain two essential elements of what is leadership; the people elements and the task elements (related to objectives). Every successful leader has to work with both of these. But I am concerned that these leadership definitions involve a "common task" or "objective". These words suggest that the end goal is already provided, clearly defined or laid down. Leadership doesn't always have the luxury of such clearly stated purposes. Sometimes leaders and followers evolve these together, with the leader consulting others to gather opinion and win support.

We prefer to think of leaders as providing direction (that is, a dream of an ideal future or a "vision") which may then be crystallised into a "common goal" and objectives, perhaps involving some of the followers in doing so. But here we are touching on the idea of leadership style. And thats for another part of the web site. So, lets have another go at defining what is leadership.

MORE DEFINITIONS

Turning now to the text books, Peter Drucker, in "The Leader of the Future", says: "The only definition of a leader is someone who has followers."

While Peter Maxwell, in "21 Irrefutable Laws of Leadership", says: "Leadership is influence - nothing more, nothing less." My own leadership definition, based upon my own experiences, studies and observation as a practitioner, is that: "A leader is someone whose direction and approach other people are willing to follow." And therefore, leadership is: "Influencing others to follow a given direction."

IMPLICATIONS FOR LEADERS

This definition of what is leadership carries a number of implications. First, within an organisation leaders are not always managers or supervisors, formally appointed by others. In fact, this is one way of distinguishing between managers and leaders; managers are appointed from above (ie, by more senior management), leaders are appointed (or anointed?) from below (ie, by their followers). To really grasp what this means, think of terms like "Ring leader" to describe someone who leads a group of people into trouble. Ring leaders are not appointed from above but from within the group. We also talk of some people as being a "Bad influence". We are concerned about people who are a bad influence because, once again, we recognise their ability to lead others into trouble. Ring leaders and bad influences are clearly not appointed, but they are most definitely followed.

Secondly, leaders don't even need to have responsibility for a team. Sometimes people are recognised as having leadership characteristics or qualities by others, who then simply choose to follow what the person says or does. Good examples are people who lead religious (such as Jesus Christ), revolutionary (such as Napoleon) or civil rights (such as Martin Luther King) movements. Another implication is that being a manager does not make you a leader. A manager may have excellent skills in organising work, creating policies and procedures, following disciplines and delivering services. But if others don't willingly follow their lead, they are not a leader. So, leaders must offer others (their followers) a cause, direction or objective that is interesting, attractive or satisfying enough for others to wish to follow. Finally, is a leader created, or is leadership defined, by giving someone a job title? No, it's defined by what a person is (their qualities), what they have learned (their skills) and what they do (their actions). Others recognise these attributes and choose, willingly, to follow.

So, to answer the question "what is leadership?", leadership is:

"Influencing others to follow a given direction."

And it can be thrilling, challenging, scary, satisfying, humbling and very rewarding!

THEORIES

EARLY WESTERN HISTORY

The search for the characteristics or traits of leaders has continued for centuries. Philosophical writings from Plato's Republic to Plutarch's Lives have explored the question "What qualities distinguish an individual as a leader?" Underlying this search was the early recognition of the importance of leadership and the assumption that leadership is rooted in the characteristics that certain individuals possess. This idea that leadership is based on individual attributes is known as the "trait theory of leadership".

A number of works in the 19th century – when the traditional authority of monarchs, lords and bishops had begun to wane – explored the trait theory at length: note especially the writings of Thomas Carlyle and of Francis Galton, whose works have prompted decades of research. In Heroes and Hero Worship (1841), Carlyle identified the talents, skills, and physical characteristics of men who rose to power. Galton's Hereditary Genius (1869) examined leadership qualities in the families of powerful men. After showing that the numbers of eminent relatives dropped off when his focus moved from first-degree to second-degree relatives, Galton concluded that leadership was inherited. In other words, leaders were born, not developed. Both of these notable works lent great initial support for the notion that leadership is rooted in characteristics of a leader.

Cecil Rhodes (1853–1902) believed that public-spirited leadership could be nurtured by identifying young people with "moral force of character and instincts to lead", and educating them in contexts (such as the collegiate environment of the University of Oxford) which further developed such characteristics. International networks of such leaders could help to promote international understanding and help "render war impossible". This vision of leadership underlay the creation of the Rhodes Scholarships, which have helped to shape notions of leadership since their creation in 1903.

RISE OF ALTERNATIVE THEORIES

In the late 1940s and early 1950s, however, a series of qualitative reviews of these prompted researchers to take a drastically different view of the driving forces behind leadership. In reviewing the extant literature, Stogdill and Mann found that while some traits were common across a number of studies, the overall evidence suggested that persons who are leaders in one situation may not necessarily be leaders in other situations. Subsequently, leadership was no longer characterized as an enduring individual trait, as situational approaches (see alternative leadership theories below) posited that individuals can be effective in certain situations, but not others. The focus then shifted away from traits of leaders to an investigation of the leader behaviours that were effective. This approach dominated much of the leadership theory and research for the next few decades

REEMERGENCE OF TRAIT THEORY

New methods and measurements were developed after these influential reviews that would ultimately reestablish the trait theory as a viable approach to the study of leadership. For example, improvements in researchers' use of the round robin research design methodology allowed researchers to see that individuals can and do emerge as leaders across a variety of situations and tasks. Additionally, during the 1980s statistical advances allowed researchers to conduct meta-analyses, in which they could quantitatively analyze and summarize the findings from a wide array of studies. This advent allowed trait theorists to create a comprehensive picture of previous leadership research rather than rely on the qualitative reviews of the past.

Equipped with new methods, leadership researchers revealed the following:

- Individuals can and do emerge as leaders across a variety of situations and tasks.
- Significant relationships exist between leadership emergence and such individual traits as:
- Intelligence
- Adjustment
- Extraversion
- Conscientiousness
- Openness to experience
- General self-efficacy

While the trait theory of leadership has certainly regained popularity, its reemergence has not been accompanied by a corresponding increase in sophisticated conceptual frameworks.

Specifically, Zaccaro (2007) noted that trait theories still:

- Focus on a small set of individual attributes such as Big Five personality traits, to the neglect of cognitive abilities, motives, values, social skills, expertise, and problem-solving skills.
- Fail to consider patterns or integrations of multiple attributes.
- Do not distinguish between those leader attributes that are generally not malleable over time and those that are shaped by, and bound to, situational influences.
- Do not consider how stable leader attributes account for the behavioural diversity necessary for effective leadership.

ATTRIBUTE PATTERN APPROACH

Considering the criticisms of the trait theory outlined above, several researchers have begun to adopt a different perspective of leader individual differences—the leader attribute pattern approach. In contrast to the traditional approach, the leader attribute pattern approach is based on theorists' arguments that the influence of individual characteristics on outcomes is best understood by considering the person as an integrated totality rather than a summation of individual variables. In other words, the leader attribute pattern approach argues that integrated constellations or combinations of individual differences may explain substantial variance in both leader emergence and leader effectiveness beyond that explained by single attributes, or by additive combinations of multiple attributes..

BEHAVIOURAL AND STYLE THEORIES

In response to the early criticisms of the trait approach, theorists began to research leadership as a set of behaviours, evaluating the behaviour of successful leaders, determining a behaviour taxonomy, and identifying broad leadership styles. David McClelland, for example, posited that leadership takes a strong personality with a well-developed positive ego. To lead, self-confidence and high self-esteem are useful, perhaps even essential.

Kurt Lewin, Ronald Lipitt, and Ralph White developed in 1939 the seminal work on the influence of leadership styles and performance. The researchers evaluated the performance of groups of eleven-year-old boys under different types of work climate. In each, the leader exercised his influence regarding the type of group decision making, praise and criticism (feedback), and the management of the group tasks (project management) according to three styles: authoritarian, democratic, and laissez-faire. The managerial grid model is also based on a behavioural theory. The model was developed by Robert Blake and Jane Mouton in 1964 and suggests five different leadership styles, based on the leaders' concern for people and their concern for goal achievement.

POSITIVE REINFORCEMENT

B.F. Skinner is the father of behaviour modification and developed the concept of positive reinforcement. Positive reinforcement occurs when a positive stimulus is presented in response to a behaviour, increasing the likelihood of that behaviour in the future. The following is an example of how positive reinforcement can be used in a business setting. Assume praise is a positive reinforcer for a particular employee. This employee does not show up to work on time every day. The manager of this employee decides to praise the employee for showing up on time every day the employee actually shows up to work on time. As a result, the employee comes to work on time more often because the employee likes to be praised. In this example, praise (the stimulus) is a positive reinforcer for this employee because the employee arrives at work on time (the behaviour) more frequently after being praised for showing up to work on time.

The use of positive reinforcement is a successful and growing technique used by leaders to motivate and attain desired behaviours from subordinates. Organizations such as Frito-Lay, 3M, Goodrich, Michigan Bell, and Emery Air Freight have all used reinforcement to increase productivity. Empirical research covering the last 20 years suggests that reinforcement theory has a 17 per cent increase in performance. Additionally, many reinforcement techniques such as the use of praise are inexpensive, providing higher performance for lower costs.

SITUATIONAL AND CONTINGENCY THEORIES

Situational theory also appeared as a reaction to the trait theory of leadership. Social scientists argued that history was more than the result of intervention of great men asCarlyle suggested. Herbert Spencer (1884) (and Karl Marx) said that the times produce the person and not the other way around.

This theory assumes that different situations call for different characteristics; according to this group of theories, no single optimal psychographic profile of a leader exists. According to the theory, "what an individual actually does when acting as a leader is in large part dependent upon characteristics of the situation in which he functions."

Some theorists started to synthesize the trait and situational approaches. Building upon the research of Lewin et al., academics began to normalize the descriptive models of leadership climates, defining three leadership styles and identifying which situations each style works better in. The authoritarian leadership style, for example, is approved in periods of crisis but fails to win the "hearts and minds" of followers in day-to-day management; the democratic leadership style is more adequate in situations that require consensus building; finally, the laissez-faire leadership style is appreciated for the degree of freedom it provides, but as the leaders do not "take charge", they can be perceived as a failure in protracted or thorny organizational problems. Thus, theorists defined the style of leadership as contingent to the situation, which is sometimes classified as contingency theory. Four contingency leadership theories appear more prominently in recent years: Fiedler contingency model, Vroom-Yetton decision model, the path-goal theory, and the Hersey-Blanchard situational theory.

The Fiedler contingency model bases the leader's effectiveness on what Fred Fiedler called situational contingency. This results from the interaction of leadership style and situational favorability. The theory defined two types of leader: those who tend to accomplish the task by developing good relationships with the group (relationship-oriented), and those who have as their prime concern carrying out the task itself (task-oriented). According to Fiedler, there is no ideal leader. Both task-oriented and relationship-oriented leaders can be effective if their leadership orientation fits the situation. When there is a good leader-member relation, a highly structured task, and high leader position power, the situation is considered a "favorable situation". Fiedler found that task-oriented leaders are more effective in extremely favorable or unfavorable situations, whereas relationship-oriented leaders perform best in situations with intermediate favorability.

Victor Vroom, in collaboration with Phillip Yetton (1973) and later with Arthur Jago (1988), developed a taxonomy for describing leadership situations, which was used in a normative decision model where leadership styles were connected to situational variables, defining which approach was more suitable to which situation. This approach was novel because it supported the idea that the same manager could rely on different group decision making approaches depending on the attributes of each situation. This model was later referred to as situational contingency theory. The path-goal theory of leadership was developed by Robert House (1971) and was based on the expectancy theory of

Victor Vroom. According to House, the essence of the theory is "the meta proposition that leaders, to be effective, engage in behaviours that complement subordinates' environments and abilities in a manner that compensates for deficiencies and is instrumental to subordinate satisfaction and individual and work unit performance". The theory identifies four leader behaviours, achievement-oriented,directive, participative, and supportive, that are contingent to the environment factors and follower characteristics. In contrast to the Fiedler contingency model, the path-goal model states that the four leadership behaviours are fluid, and that leaders can adopt any of the four depending on what the situation demands. The path-goal model can be classified both as a contingency theory, as it depends on the circumstances, and as a transactional leadership theory, as the theory emphasizes the reciprocity behaviour between the leader and the followers.

The situational leadership model proposed by Hersey and Blanchard suggests four leadership-styles and four levels of follower-development. For effectiveness, the model posits that the leadership-style must match the appropriate level of follower-development. In this model, leadership behaviour becomes a function not only of the characteristics of the leader, but of the characteristics of followers as well.

FUNCTIONAL THEORY

Functional leadership theory (Hackman and Walton, 1986; McGrath, 1962; Adair, 1988; Kouzes and Posner, 1995) is a particularly useful theory for addressing specific leader behaviours expected to contribute to organizational or unit effectiveness. This theory argues that the leader's main job is to see that whatever is necessary to group needs is taken care of; thus, a leader can be said to have done their job well when they have contributed to group effectiveness and cohesion (Fleishman et al., 1991; Hackman and Wageman, 2005; Hackman and Walton, 1986). While functional leadership theory has most often been applied to team leadership (Zaccaro, Rittman, and Marks, 2001), it has also been effectively applied to broader organizational leadership as well. In summarizing literature on functional leadership, Klein, Zeigert, Knight, and Xiao (2006) observed five broad functions a leader performs when promoting organization's effectiveness. These functions include environmental monitoring, organizing subordinate activities, teaching and coaching subordinates, motivating others, and intervening actively in the group's work.

A variety of leadership behaviours are expected to facilitate these functions. In initial work identifying leader behaviour, Fleishman (1953) observed that subordinates perceived their supervisors' behaviour in terms of two broad categories referred to as consideration and initiating structure. Consideration includes behaviour involved in fostering effective relationships. Examples of such behaviour would include showing concern for a subordinate or acting in a supportive manner towards others. Initiating structure involves the actions of the leader focused specifically on task accomplishment. This could include role clarification, setting performance standards, and holding subordinates accountable to those standards.

INTEGRATED PSYCHOLOGICAL THEORY

The Integrated Psychological theory of leadership is an attempt to integrate the strengths of the older theories (*i.e.* traits, behavioural/styles, situational and functional) while addressing their limitations, largely by introducing a new element – the need for leaders to develop their leadership presence, attitude towards others and behavioural flexibility by practicing psychological mastery. It also offers a foundation for leaders wanting to apply the philosophies of servant leadership and authentic leadership. Integrated Psychological theory began to attract attention after the publication of James Scouller's Three Levels of Leadership model (2011). Scouller argued that the older theories offer only limited assistance in developing a person's ability to lead effectively.

He pointed out, for example, that:

- Traits theories, which tend to reinforce the idea that leaders are born not made, might help us select leaders, but they are less useful for developing leaders.
- An ideal style (*e.g.* Blake and Mouton's team style) would not suit all circumstances.
- Most of the situational/contingency and functional theories assume that leaders can change their behaviour to meet differing circumstances or widen their behavioural range at will, when in practice many find it hard to do so because of unconscious beliefs, fears or ingrained habits. Thus, he argued, leaders need to work on their inner psychology.
- None of the old theories successfully address the challenge of developing "leadership presence"; that certain "something" in leaders that commands attention, inspires people, wins their trust and makes followers want to work with them.

Scouller therefore proposed the Three Levels of Leadership model, which was later categorized as an "Integrated Psychological" theory on the Businessballs education web site. In essence, his model aims to summarize what leaders have to do, not only to bring leadership to their group or organization, but also to develop themselves technically and psychologically as leaders.

The three levels in his model are Public, Private and Personal leadership:

- The first two – public and private leadership – are "outer" or behavioural levels. These are the behaviours that address what Scouller called "the four dimensions of leadership". These dimensions are: (1) a shared, motivating group purpose; (2) action, progress and results; (3) collective unity or team spirit; (4) individual selection and motivation.Public leadership focuses on the 34 behaviours involved in influencing two or more people simultaneously. Private leadership covers the 14 behaviours needed to influence individuals one to one.

- The third – personal leadership – is an "inner" level and concerns a person's growth towards greater leadership presence, knowhow and skill. Working on one's personal leadership has three aspects: (1) Technical knowhow and skill (2) Developing the right attitude towards other people – which is the basis of servant leadership (3) Psychological self-mastery – the foundation for authentic leadership.

Scouller argued that self-mastery is the key to growing one's leadership presence, building trusting relationships with followers and dissolving one's limiting beliefs and habits, thereby enabling behavioural flexibility as circumstances change, while staying connected to one's core values (that is, while remaining authentic). To support leaders' development, he introduced a new model of the human psyche and outlined the principles and techniques of self-mastery, which include the practice of mindfulness meditation.

TRANSACTIONAL AND TRANSFORMATIONAL THEORIES

Bernard Bass and colleagues developed the idea of two different types of leadership, transactional that involves exchange of labour for rewards and transformational which is based on concern for employees, intellectual stimulation, and providing a group vision. The transactional leader (Burns, 1978) is given power to perform certain tasks and reward or punish for the team's performance. It gives the opportunity to the manager to lead the group and the group agrees to follow his lead to accomplish a predetermined goal in exchange for something else. Power is given to the leader to evaluate, correct, and train subordinates when productivity is not up to the desired level, and reward effectiveness when expected outcome is reached.

LEADER–MEMBER EXCHANGE THEORY

Another theory that addresses a specific aspect of the leadership process is the leader–member exchange (LMX) theory, which evolved from an earlier theory called the vertical dyad linkage (VDL) model. Both of these models focus on the interaction between leaders and individual followers. Similar to the transactional approach, this interaction is viewed as a fair exchange whereby the leader provides certain benefits such as task guidance, advice, support, and/ or significant rewards and the followers reciprocate by giving the leader respect, cooperation, commitment to the task and good performance. However, LMX recognizes that leaders and individual followers will vary in the type of exchange that develops between them. LMX theorizes that the type of exchanges between the leader and specific followers can lead to the creation of in-groupsand out-groups. In-group members are said to have high-quality exchanges with the leader, while out-group members have low-quality exchanges with the leader.

IN-GROUP MEMBERS

In-group members are perceived by the leader as being more experienced, competent, and willing to assume responsibility than other followers. The leader begins to rely on these individuals to help with especially challenging tasks. If the follower responds well, the leader rewards him/her with extra coaching, favorable job assignments, and developmental experiences. If the follower shows high commitment and effort followed by additional rewards, both parties develop mutual trust, influence, and support of one another. Research shows the in-group members usually receive higher performance evaluations from the leader, higher satisfaction, and faster promotions than out-group members. In-group members are also likely to build stronger bonds with their leaders by sharing the same social backgrounds and interests.

OUT-GROUP MEMBERS

Out-group members often receive less time and more distant exchanges than their in-group counterparts. With out-group members, leaders expect no more than adequate job performance, good attendance, reasonable respect, and adherence to the job description in exchange for a fair wage and standard benefits. The leader spends less time with out-group members, they have fewer developmental experiences, and the leader tends to emphasize his/her formal authority to obtain compliance to leader requests. Research shows that out-group members are less satisfied with their job and organization, receive lower performance evaluations from the leader, see their leader as less fair, and are more likely to file grievances or leave the organization.

EMOTIONS

Leadership can be perceived as a particularly emotion-laden process, with emotions entwined with the social influence process. In an organization, the leader's mood has some effects on his/her group.

These effects can be described in three levels:

1. The mood of individual group members. Group members with leaders in a positive mood experience more positive mood than do group members with leaders in a negative mood. The leaders transmit their moods to other group members through the mechanism of emotional contagion. Mood contagion may be one of the psychological mechanisms by which charismatic leaders influence followers.
2. The affective tone of the group. Group affective tone represents the

consistent or homogeneous affective reactions within a group. Group affective tone is an aggregate of the moods of the individual members of the group and refers to mood at the group level of analysis. Groups with leaders in a positive mood have a more positive affective tone than do groups with leaders in a negative mood.

3. Group processes like coordination, effort expenditure, and task strategy. Public expressions of mood impact how group members think and act. When people experience and express mood, they send signals to others. Leaders signal their goals, intentions, and attitudes through their expressions of moods. For example, expressions of positive moods by leaders signal that leaders deem progress towards goals to be good. The group members respond to those signals cognitively and behaviourally in ways that are reflected in the group processes.

In research about client service, it was found that expressions of positive mood by the leader improve the performance of the group, although in other sectors there were other findings.

Beyond the leader's mood, her/his behaviour is a source for employee positive and negative emotions at work. The leader creates situations and events that lead to emotional response. Certain leader behaviours displayed during interactions with their employees are the sources of these affective events. Leaders shape workplace affective events. Examples – feedback giving, allocating tasks, resource distribution. Since employee behaviour and productivity are directly affected by their emotional states, it is imperative to consider employee emotional responses to organizational leaders. Emotional intelligence, the ability to understand and manage moods and emotions in the self and others, contributes to effective leadership within organizations.

NEO-EMERGENT THEORY

The neo-emergent leadership theory (from the Oxford school of leadership) sees leadership as created through the emergence of information by the leader or other stakeholders, not through the true actions of the leader himself. In other words, the reproduction of information or stories form the basis of the perception of leadership by the majority. It is well known that the naval hero Lord Nelson often wrote his own versions of battles he was involved in, so that when he arrived home in England he would receive a true hero's welcome. In modern society, the press, blogs and other sources report their own views of leaders, which may be based on reality, but may also be based on a political command, a payment, or an inherent interest of the author, media, or leader. Therefore, one can argue that the perception of all leaders is created and in fact does not reflect their true leadership qualities at all.

STYLES

A leadership style is a leader's style of providing direction, implementing plans, and motivating people. It is the result of the philosophy, personality, and experience of the leader. Rhetoric specialists have also developed models for understanding leadership. Different situations call for different leadership styles. In an emergency when there is little time to converge on an agreement and where a designated authority has significantly more experience or expertise than the rest of the team, an autocratic leadership style may be most effective; however, in a highly motivated and aligned team with a homogeneous level of expertise, a more democratic or laissez-faire style may be more effective. The style adopted should be the one that most effectively achieves the objectives of the group while balancing the interests of its individual members.

AUTOCRATIC OR AUTHORITARIAN

Under the autocratic leadership style, all decision-making powers are centralized in the leader, as with dictators. Leaders do not entertain any suggestions or initiatives from subordinates. The autocratic management has been successful as it provides strong motivation to the manager. It permits quick decision-making, as only one person decides for the whole group and keeps each decision to him/herself until he/she feels it needs to be shared with the rest of the group.

PARTICIPATIVE OR DEMOCRATIC

The democratic leadership style consists of the leader sharing the decision-making abilities with group members by promoting the interests of the group members and by practicing social equality. This has also been called shared leadership.

TASK-ORIENTED AND RELATIONSHIP-ORIENTED

Task-oriented leadership is a style in which the leader is focused on the tasks that need to be performed in order to meet a certain production goal. Task-oriented leaders are generally more concerned with producing a step-by-step solution for given problem or goal, strictly making sure these deadlines are met, results and reaching target outcomes. Relationship-oriented leadership is a contrasting style in which the leader is more focused on the relationships amongst the group and is generally more concerned with the overall well-being and satisfaction of group members. Relationship-oriented leaders emphasize communication within the group, shows trust and confidence in group members, and shows appreciation for work done.

Task-oriented leaders are typically less concerned with the idea of catering to group members, and more concerned with acquiring a certain solution to meet a production goal. For this reason, they typically are able to make sure that deadlines are met, yet their group members' well-being may suffer. Relationship-oriented leaders are focused on developing the team and the relationships in it. The positives to having this kind of environment are that team members are more motivated and have support, however, the emphasis on relations as opposed to getting a job done might make productivity suffer.

SEX DIFFERENCES

Another factor that covaries with leadership style is whether the person is male or female. When men and women come together in groups, they tend to adopt different leadership styles. Men generally assume an agentic leadership style. They are task-oriented, active, decision focused, independent and goal oriented. Women, on the other hand, are generally more communal when they assume a leadership position; they strive to be helpful towards others, warm in relation to others, understanding, and mindful of others' feelings. In general, when women are asked to describe themselves to others in newly formed groups, they emphasize their open, fair, responsible, and pleasant communal qualities. They give advice, offer assurances, and manage conflicts in an attempt to maintain positive relationships among group members. Women connect more positively to group members by smiling, maintaining eye contact and respond tactfully to others' comments. Men, conversely, describe themselves as influential, powerful and proficient at the task that needs to be done. They tend to place more focus on initiating structure within the group, setting standards and objectives, identifying roles, defining responsibilities and standard operating procedures, proposing solutions to problems, monitoring compliance with procedures, and finally, emphasizing the need for productivity and efficiency in the work that needs to be done. As leaders, men are primarily task-oriented, but women tend to be both task- and relationship-oriented. However, it is important to note that these sex differences are only tendencies, and do not manifest themselves within men and women across all groups and situations.

PERFORMANCE

In the past, some researchers have argued that the actual influence of leaders on organizational outcomes is overrated and romanticized as a result of biased attributions about leaders. Despite these assertions, however, it is largely recognized and accepted by practitioners and researchers that leadership is important, and research supports the notion that leaders do contribute to key organizational outcomes. To facilitate successful performance it is important to understand and accurately measure leadership performance.

Job performance generally refers to behaviour that is expected to contribute to organizational success. Campbell identified a number of specific types of performance dimensions; leadership was one of the dimensions that he identified. There is no consistent, overall definition of leadership performance.

Many distinct conceptualizations are often lumped together under the umbrella of leadership performance, including outcomes such as leader effectiveness, leader advancement, and leader emergence (Kaiser et al., 2008). For instance, leadership performance may be used to refer to the career success of the individual leader, performance of the group or organization, or even leader emergence. Each of these measures can be considered conceptually distinct. While these aspects may be related, they are different outcomes and their inclusion should depend on the applied or research focus. A toxic leader is someone who has responsibility over a group of people or an organization, and who abuses the leader–follower relationship by leaving the group or organization in a worse-off condition than when he/she joined it.

TRAITS

Most theories in the 20th century argued that great leaders were born, not made. Current studies have indicated that leadership is much more complex and cannot be boiled down to a few key traits of an individual. Years of observation and study have indicated that one such trait or a set of traits does not make an extraordinary leader. What scholars have been able to arrive at is that leadership traits of an individual do not change from situation to situation; such traits include intelligence, assertiveness, or physical attractiveness. However, each key trait may be applied to situations differently, depending on the circumstances. The following summarizes the main leadership traits found in research by Jon P. Howell, business professor at New Mexico State University and author of the book Snapshots of Great Leadership.

Determination and drive include traits such as initiative, energy, assertiveness, perseverance and sometimes dominance. People with these traits often tend to wholeheartedly pursue their goals, work long hours, are ambitious, and often are very competitive with others. Cognitive capacity includes intelligence, analytical and verbal ability, behavioural flexibility, and good judgement. Individuals with these traits are able to formulate solutions to difficult problems, work well under stress or deadlines, adapt to changing situations, and create well-thought-out plans for the future. Howell provides examples of Steve Jobs and Abraham Lincoln as encompassing the traits of determination and drive as well as possessing cognitive capacity, demonstrated by their ability to adapt to their continuously changing environments.

Self-confidence encompasses the traits of high self-esteem, assertiveness, emotional stability, and self-assurance. Individuals that are self-confident do not doubt themselves or their abilities and decisions; they also have the ability to project this self-confidence onto others, building their trust and commitment. Integrity is demonstrated in individuals who are truthful, trustworthy, principled, consistent, dependable, loyal, and not deceptive. Leaders with integrity often share these values with their followers, as this trait is mainly an ethics issue. It is often said that these leaders keep their word and are honest and open with their cohorts. Sociability describes individuals who are friendly, extroverted, tactful, flexible, and interpersonally competent. Such a trait enables leaders to be accepted well by the public, use diplomatic measures to solve issues, as well as hold the ability to adapt their social persona to the situation at hand. According to Howell, Mother Teresa is an exceptional example that embodies integrity, assertiveness, and social abilities in her diplomatic dealings with the leaders of the world. Few great leaders encompass all of the traits listed above, but many have the ability to apply a number of them to succeed as front-runners of their organization or situation.

THE ONTOLOGICAL-PHENOMENOLOGICAL MODEL FOR LEADERSHIP

One of the more recent definitions of leadership comes from Werner Erhard, Michael C. Jensen, Steve Zaffron, and Kari Granger who describe leadership as "an exercise in language that results in the realization of a future that wasn't going to happen anyway, which future fulfills (or contributes to fulfilling) the concerns of the relevant parties...". This definition ensures that leadership is talking about the future and includes the fundamental concerns of the relevant parties. This differs from relating to the relevant parties as "followers" and calling up an image of a single leader with others following. Rather, a future that fulfills on the fundamental concerns of the relevant parties indicates the future that wasn't going to happen is not the "idea of the leader", but rather is what emerges from digging deep to find the underlying concerns of those who are impacted by the leadership.

CONTEXTS

Organizations

An organization that is established as an instrument or means for achieving defined objectives has been referred to as a formal organization. Its design specifies how goals are subdivided and reflected in subdivisions of the organization. Divisions, departments, sections, positions, jobs, and tasks make up this work structure. Thus, the formal organization is expected to behave impersonally in regard to relationships with clients or with its members. According to Weber's definition, entry and subsequent advancement is by merit or seniority. Employees receive a salary and enjoy a degree of tenure that safeguards them from the arbitrary influence of superiors or of powerful clients. The higher one's position in the hierarchy, the greater one's presumed expertise in adjudicating problems that may arise in the course of the work carried out at lower levels of the organization. It is this bureaucratic structure that forms the basis for the appointment of heads or chiefs of administrative subdivisions in the organization and endows them with the authority attached to their position. In contrast to the appointed head or chief of an administrative unit, a leader emerges within the context of the informal organization that underlies the formal structure. The informal organization expresses the personal objectives and goals of the individual membership. Their objectives and goals may or may not coincide with those of the formal organization. The informal organization represents an extension of the social structures that generally characterize human life — the spontaneous emergence of groups and organizations as ends in themselves. In prehistoric times, humanity was preoccupied with personal security, maintenance, protection, and survival. Now humanity spends a major portion of waking hours working for organizations. The need to identify with a community that provides security, protection, maintenance, and a feeling of belonging has continued unchanged from prehistoric times. This need is met by the informal organization and its emergent, or unofficial, leaders.

Leaders emerge from within the structure of the informal organization. Their personal qualities, the demands of the situation, or a combination of these and other factors attract followers who accept their leadership within one or several overlay structures. Instead of the authority of position held by an appointed head or chief, the emergent leader wields influence or power. Influence is the ability of a person to gain co-operation from others by means of persuasion or control over rewards. Power is a stronger form of influence because it reflects a person's ability to enforce action through the control of a means of punishment.

A leader is a person who influences a group of people towards a specific result. It is not dependent on title or formal authority. (Elevos, paraphrased from Leaders, Bennis, and Leadership Presence, Halpern and Lubar.) Ogbonnia (2007) defines an effective leader "as an individual with the capacity to consistently succeed in a given condition and be viewed as meeting the expectations of an organization or society."

Leaders are recognized by their capacity for caring for others, clear communication, and a commitment to persist. An individual who is appointed to a managerial position has the right to command and enforce obedience by virtue of the authority of their position. However, she or he must possess adequate personal attributes to match this authority, because authority is only potentially available to him/her. In the absence of sufficient personal competence, a manager may be confronted by an emergent leader who can challenge her/his role in the organization and reduce it to that of a figurehead. However, only authority of position has the backing of formal sanctions. It follows that whoever wields personal influence and power can legitimize this only by gaining a formal position in the hierarchy, with commensurate authority. Leadership can be defined as one's ability to get others to willingly follow. Every organization needs leaders at every level.

MANAGEMENT

Over the years the philosophical terminology of "management" and "leadership" have, in the organizational context, been used both as synonyms and with clearly differentiated meanings. Debate is fairly common about whether the use of these terms should be restricted, and generally reflects an awareness of the distinction made by Burns (1978) between "transactional" leadership (characterized by *e.g.* emphasis on procedures, contingent reward, management by exception) and "transformational" leadership (characterized by *e.g.* charisma, personal relationships, creativity).

GROUP

In contrast to individual leadership, some organizations have adopted group leadership. In this situation, more than one person provides direction to the group as a whole. Some organizations have taken this approach in hopes of increasing creativity, reducing costs, or downsizing. Others may see the traditional leadership of a boss as costing too much in team performance. In some situations, the team members best able to handle any given phase of the project become the temporary leaders. Additionally, as each team member has the opportunity to experience the elevated level of empowerment, it energizes staff and feeds the cycle of success. Leaders who demonstrate persistence, tenacity, determination, and synergistic communication skills will bring out the same qualities in their groups. Good leaders use their own inner mentors to energize their team and organizations and lead a team to achieve success.

ACCORDING TO THE NATIONAL SCHOOL BOARDS ASSOCIATION (USA)

These Group Leaderships or Leadership Teams have specific characteristics:

CHARACTERISTICS OF A TEAM

- There must be an awareness of unity on the part of all its members.
- There must be interpersonal relationship. Members must have a chance to contribute, and learn from and work with others.
- The members must have the ability to act together towards a common goal.

Ten characteristics of well-functioning teams:

- *Purpose:* Members proudly share a sense of why the team exists and are invested in accomplishing its mission and goals.
- *Priorities:* Members know what needs to be done next, by whom, and by when to achieve team goals.
- *Roles:* Members know their roles in getting tasks done and when to allow a more skillful member to do a certain task.

- *Decisions:* Authority and decision-making lines are clearly understood.
- *Conflict:* Conflict is dealt with openly and is considered important to decision-making and personal growth.
- *Personal traits:* members feel their unique personalities are appreciated and well utilized.
- *Norms:* Group norms for working together are set and seen as standards for every one in the groups.
- *Effectiveness:* Members find team meetings efficient and productive and look forward to this time together.
- *Success:* Members know clearly when the team has met with success and share in this equally and proudly.
- *Training:* Opportunities for feedback and updating skills are provided and taken advantage of by team members.

SELF-LEADERSHIP

Self-leadership is a process that occurs within an individual, rather than an external act. It is an expression of who we are as people.

PRIMATES

Mark van Vugt and Anjana Ahuja in Naturally Selected: The Evolutionary Science of Leadership present evidence of leadership in non-human animals, from ants and bees to baboons and chimpanzees. They suggest that leadership has a long evolutionary history and that the same mechanisms underpinning leadership in humans can be found in other social species, too. Richard Wrangham and Dale Peterson, in Demonic Males: Apes and the Origins of Human Violence, present evidence that only humans andchimpanzees, among all the animals living on Earth, share a similar tendency for a cluster of behaviours: violence, territoriality, and competition for uniting behind the one chief male of the land. This position is contentious. Many animals beyond apes are territorial, compete, exhibit violence, and have a social structure controlled by a dominant male (lions, wolves, etc.), suggesting Wrangham and Peterson's evidence is not empirical. However, we must examine other species as well, including elephants (which are matriarchal and follow an alpha female), meerkats (who are likewise matriarchal), and many others.

By comparison, bonobos, the second-closest species-relatives of humans, do not unite behind the chief male of the land. The bonobos show deference to an alpha or top-ranking female that, with the support of her coalition of other females, can prove as strong as the strongest male. Thus, if leadership amounts to getting the greatest number of followers, then among the bonobos, a female almost always exerts the strongest and most effective leadership. However, not all scientists agree on the allegedly peaceful nature of the bonobo or its reputation as a "hippie chimp".

HISTORICAL VIEWS

Sanskrit literature identifies ten types of leaders. Defining characteristics of the ten types of leaders are explained with examples from history and mythology. Aristocratic thinkers have postulated that leadership depends on one's "blue blood" or genes. Monarchy takes an extreme view of the same idea, and may prop up its assertions against the claims of mere aristocrats by invoking divine sanction. Contrariwise, more democratically inclined theorists have pointed to examples of meritocratic leaders, such as the Napoleonicmarshals profiting from careers open to talent. In the autocratic/ paternalistic strain of thought, traditionalists recall the role of leadership of the Roman pater familias. Feminist thinking, on the other hand, may object to such models as patriarchal and posit against them emotionally attuned, responsive, and consensualempathetic guidance, which is sometimes associated with matriarchies.

Comparable to the Roman tradition, the views of Confucianism on "right living" relate very much to the ideal of the (male) scholar-leader and his benevolent rule, buttressed by a tradition of filial piety. Leadership is a matter of intelligence, trustworthiness, humaneness, courage, and discipline... Reliance on intelligence alone results in rebelliousness. Exercise of humaneness alone results in weakness. Fixation on trust results in folly. Dependence on the strength of courage results in violence. Excessive discipline and sternness in command result in cruelty. When one has all five virtues together, each appropriate to its function, then one can be a leader. — Sun Tzu

Machiavelli's The Prince, written in the early 16th century, provided a manual for rulers ("princes" or "tyrants" in Machiavelli's terminology) to gain and keep power. In the 19th century the elaboration of anarchist thought called the whole concept of leadership into question. One response to this denial of élitism came with Leninism, which demanded an élite group of disciplined cadres to act as the vanguard of a socialist revolution, bringing into existence the dictatorship of the proletariat. Other historical views of leadership have addressed the seeming contrasts between secular and religious leadership. The doctrines of Caesaro-papism have recurred and had their detractors over several centuries. Christian thinking on leadership has often emphasized stewardship of divinely provided resources—human and material—and their deployment in accordance with a Divine plan. Compare servant leadership. For a more general take on leadership in politics, compare the concept of the statesperson.

MYTHS

Leadership, although largely talked about, has been described as one of the least understood concepts across all cultures and civilizations. Over the years, many researchers have stressed the prevalence of this misunderstanding, stating that the existence of several flawed assumptions, or myths, concerning leadership often interferes with individuals' conception of what leadership is all about.

LEADERSHIP IS INNATE

According to some, leadership is determined by distinctive dispositional characteristics present at birth (*e.g.*, extraversion; intelligence; ingenuity). However, according to Forsyth (2009) there is evidence to show that leadership also develops through hard work and careful observation. Thus, effective leadership can result from nature (*i.e.*, innate talents) as well as nurture (*i.e.*, acquired skills).

LEADERSHIP IS POSSESSING POWER OVER OTHERS

Although leadership is certainly a form of power, it is not demarcated by power over people – rather, it is a power with people that exists as a reciprocal relationship between a leader and his/her followers. Despite popular belief, the use of manipulation, coercion, and domination to influence others is not a requirement for leadership. In actuality, individuals who seek group consent and strive to act in the best interests of others can also become effective leaders (*e.g.*, class president; court judge).

LEADERS ARE POSITIVELY INFLUENTIAL

The validity of the assertion that groups flourish when guided by effective leaders can be illustrated using several examples. For instance, according to Baumeister et al. (1988), the bystander effect (failure to respond or offer assistance) that tends to develop within groups faced with an emergency is significantly reduced in groups guided by a leader.Moreover, it has been documented that group performance, creativity, and efficiency all tend to climb in businesses with designated managers or CEOs. However, the difference leaders make is not always positive in nature. Leaders sometimes focus on fulfilling their own agendas at the expense of others, including his/her own followers (*e.g.*,Pol Pot; Josef Stalin). Leaders who focus on personal gain by employing stringent and manipulative leadership styles often make a difference, but usually do so through negative means.

LEADERS ENTIRELY CONTROL GROUP OUTCOMES

In Western cultures it is generally assumed that group leaders make all the difference when it comes to group influence and overall goal-attainment. Although common, this romanticized view of leadership (*i.e.*, the tendency to overestimate the degree of control leaders have over their groups and their groups' outcomes) ignores the existence of many other factors that influence group dynamics. For example, group cohesion, communication patterns among members, individual personality traits, group context, the nature or orientation of the work, as well as behavioural norms and established standards influence group functionality in varying capacities. For this reason, it is unwarranted to assume that all leaders are in complete control of their groups' achievements.

ALL GROUPS HAVE A DESIGNATED LEADER

Despite preconceived notions, not all groups need have a designated leader. Groups that are primarily composed of women, are limited in size, are free from stressful decision-making, or only exist for a short period of time (*e.g.*, student work groups; pub quiz/trivia teams) often undergo a diffusion of responsibility, where leadership tasks and roles are shared amongst members.

GROUP MEMBERS RESIST LEADERS

Although research has indicated that group members' dependence on group leaders can lead to reduced self-reliance and overall group strength, most people actually prefer to be led than to be without a leader. This "need for a leader" becomes especially strong in troubled groups that are experiencing some sort of conflict. Group members tend to be more contented and productive when they have a leader to guide them. Although individuals filling leadership roles can be a direct source of resentment for followers, most people appreciate the contributions that leaders make to their groups and consequently welcome the guidance of a leader.

ACTION-ORIENTED ENVIRONMENTS

In most cases these teams are tasked to operate in remote and changeable environments with limited support or backup (action environments). Leadership of people in these environments requires a different set of skills to that of front line management. These leaders must effectively operate remotely and negotiate the needs of the individual, team, and task within a changeable environment. This has been termed action oriented leadership. Some examples of demonstrations of action oriented leadership include extinguishing a rural fire, locating a missing person, leading a team on an outdoor expedition, or rescuing a person from a potentially hazardous environment.

Other examples include modern technology deployments of small/medium-sized IT teams into client plant sites. Leadership of these teams requires hands on experience and a lead-by-example attitude to empower team members to make well thought out and concise decisions independent of executive management and/or home base decision makers. Zachary Hansen was an early adopter of Scrum/Kanban branch development methodologies during the mid 90's to alleviate the dependency that field teams had on trunk based development. This method of just-in-time action oriented development and deployment allowed remote plant sites to deploy up-to-date software patches frequently and without dependency on core team deployment schedules satisfying the clients need to rapidly patch production environment bugs as needed.

CRITICAL THOUGHT

Noam Chomsky and others have brought critical thinking to the very concept of leadership and have provided an analysis that asserts that people abrogate their responsibility to think and will actions for themselves. While the conventional view of leadership is rather satisfying to people who "want to be told what to do", these critics say that one should question why they are being subjected to a will or intellect other than their own if the leader is not a Subject Matter Expert (SME).

The fundamentally anti-democratic nature of the leadership principle is challenged by the introduction of concepts such as autogestion, employeeship, common civic virtue, etc., which stress individual responsibility and/or group authority in the work place and elsewhere by focusing on the skills and attitudes that a person needs in general rather than separating out leadership as the basis of a special class of individuals.

Similarly, various historical calamities are attributed to a misplaced reliance on the principle of leadership.

EXECUTIVES

Executives are energetic, outgoing, and competitive. They can be visionary, hard-working, and decisive. However, managers need to be aware of unsuccessful executives who once showed management potential but who are later dismissed or retired early. They typically fail because of personality factors rather than job performances.

Terms fallacies in their thinking are:

- *Unrealistic optimism fallacy:* Believing they are so smart that they can do whatever they want
- *Egocentrism fallacy:* Believing they are the only ones who matter, that the people who work for them don't count
- *Omniscience fallacy:* Believing they know everything and seeing no limits to their knowledge
- *Omnipotence fallacy:* Believing they are all powerful and therefore entitled to do what they want
- *Invulnerability fallacy:* Believing they can get away with doing what they want because they are too clever to get caught; even if they are caught, believing they will go unpunished because of their importance.

2

Leadership Development

Leadership development refers to any activity that enhances the quality of leadership within an individual or organization. These activities have ranged from MBA style programmes offered at university business schools to action learning, high-ropes courses and executive retreats.

DEVELOPING INDIVIDUAL LEADERS

Traditionally, leadership development has focused on developing the leadership abilities and attitudes of individuals. LEAD is an annual leadership event platform dedicated to creating #AWorldInspired. World class, inspirational speakers have included, 42nd President of the USA, Bill Clinton, leadership coach, Marshall Goldsmith and youth leadership guru, Craig Kielburger.

Just as people are not all born with the ability or desire to play football (soccer) like Zinedine Zidane or to sing like Luciano Pavarotti, people are not all born with the ability to lead. Different personal traits and characteristics can help or hinder a person's leadership effectiveness and require formalized programmes for developing leadership competencies Classroom-style training and associated reading is effective in helping leaders to know more about what is involved in leading well. However, knowing what to do and doing what one knows are two very different outcomes; management expert Henry Mintzberg is one person to highlight this dilemma. It is estimated that as little as 15 per cent of learning from traditional classroom-style training results in sustained behavioural change within workplaces.

The success of leadership development efforts has been linked to three variables:

1. Individual learner characteristics
2. The quality and nature of the leadership development programme
3. Genuine support for behavioural change from the leader's supervisor

Military officer-training academies, such as the Royal Military Academy Sandhurst, go to great lengths to accept only candidates who show the highest potential to lead well.Personal characteristics that are associated with successful leadership development include leader motivation to learn, a high achievement drive and personality traits such as openness to experience, an internal focus of control, and self-monitoring.In order to develop individual leaders, supervisors or superiors must conduct an individual assessment.

Development is also more likely to occur when the design of the development programme:

- Integrates a range of developmental experiences over a set period of time (*e.g.* 6–12 months). These experiences may include 360 degree feedback, experiential classroom style programmes, business school style coursework, executive coaching, reflective journaling, mentoring and more.
- Involves goal-setting, following an assessment of key developmental needs and then an evaluation of the achievement of goals after a given time period

Among key concepts in leadership development one may find:

- *Experiential learning:* Positioning the individual in the focus of the learning process, going through the four stages of experiential learning as formulated by David A. Kolb: 1. concrete experience 2. observation and reflection 3. forming abstract concept 4. testing in new situations.
- *Self efficacy:* The right training and coaching should bring about 'Self efficacy' in the trainee, as Albert Bandura formulated: a person's belief about his capabilities to produce effects
- *Visioning:* Developing the ability to formulate a clear image of the aspired future of an organization unit.
- *Attitude:* Attitude plays a major role in being a leader.

A good personal leadership development programme should enable one to develop a plan that helps one gain essential leadership skills required for roles across a wide spectrum from a youth environment to the corporate world.

DEVELOPING LEADERSHIP AT A COLLECTIVE LEVEL

More recently, organizations have come to understand that leadership can also be developed by strengthening the connection between, and alignment of, the efforts of individual leaders and the systems through which they influence organizational operations. This has led to a differentiation between leader development and leadership development. Leadership development can build on the development of individuals (including followers) to become leaders. In addition, it also needs to focus on the interpersonal linkages between the individuals in the team.

In the belief that the most important resource that an organization possesses is the people that comprise the organization, some organizations address the development of these resources (even including the leadership).

In contrast, the concept of "Employeeship" recognizes that what it takes to be a good leader is not too dissimilar to what it takes to be a good employee. Therefore, bringing the notional leader together with the team to explore these similarities (rather than focusing on the differences) brings positive results. This approach has been particularly successful in Sweden where the power distance between manager and team is small.

SUCCESSION PLANNING

The development of "high potentials" to effectively take over the current leadership when their time comes to exit their positions is known as succession planning. This type of leadership development usually requires the extensive transfer of an individual between departments. In many multinationals, it usually requires international transfer and experience to build a future leader. Succession planning requires a sharp focus on organization's future and vision, in order to align leadership development with the future the firm aspires to create. Thus successive leadership development is based not only on knowledge and history but also on a dream. For such a plan to be successful, a screening of future leadership should be based not only on "what we know and have" but also on "what we aspire to become". Persons involved in succession planning should be current leadership representing the vision and HR executives having to translate it all into a programme. According to Meir Jacob and Amit Cohen (1995) three critical dimensions should be considered: 1. Skills and knowledge 2. Role perception and degree of acceptance of leading role 3. Self-efficacy (Albert Bandura). These three dimensions should be a basis of any leadership succession programme.

EXECUTIVE DEVELOPMENT

Executive development is the whole of activities aimed at developing the skills and competencies of those that (will) have executive positions in organisations. While "executive" and "manager" and "leader" are often used interchangeably, "executive" is commonly used to signify the top 5 per cent to 10 per cent of the organization. Similarly, "development" and "training" and "education" are often used as synonyms, however "development" is generally seen as the more encompassing of the three in terms of activities that build skills and competencies.

While it is typical to find organizations that have dedicated corporate training and development people and processes, it is not always the case that an organization will have a dedicated executive development set of activities. In some organizations (typically large multi-nationals), there is a separate executive development team, in other organizations executive development is handled as one of many activities by the larger corporate training group, and in yet other scenarios there is no executive development activity to speak of.

In contrast to other corporate training and development activities, which have as their core purpose to build tactical skills for employees, executive development plays a different role for the organization. Indeed some executive development is conducted for the purpose of building tactical skills (sometimes referred to as "hard skills" such as business fundamentals- finance, marketing, operations and also "soft skills" such as communication and team building), yet executive development is also used to evaluate future potential future executives as well as a mechanism for the CEO and the executive team to cascade their strategies, goals, and even elements of the culture to the rest of the management team and ultimately the organization. In the best of cases, executive development not only helps an organization execute its key strategies, it can also help provide input to the strategy creation process. In this way, executive development is much more strategic than typical corporate training and development which is used for most employees of an organization.

PHILOSOPHIES AND PRACTICES

There is a wide range of practices in the field of executive development today. On one hand, there are organizations that have for many years, if not decades, had very thorough executive development functions that conduct a wide variety of high profile and highly regarded set of activities (GE's Crotonville is the classic example). On the other end of the spectrum, there are some organizations that have curtailed many of the executive development activities and spending in the wake of the economic crisis of 2008/2009. As one looks across different companies, and against the backdrop of different periods, there exists a wide variety of executive development activity.

Also, the main philosophy of executive development is quite different depending on the organization. For some, the development process has and continues to play a very strategic role in the organization- it is with and through executive development activities that organizational strategies are formed, communicated, and reinforced with senior management. In other organizations, development of executives is seen as an inherently positive activity, which, akin to insurance, is probably better to have than not. In organizations where development has not had an opportunity to prove its value, it may be seen as a waste of time and rarely something that the organization commits its leaders' precious time towards.

REPORTING AND STRUCTURE

Most often the executive development function reports into the head of Talent Management, the head of HR, or into the Chief Learning Officer (CLO). In rare cases, it reports into an operating executive (*i.e.* COO). Executive development can be very effective under any reporting structure – what is key is executive level sponsorship and access to senior line leaders who can help ensure development is aligned with and supports the company's strategy.

Most often, the head of executive development will have additional resources working alongside him/her. These may be in the form of direct reports, and/or HR business partners and shared resources in the Talent Management function. While the majority of executive development professionals are the more senior talent management professionals in the organization (based on expertise, education such as graduate degree, and tenure), in some cases and perhaps more frequently organizations are putting "outsiders" in charge of executive development who have not spent the bulk of their career in Talent Management or Human Resources (some examples include CBS Corporation and the U.S. Navy). Among the reasons for this are to bring a fresh perspective into the role and to bring strategy and operational expertise into the function. On the supplier side, there exists a rich ecosystem of development professionals; essentially any part of the executive development process can be procured from an outside firm or set of individual consultants and coaches.

PRIMARY ACTIVITIES

Executive Development activities generally fall into two broad categories: Assessment and Development as outlined below.

ASSESSMENT

- *Capability Requirements* – Provide input into the organization's strategy formulation process by identifying what is required of executives from a capability perspective
- *Capability Assessment* – Measure existing capabilities against required capabilities
- *Gap Analysis* – Identify gap between requirements and current assessment, with an eye towards what capabilities can be "built" (development) vs. "bought" external hiring

DEVELOPMENT

- *Segment executive population*– Create groupings of executives, by level, geography, business unit, or other affiliation (C-suite track, high potential's, critical roles etc.)
- *Architect* – Create development activities and experiences for the different segmentations
- *Deliver* – Coordinate across the ecosystem of internal and external partners to deliver development experiences and manage execution of executive development initiatives, etc.
- *Measure and Refine* – Conduct post activity ROI (typically Kirkpatrick Level I-IV), make course corrections, summarize and report results

Some of the adjacent Talent Management activities that executive development may have involvement with include the succession planning process (typically not CEO or CEO -1, but below), executive onboarding (ideally both external hiring and internal changes), structuring on the job developmental assignments, and working with alumni of development programmes, and alumni of the organization.

DEVELOPMENTAL OPTIONS

Executive development professionals have a wide variety of activities they can choose to deploy including in order of most commonly found:

- OTJ (On the job) stretch assignments, line and staff roles, rotational assignments
- Executive coaching
- Mentoring
- Custom workshops and activities
- Action learning
- Business school open enrollment courses
- Online courses and resources

BEST PRACTICES

The following are a set of best practices most often found in organizations that have long standing development activities which are highly regarded in and outside of the organization.

- *Articulate a clear and compelling vision* – Leaders have many competing priorities, and need a compelling set of reasons to support development activities. The development team needs to build a compelling case and consistent themes across its development strategy.
- *Build support across key sponsors* - Executive development professionals need to have a deep set of contacts both inside of the organization and across many functions and outside with thought leaders and experts. Many organizations have found that Advisory Boards, which seek to create a formal process of soliciting the input from stakeholders as highly effective. Relationships with internal executives, who are increasingly used as "faculty" to delivery development, are important to nurture. A strong professional network is the "currency" of the development professional.
- *Ground development in business challenges* – When in doubt, development that is rooted in solving current and significant business challenges will always prevail over development that is designed to round out a leader or a group of professionals.
- *Shorten the timeline* – Especially in light of budget cutbacks that are all too common in organizations today, it is important that development is focused on solving current operating cycle issues and challenges. Development plans that span many quarters risk never being fully implemented.

- *Market successes* – Successful development professionals, like any other professionals in the organization, are quite good at highlighting their impact for the organization and making sure to create "buzz" for their work and activities. Whether through formal ROI studies or informal anecdotal reviews that are circulated to strategic individuals, it is key to promote success.

EXECUTIVE DEVELOPMENT 2.0

Below are key factors that are impacting the field of executive development:

- *Time frame* – The speed with which organizations need to revise strategies, launch new products and services, expand their global footprint, etc. continues to accelerate; more rapid means of enabling the organization and its leaders to make these changes are required from the development function.
- *Share of mind* – Executives are incredibly taxed with an increasing set of responsibilities; mid-level management has been reduced and the number of stakeholders (community, environment, government, etc.) has increased, all putting incredible pressure on leaders. Development that is not of immediate value risks elimination.
- *Budget* – The current economic situation has put great pressure on all expenses across the organization, executive development is no exception. Centralized development budgets are all targets, while certain activities such as executive coaching that may be paid out of a business unit budget may be more insulated from cutbacks.
- *"Bottom line" HR* – As many organizations have become more results oriented and quantitative for all support functions, there is increased pressure for HR and all of its components to "raise its game" and prove in business terms its impact.

These factors are creating a new operating context for executive development professionals. In response to this new environment, The Institute of Executive Development has articulated a vision of what *Executive Development 2.0 will look like:*

- The purpose of the function is to drive the organizational strategy (not solely build skills)
- The content will be based on current business imperatives
- The timeline is focused on the immediate 12 months, not longer
- The format will include more on the job and action learning (vs. formal workshops and programmes)
- The audience will include stakeholders such as customers and partners
- The budget will be measured more in terms of investment of executive's time (vs. funds)

While executive development continues to become enriched by many approaches, one approach, adult development and its subfield Positive Adult Development is beginning to create opportunities for what has been essentially reserved for academic research to become an increasing part of executive practices.

ORGANIZATION DEVELOPMENT

Organization development (OD) is a deliberately planned, organization-wide effort to increase an organization's effectiveness and/or efficiency, and/or to enable the organization to achieve its strategic goals. OD theorists and practitioners define OD in various ways. Its multiplicity of definitions reflects the complexity of the discipline and is responsible for its lack of understanding. For example, Vasudevan has referred to OD being about promoting organizational readiness to meet change, and it has been said that OD is a systemic learning and development strategy intended to change the basics of beliefs, attitudes and relevance of values, and structure of the current organization to better absorb disruptive technologies, shrinking or exploding market opportunities and ensuing challenges and chaos.

It is worth understanding what OD is not. It is not training, personal development, team development or team building, human-resource development (HRD), learning and development (LandD) or a part of HR - although it is often mistakenly understood as some or all of these. OD interventions are about change and so involve people - but OD also develops processes, systems and structures.

The primary purpose of OD is to develop the organization, not to train or develop the staff.

OVERVIEW

Organization development is an ongoing, systematic process of implementing effective organizational change. OD is known as both a field of science focused on understanding and managing organizational change and as a field of scientific study and enquiry. It is interdisciplinary in nature and draws on sociology, psychology, particularly industrial and organizational psychology, and theories of motivation, learning, and personality. Although behavioural science has provided the basic foundation for the study and practice of OD, new and emerging fields of study have made their presence felt. Experts in systems thinking and organizational learning, structure of intuition in decision making, and coaching (to name a few) whose perspective is not steeped in just the behavioural sciences, but a much more multi-disciplinary and inter-disciplinary approach, have emerged as OD catalysts or tools.

Organization development is a growing field that is responsive to many new approaches.

HISTORY

Kurt Lewin (1898–1947) is widely recognized as the founding father of OD, although he died before the concept became current in the mid-1950s. From Lewin came the ideas of group dynamics and action research which underpin the basic OD process as well as providing its collaborative consultant/client ethos. Institutionally, Lewin founded the "Research Center for Group Dynamics" (RCGD) at MIT, which moved to Michigan after his death. RCGD colleagues were among those who founded the National Training Laboratories (NTL), from which the T-groups and group-based OD emerged.

Kurt Lewin played a key role in the evolution of organization development as it is known today. As early as World War II, Lewin experimented with a collaborative change process (involving himself as consultant and a client group) based on a three-step process of planning, taking action, and measuring results. This was the forerunner of action research, an important element of OD, which will be discussed later. Lewin then participated in the beginnings of laboratory training, or T-groups, and, after his death in 1947, his close associates helped to develop survey-research methods at the University of Michigan. These procedures became important parts of OD as developments in this field continued at the National Training Laboratories and in growing numbers of universities and private consulting firms across the country. Two of the leading universities offering doctoral leveldegrees in OD are Benedictine University and the Fielding Graduate University.

Douglas McGregor and Richard Beckhard while "consulting together at General Mills in the 1950s, the two coined the term organization development (OD) to describe an innovative bottoms-up change effort that fit no traditional consulting categories" (Weisbord, 1987, p. 112).

The failure of off-site laboratory training to live up to its early promise was one of the important forces stimulating the development of OD. Laboratory training is learning from a person's "here and now" experience as a member of an ongoing training group. Such groups usually meet without a specific agenda. Their purpose is for the members to learn about themselves from their spontaneous "here and now" responses to an ambiguous hypothetical situation. Problems of leadership, structure, status, communication, and self-serving behaviour typically arise in such a group. The members have an opportunity to learn something about themselves and to practice such skills as listening, observing others, and functioning as effective group members. Herbert A. Shepard conducted the first large-scale experiments in Organization Development in the late fifties.

As formerly practiced (and occasionally still practiced for special purposes), laboratory training was conducted in "stranger groups," or groups composed of individuals from different organizations, situations, and backgrounds. A major difficulty developed, however, in transferring knowledge gained from these "stranger labs" to the actual situation "back home". This required a transfer between two different cultures, the relatively safe and protected environment of the T-group (or training group) and the give-and-take of the organizational environment with its traditional values. This led the early pioneers in this type of learning to begin to apply it to "family groups" — that is, groups located within an organization. From this shift in the locale of the training site and the realization that culture was an important factor in influencing group members (along with some other developments in the behavioural sciences) emerged the concept of organization development.

CORE VALUES

Underlying Organization Development are humanistic values.

Margulies and Raia (1972) articulated the humanistic values of OD as follows:

1. Providing opportunities for people to function as human beings rather than as resources in the productive process.
2. Providing opportunities for each organization member, as well as for the organization itself, to develop to their full potential.
3. Seeking to increase the effectiveness of the organization in terms of all of its goals.
4. Attempting to create an environment in which it is possible to find exciting and challenging work.
5. Providing opportunities for people in organizations to influence the way in which they relate to work, the organization, and the environment.
6. Treating each human being as a person with a complex set of needs, all of which are important to their work and their life.

Differentiating OD from other change efforts such as-

1. Operation management 2. Training and Development 3. Technological innovations....etc.

OBJECTIVES

The objectives of OD are:

1. To increase the level of inter-personal trust among employees.
2. To increase employees' level of satisfaction and commitment.
3. To confront problems instead of neglecting them.
4. To effectively manage conflict.
5. To increase cooperation and collaboration among the employees.
6. To increase the organization's problem solving.
7. To put in place processes that will help improve the ongoing operation of the organization on a continuous basis.

As objectives of organizational development are framed keeping in view specific situations, they vary from one situation to another. In other words, these programmes are tailored to meet the requirements of a particular situation.

But broadly speaking, all organizational development programmes try to achieve the following objectives:

1. Making individuals in the organization aware of the vision of the organization. Organizational development helps in making employees align with the vision of the organization.
2. Encouraging employees to solve problems instead of avoiding them.
3. Strengthening inter-personnel trust, cooperation, and communication for the successful achievement of organizational goals.
4. Encouraging every individual to participate in the process of planning, thus making them feel responsible for the implementation of the plan.
5. Creating a work atmosphere in which employees are encouraged to work and participate enthusiastically.
6. Replacing formal lines of authority with personal knowledge and skill.
7. Creating an environment of trust so that employees willingly accept change.

According to organizational development thinking, organization development provides managers with a vehicle for introducing change systematically by applying a broad selection of management techniques. This, in turn, leads to greater personal, group, and organizational effectiveness.

CHANGE AGENT

A change agent in the sense used here is not a technical expert skilled in such functional areas as accounting, production, or finance. The change agent is a behavioural scientist who knows how to get people in an organization involved in solving their own problems. A change agent's main strength is a comprehensive knowledge of human behaviour, supported by a number of intervention techniques (to be discussed later). The change agent can be either external or internal to the organization. An internal change agent is usually a staff person who has expertise in the behavioural sciences and in the intervention technology of OD. Beckhard reports several cases in which line people have been trained in OD and have returned to their organizations to engage in successful change assignments. In the natural evolution of change mechanisms in organizations, this would seem to approach the ideal arrangement.

Researchers at the University of Oxford found that leaders can be effective change agents within their own organizations if they are strongly committed to 'knowledge leadership' targeted towards organizational development. In their three-year study of UK health care organizations, the researchers identified three different mechanisms through which knowledge leaders actively 'transposed', 'appropriated' or 'contended' change concepts, effectively translating and embedding these in organizational practice. Qualified change agents can be found on some university faculties, or they may be private consultants associated with such organizations as the National Training Laboratories Institute for Applied Behavioural Science (Washington, D.C.) University Associates (San Diego, California), the Human Systems Intervention graduate programme in the Department of Applied Human Sciences (Concordia University, Montreal, Canada), Navitus (Pvt) Ltd (Pakistan), MaxFoster Global and similar organizations. The change agent may be a staff or line member of the organization who is schooled in OD theory and technique. In such a case, the "contractual relationship" is an in-house agreement that should probably be explicit with respect to all of the conditions involved except the fee.

SPONSORING ORGANIZATION

The initiative for OD programmes often comes from an organization that has a problem or anticipates facing a problem. This means that top management or someone authorized by top management is aware that a problem exists and has decided to seek help in solving it. There is a direct analogy here to the practice of psychotherapy: The client orpatient must actively seek help in finding a solution to his problems. This indicates a willingness on the part of the client organization to accept help and assures the organization that management is actively concerned.

APPLIED BEHAVIOURAL SCIENCE

One of the outstanding characteristics of OD that distinguishes it from most other improvement programmes is that it is based on a "helping relationship." Some believe that the change agent is not a physician to the organization's ills; that s/he does not examine the "patient," make a diagnosis, and write a prescription. Nor does she try to teach organizational members a new inventory of knowledge which they then transfer to the job situation. Using theory and methods drawn from such behavioural sciences asindustrial/organizational psychology, industrial sociology, communication, cultural anthropology, administrative theory, organizational behaviour, economics, and political science, the change agent's main function is to help the organization define and solve its own problems. The basic method used is known as action research. This approach, which is described in detail later, consists of a preliminary diagnosis, collecting data, feedback of the data to the client, data exploration by the client group, action planning based on the data, and taking action.

SYSTEMS CONTEXT

THE HOLISTIC AND FUTURISTIC VIEW OF ORGANIZATION

OD deals with a total system — the organization as a whole, including its relevant environment — or with a subsystem or systems — departments or work groups — in the context of the total system. Parts of systems — for example, individuals, cliques, structures, norms, values, and products — are not considered in isolation; the principle of interdependency — that change in one part of a system affects the other parts — is fully recognized. Thus, OD interventions focus on the total culture and cultural processes of organizations. The focus is also on groups, since the relevant behaviour of individuals in organizations and groups is generally a product of the influences of groups rather than of personalities.

IMPROVED ORGANIZATIONAL PERFORMANCE

The objective of OD is to improve the organization's capacity to handle its internal and external functioning and relationships. This includes improved interpersonal and group processes, more effective communication, enhanced ability to cope with organizational problems of all kinds. It also involves more effective decision processes, more appropriate leadership styles, improved skill in dealing with destructive conflict, as well as developing improved levels of trust and cooperation among organizational members. These objectives stem from a value system based on an optimistic view of the nature of man — that man in a supportive environment is capable of achieving higher levels of development and accomplishment. Essential to organization development and effectiveness is the scientific method — enquiry, a rigorous search for causes, experimental testing of hypotheses, and review of results.

Self-managing work groups allows the members of a work team to manage, control, and monitor all facets of their work, from recruiting, hiring, and new employees to deciding when to take rest breaks. An early analysis of the first-self-managing work groups yielded the following behavioural characteristics:

- Employees assume personal responsibility and accountability for outcomes of their work.
- Employees monitor their own performance and seek feedback on how well they are accomplishing their goals.
- Employees manage their performance and take corrective action when necessary to improve their and the performance of other group members.
- Employees seek guidance, assistance, and resources from the organization when they do not have what they need to do the job.
- Employees help members of their work group and employees in other groups to improve job performance and raise productivity for the organization as a whole.

ORGANIZATIONAL SELF-RENEWAL

The ultimate aim of OD practitioners is to "work themselves out of a job" by leaving the client organization with a set of tools, behaviours, attitudes, and an action plan with which to monitor its own state of health and to take corrective steps towards its own renewal and development. This is consistent with the systems concept of feedback as a regulatory and corrective mechanism.

UNDERSTANDING ORGANIZATIONS

Weisbord presents a six-box model for understanding organizations:

1. *Purposes:* The organization members are clear about the organization's mission and purpose and goal agreements, whether people support the organization's purpose.
2. *Structure:* How is the organization's work divided up? The question is whether there is an adequate fit between the purpose and the internal structure.
3. *Relationship:* Between individuals, between units or departments that perform different tasks, and between the people and requirements of their jobs.
4. *Rewards:* The consultant should diagnose the similarities between what the organization formally rewarded or punished members for.
5. *Leadership:* Is to watch for blips among the other boxes and maintain balance among them.
6. *Helpful mechanism:* Is a helpful organization that must attend to in order to survive which as planning, control, budgeting, and other information systems that help organization member accomplish.

MODERN DEVELOPMENT

In recent years, serious questioning has emerged about the relevance of OD to managing change in modern organizations. The need for "reinventing" the field has become a topic that even some of its "founding fathers" are discussing critically.

With this call for reinvention and change, scholars have begun to examine organization development from an emotion-based standpoint. For example, deKlerk (2007) writes about how emotional trauma can negatively affect performance. Due to downsizing, outsourcing, mergers, restructuring, continual changes, invasions of privacy, harassment, and abuses of power, many employees experience the emotions of aggression, anxiety, apprehension, cynicism, and fear, which can lead to performance decreases. deKlerk (2007) suggests that in order to heal the trauma and increase performance, O.D. practitioners must acknowledge the existence of the trauma, provide a safe place for employees to discuss their feelings, symbolize the trauma and put it into perspective, and then allow for and deal with the emotional responses. One method of achieving this is by having employees draw pictures of what they feel about the situation, and then having them explain their drawings with each other. Drawing pictures is beneficial because it allows employees to express emotions they normally would not be able to put into words. Also, drawings often prompt active participation in the activity, as everyone is required to draw a picture and then discuss its meaning.

The use of new technologies combined with globalization has also shifted the field of organization development. Roland Sullivan (2005) defined Organization Development with participants at the 1st Organization Development Conference for Asia in Dubai-2005 as "Organization Development is a transformative leap to a desired vision where strategies and systems align, in the light of local culture with an innovative and authentic leadership style using the support of high tech tools. Bob Aubrey (2015) introduced KDIs (Key Development Indicators) to help organisations go beyond performance and align strategy, organisations and individuals and argued that fundamental challenges such as robotics, artificial intelligence and genetics prefigure a regeneration of the field.

ACTION RESEARCH

Wendell L French and Cecil Bell defined organization development (OD) at one point as "organization improvement through action research". If one idea can be said to summarize OD's underlying philosophy, it would be action research as it was conceptualized by Kurt Lewin and later elaborated and expanded on by other behavioural scientists. Concerned with social change and, more particularly, with effective, permanent social change, Lewin believed that the motivation to change was strongly related to action: If people are active in decisions affecting them, they are more likely to adopt new ways. "Rational social management", he said, "proceeds in a spiral of steps, each of which is composed of a circle of planning, action, and fact-finding about the result of action".

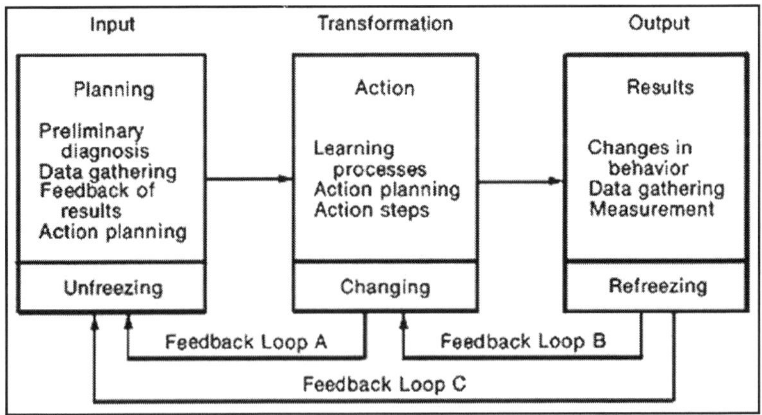

Fig. Systems Model of Action-Research Process.

Lewin's description of the process of change involves three steps:

"Unfreezing": Faced with a dilemma or disconfirmation, the individual or group becomes aware of a need to change.

"Changing": The situation is diagnosed and new models of behaviour are explored and tested.

"Refreezing": Application of new behaviour is evaluated, and if reinforced, adopted.

The steps and processes involved in planned change through action research. Action research is depicted as a cyclical process of change. The cycle begins with a series of planning actions initiated by the client and the change agent working together. The principal elements of this stage include a preliminary diagnosis, data gathering, feedback of results, and joint action planning. In the language of systems theory, this is the input phase, in which the client system becomes aware of problems as yet unidentified, realizes it may need outside help to effect changes, and shares with the consultant the process of problem diagnosis.

The second stage of action research is the action, or transformation, phase. This stage includes actions relating to learning processes (perhaps in the form of role analysis) and to planning and executing behavioural changes in the client organization. The feedback at this stage would move via Feedback Loop A and would have the effect of altering previous planning to bring the learning activities of the client system into better alignment with change objectives. Included in this stage is action-planning activity carried out jointly by the consultant and members of the client system. Following the workshop or learning sessions, these action steps are carried out on the job as part of the transformation stage.

The third stage of action research is the output, or results, phase. This stage includes actual changes in behaviour (if any) resulting from corrective action steps taken following the second stage. Data are again gathered from the client system so that progress can be determined and necessary adjustments in learning activities can be made.

Minor adjustments of this nature can be made in learning activities via Feedback Loop B. Major adjustments and reevaluations would return the OD project to the first, or planning, stage for basic changes in the programme. The action-research model follows Lewin's repetitive cycle of planning, action, and measuring results. It also illustrates other aspects of Lewin's general model of change. As indicated in the diagram, the planning stage is a period of unfreezing, or problem awareness.The action stage is a period of changing, that is, trying out new forms of behaviour in an effort to understand and cope with the system's problems. (There is inevitable overlap between the stages, since the boundaries are not clear-cut and cannot be in a continuous process). The results stage is a period of refreezing, in which new behaviours are tried out on the job and, if successful and reinforcing, become a part of the system's repertoire of problem-solving behaviour.

Action research is problem centered, client centered, and action oriented. It involves the client system in a diagnostic, active-learning, problem-finding, and problem-solving process. Data are not simply returned in the form of a written report but instead are fed back in open joint sessions, and the client and the change agent collaborate in identifying and ranking specific problems, in devising methods for finding their real causes, and in developing plans for coping with them realistically and practically. Scientific method in the form of data gathering, forming hypotheses, testing hypotheses, and measuring results, although not pursued as rigorously as in the laboratory, is nevertheless an integral part of the process. Action research also sets in motion a long-range, cyclical, self-correcting mechanism for maintaining and enhancing the effectiveness of the client's system by leaving the system with practical and useful tools for self-analysis and self-renewal.

OD INTERVENTIONS

"Interventions" are principal learning processes in the "action" stage of organization development. Interventions are structured activities used individually or in combination by the members of a client system to improve their social or task performance. They may be introduced by a change agent as part of an improvement programme, or they may be used by the client following a programme to check on the state of the organization's health, or to effect necessary changes in its own behaviour. "Structured activities" mean such diverse procedures as experiential exercises, questionnaires, attitude surveys, interviews, relevant group discussions, and even lunchtime meetings between the change agent and a member of the client organization. Every action that influences an organization's improvement programme in a change agent-client system relationship can be said to be an intervention.

There are many possible intervention strategies from which to choose. Several assumptions about the nature and functioning of organizations are made in the choice of a particular strategy.

Beckhard lists six such assumptions:

1. The basic building blocks of an organization are groups (teams). Therefore, the basic units of change are groups, not individuals.
2. An always relevant change goal is the reduction of inappropriate competition between parts of the organization and the development of a more collaborative condition.
3. Decision making in a healthy organization is located where the information sources are, rather than in a particular role or level of hierarchy.
4. Organizations, subunits of organizations, and individuals continuously manage their affairs against goals. Controls are interim measurements, not the basis of managerial strategy.
5. One goal of a healthy organization is to develop generally open communication, mutual trust, and confidence between and across levels.

6. People support what they help create. People affected by a change must be allowed active participation and a sense of ownership in the planning and conduct of the change.

Interventions range from those designed to improve the effectiveness of individuals through those designed to deal with teams and groups, intergroup relations, and the total organization. There are interventions that focus on task issues (what people do), and those that focus on process issues (how people go about doing it). Finally, interventions may be roughly classified according to which change mechanism they tend to emphasize: for example, feedback, awareness of changing cultural norms, interaction andcommunication, conflict, and education through either new knowledge or skill practice.

One of the most difficult tasks confronting the change agent is to help create in the client system a safe climate for learning and change. In a favorable climate, human learning builds on itself and continues indefinitely during man's lifetime. Out of new behaviour, new dilemmas and problems emerge as the spiral continues upward to new levels. In an unfavorable climate, in contrast, learning is far less certain, and in an atmosphere of psychological threat, it often stops altogether. Unfreezing old ways can be inhibited inorganizations because the climate makes employees feel that it is inappropriate to reveal true feelings, even though such revelations could be constructive. In an inhibited atmosphere, therefore, necessary feedback is not available. Also, trying out new ways may be viewed as risky because it violates established norms. Such an organization may also be constrained because of the law of systems: If one part changes, other parts will become involved. Hence, it is easier to maintain the status quo. Hierarchical authority,specialization, span of control, and other characteristics of formal systems also discourage experimentation. The change agent must address himself to all of these hazards and obstacles.

Some of the things which will help him are:

1. A real need in the client system to change
2. Genuine support from management
3. Setting a personal example: listening, supporting behaviour
4. A sound background in the behavioural sciences
5. A working knowledge of systems theory"
6. A belief in man as a rational, self-educating being fully capable of learning better ways to do things.

A few examples of interventions include team building, coaching, Large Group Interventions, mentoring, performance appraisal, downsizing, TQM, and leadership development.

LEADERSHIP STUDIES

Leadership studies is a multidisciplinary academic field of study that focuses on leadership in organizational contexts and in human life. Leadership studies has origins in thesocial sciences (*e.g.*, sociology, anthropology, psychology), in humanities (*e.g.*, history and philosophy), as well as in professional and applied fields of study (*e.g.*, managementand education). The field of leadership studies is closely linked to the field of organizational studies.

As an academic area of enquiry, the study of leadership has been of interest to scholars from a wide variety of disciplinary backgrounds. Today, there are numerous academic programmes (spanning several academic colleges and departments) related to the study of leadership. Leadership degree programmes generally relate to: aspects of leadership, leadership studies, and organizational leadership (although there are a number of leadership-oriented concentrations in other academic areas).

LEADERSHIP IN HIGHER EDUCATION

Leadership has become one of the fastest growing academic fields in higher education At all levels, undergraduate through doctoral, an increasing number of colleges and universities have begun developing not only individual courses, but entire degree programmes specifically devoted to the study of leadership.

Even among some of the more established and traditional academic disciplines such as engineering, education, and medicine, specialization and concentration areas have been developed around the study of leadership. Most of these academic programmes have been designed to be multidisciplinary in nature—drawing upon theories and applications from related fields such as sociology, psychology, philosophy, and management. Such an approach, Rost (1991) has argued "allows scholars and practitioners to think radically new thoughts about leadership that are not possible from a unidisciplinary approach".

HISTORY OF LEADERSHIP AS A FIELD OF STUDY

The study of leadership can be dated back to Plato, Sun Tzu and Machiavelli; however, leadership has only become the focus of contemporary academic studies in the last 60 years, and particularly more so in the last two decades. Contemporary leadership scholars and researchers have often been questioned about the nature of their work, and its place within the academy, but much of the confusion surrounding leadership as a field of study may be attributed to a lack of understanding regarding transdisciplinary, inter-, and multi- disciplinary academic fields of study in general.

The discipline (which encompasses a host of sub-fields) is filled with definitions, theories, styles, functions, competencies, and historical examples of successful and diverse leaders. Collectively, the research findings on leadership provide a far more sophisticated and complex view of the phenomenon than most of the simplistic views presented in the popular press.

Some of the earliest studies on leadership include:

- The Ohio State Leadership Studies which began in the 1940s and focused on how leaders could satisfy common group needs. The findings indicated that the two most important dimensions in leadership included: "initiating structure", and "consideration". These characteristics could be either high or low and were independent of one another. The research was based on questionnaires to leaders and subordinates. These questionnaires are known as the Leader Behaviour Description Questionnaire (LBDQ) and the Supervisor Behaviour Description Questionnaire (SBDQ). By 1962, the LBDQ was on version XII.

- The Michigan Studies of Leadership which began in the 1950s and indicated that leaders could be classified as either "employee centered," or "job centered." These studies identified three critical characteristics of effective leaders: task oriented behaviour, relationship-oriented behaviour, and participative leadership.
- McGregors Theory X & Theory Y developed by Douglas McGregor in the 1960s at MIT Sloan School of Management. These theories described employee motivation in the workforce. Both theories begin with the premise that the role of management is to assemble the factors of production, including people, for the economic benefit of the firm. Beyond this point, the two theories of management diverge.
- Blake and Mouton Managerial Grid (1964)-updated in 1991 to the Blake and McCanse Leadership Grid-developed the orientation of "task orientation" and "people orientation" in leader behaviour. They developed the leadership grid which focused on concern for results (on the one axis) and concern for people (on the other axis).

In addition to these studies, leadership has been examined from an academic perspective through several theoretical lenses:

- *Trait and Behavioural theories of Leadership:* Attempt to describe the types of behaviour and personality tendencies associated with effective leadership.
- *Situational and Contingency theories of Leadership:* Incorporate environmental and situational considerations into leader behaviour.
- *Functional Leadership theory:* Suggests that a leader's primary responsibility is to see that whatever is necessary in relation to group needs is taken care of.
- *Information-Processing Leadership theory:* Focuses on the role of social perception in identifying leadership abilities.
- *Self Leadership theory:* Although behaviourally oriented, the essence of self leadership theory is that behaviours are directed towards the attainment of super-ordinate goals.
- *Transactional and Transformational theories of Leadership:* The transactional leader focuses on managerial reward and contingent

valuation. The transformational leader focuses on motivation and goal attainment.

The first doctoral programme in Leadership Studies was established at the University of San Diego in the School of Leadership and Education Sciences in 1979. The first undergraduate school of Leadership Studies was established at the University of Richmond (The Jepson School) in 1992. The Jepson School of Leadership Studies at the University of Richmond studies leadership as a process that can be taught. The growth of transpersonal psychology means that this field has relevance to Transpersonal business studies.

RESEARCH ON DIFFERENT TYPES OF LEADERSHIP

Empirical, meta-analytic, and theoretical studies have been conducted on various types of leadership. Some of the styles of leadership studied include:

- Ambidextrous leadership
- Democratic Leadership
- Innovation leadership
- Transactional leadership
- Transformational leadership

RESEARCH METHODS IN THE STUDY OF LEADERSHIP

Leadership has been studied using quantitative, qualitative, and mixed methods (a combination of quantitative and qualitative) research methodologies. From a quantitative psychology orientation, statistical and mathematical modeling has been used in the development of leadership scales and in testing established leader evaluation tools. Survey methodology has also been widely used in leadership research. As such, traditional methods of analysis in survey research have also extended to the analysis of survey research within the study of leadership (*e.g.*, cross-tabulations, ANOVAs, regression analysis, log-linear analysis, factor analysis, etc.). From a qualitative orientation, leadership research has included a host of research techniques: phenomenology, ethnography, grounded theory, interviews, case studies, historiography, etc.

"Coaches and coaching psychologists are increasingly using the lessons and tools of positive psychology in their practice (Biswas-Diener, 2010)." An example of leadership research done was by P. Alex Linley and Gurpal Minhas researching the strengths that may be found in more effective strengthspotters; the people who are skilled in the identification and development of strengths in others. The study consisted of an online survey used to collect data on the Strengthspotting Scale, together with an assessment of 60 different strengths using the Realise2 model. There were 528 respondents to retrieve data from and the results showed that the four strengths connector, enabler, esteem builder and feedback were found across the Strengthspotting Scale. "The strengths of Connector, Enabler and Feedback were significant predictors for each strengthspotting domain, suggesting that these may be the essence of the personal characteristics of an effective strengthspotter".

ACADEMIC PROGRAMMES

There are a considerable number of doctoral, masters, and undergraduate degree programmes related to the study of leadership. Given that the study of leadership is interdisciplinary, leadership-related degree programmes are often situated within various colleges, schools, and departments across different university campuses (*e.g.*, Schools of Education at some universities, Business Schools at other universities, and Graduate and Professional Schools at still other universities). As such, at the doctoral level leadership related degree programmes primarily include: Ph.D., Ed.D., and executive doctoral degrees (depending on the situation of the programme within the university). At the masters level leadership related degree programmes primarily include: Master of Science, Master of Arts, and executive Masters degrees. At the undergraduate level leadership related degree programmes primarily include: Bachelor of Science and Bachelor of Arts degrees as well as leadership certificate and minor programmes.

3

Effective Educational Leadership Development

"The school itself needs to become a major focus for the professional development of the professional staff - and this includes the principal of the school as well". It must be recognised that learning to teach and to lead is a lifelong professional activity, not something one completes in a leadership development programme. These programmes provide an initiation not a culmination, and in order to get better at their work educational leaders need to have constructive feedback regarding their daily work. Traditionally schools have been structured in ways that isolate staff; instead structures need to be created which make it possible for teachers, principals and superintendents to see and to talk with each other about their work.

A positive climate for adult learning is essential for leadership development programmes. The Indiana Principal Leadership Academy provided a safe, supportive environment for learning. Considerable attention was given during the programme, particularly during the early stages, to building a sense of teamwork and camaraderie. In the British Local Education Authority programme participants commented on the "loyalty, mutual trust and self-confidence the process engendered".

Educators felt strongly about the benefits derived from being able to practice new behaviours in a safe environment before trying them in a real-life setting. Peer interaction, feedback and mentoring were noted as strengths. Principals responded that they might have derived additional benefits from their training programme if they had been encouraged to take even more risks during their programme. "An ideal learning environment will be sensitive to the varying levels of readiness manifested by school leadership candidates and recognise the particular needs of adult learners working in a variety of social contexts".

Leadership development programmes require the deliberate creation of support networks. Building a network for programme participants promotes continuing professional and personal development, develops a trusted peer group, and creates time for reading, reflection and thoughtful discussion. Such networks require a professional focus, variety and relevance in topics, a confidential environment for substantive discourse, and leadership opportunities for all participants.

Researchers have advocated the notions of situated cognition and cognitive apprenticeship as a way of improving the quality of administrative training programmes by placing greater emphasis on the social and cultural context in which learning takes place. Learning is viewed as active, collaborative and authentic, and the focus is on the processes educational leaders use in actual practice to solve real-life problems. Use of authentic problems and settings promotes transfer of knowledge from the instructional setting to the real-life administrative setting. For transfer of knowledge and skills which are subject to routine and frequent use, it is helpful to provide many opportunities for practice across a wide variety of problem types, feedback about the adequacy of performance, and additional opportunities for guided practice.

Coaching during the process of implementation enables the learner to practice new skills and strategies with an expert's support and guidance. The skilled coach already possesses sophisticated cognitive structures to guide performance and the knowledge of how best to provide feedback. "As a consequence, such a person is likely to facilitate improvement in the learner's guiding schema and actual performance much faster than if the learner has available only his or her own analysis of performance discrepancies". Coaching can provide the learner with the confidence to undertake new initiatives as well as with the technical assistance needed to do so successfully.

"Moreover, unless principals acquire skill mastery, they may do more harm than good during the implementation process". Coaching also supports the adaptation of programme content to the needs of the local school. This function is of particular importance when the programme is general in nature and the settings for implementation vary widely among participants. In addition coaching provides a limited form of accountability. The awareness that a colleague or instructor will be coming to coach provides additional impetus for a learner to engage in implementation.

Other cognitive and metacognitive processes also need attention. Effective educational leadership is a highly complex process which is "grossly underestimated by behaviourally-based recipes for administrative success". Actions unique to individual leaders may explain a much greater proportion of their effectiveness than the relatively small number of actions that research suggests they have in common. Efforts to improve the effectiveness of educational leaders may more productive if more consideration were given to improve the quality of thinking and problem solving rather than simply focussing on actions or behaviours. Such cognitive orientations are compatible with adult learning theory and with the notion of reflective practice. The leadership profiles from Ontario, the Northwest Territories and Western Australia described patterns of professional growth for educational leaders: from a tendency towards reactive responses to proactive responses; from reliance on personal preferences in decision making to a focus on consensus to an outcomes-based or consequences focus to a sensitivity to, and accommodation of, multiple environmental influences; from rigid adherence to fixed procedure to procedural flexibility to philosophical or conceptual fidelity; from in-school focus to interschool focus to school-within-the-greater-community focus; and from a limited repertoire to a broad repertoire of strategies.

These patterns are an illustration of the developmental nature of leadership which requires consideration in programme design. In a redesigned leadership development programme Behar-Horenstein (1995) recommended the following characteristics: use of performance-based competencies; generation of knowledge that promotes the development of a reflective practitioner; a focus on cognitive and metacognitive processes; instructional methods that emulate the modelling, coaching and scaffolding concepts integral to cognitive apprenticeship; group discussion activities that encourage students to link their experiences to conceptual knowledge; learning activities that challenge students to use problem-solving skills and demonstrate their theoretical knowledge; and a greater emphasis on curriculum, instruction and teaching processes rather than the administrative and managerial functions.

Based on my leadership experiences and on recommendations from a variety of print and electronic sources, these characteristics seem appropriate.

I would also recommend additional characteristics for leadership development programmes:

- Appropriate both before being selected to leadership roles and while in leadership roles
- Personally relevant, individualised and developmental
- Conducted in a safe environment which promotes creative thought, taking risks and sharing information
- Practice-based and problem-based
- Local, national and international perspectives presented with with both electronic and face-to-face interaction
- Academically challenging, rigorous and well supervised.

From my perspective as a practising principal, a well-designed leadership development programme would provide the opportunity to grow personally and professionally; to do creative, excellent work for the employing school district; and to receive the additional benefit of recognised leadership credentials.

FORMATS FOR AN EFFECTIVE EDUCATIONAL LEADERSHIP DEVELOPMENT PROGRAMME

Instructional formats for leadership development programmes have included team teaching, collegial support teams, field-based experiences, small group and individual projects, readings, lectures, and self-directed learning contracts. Although specific activities varied from cohort to cohort, the Indiana Principal Leadership Academy staff attempted to cover the same content and achieve the same goals using a variety of strategies and formats. The principals generally expressed a preference for initial presentation of content, followed by collegial groups focused on discovering the practical applications.

Working in collegial groups and sharing both problems and ideas with peers has been cited as important as the content of the leadership training. The sharing of work-related problems in facilitated groups was a central feature for the majority of participants and group facilitators in the British Local Education Authority programme. "The perceived success of the groups was generally expressed in terms of the opportunity to explore important issues of practical concern with experienced colleagues from other schools and the effectiveness of the suggested solutions to these issues".

Many of the changes in practice which were considered or implemented by participants were influenced by the work in small groups. Most problems which are perceived by school administrators to be ill-structured are defined as such because of their social complexity rather than their technical character. Further, most such problems have to be solved by administrators in some form of collaboration with others.

"It is particularly important, for these reasons, to understand the significance of the social context for administrative problem-solving". Directed social interaction has the potential to improve individual problem-solving expertise because of the group modelling of more expert processes and provision of socially compelling, insightful feedback.

Mentorships are essential in leadership development programmes. "Effective leaders serve as mentors to their organisations and foster the development of people within them". A mentor shares the responsibility for another person's developmental journey by providing support, challenge and vision. Mentors provide a climate of trust which allows the learner to feel safe enough to risk new perspectives and behaviours. Both persons must understand that the freedom to fail is a precondition for growth and development. Mentors introduce tension by raising challenging questions or tasks which they consider appropriate for the learner. Finally, mentors offer direction and vision by providing larger perspectives. The value of mentoring has been recognised in administrator induction programmes in California, Ohio and North Carolina. Maine also has adopted legislation which required mentoring or some other formal support system as part of the recertification process for all school administrators. While programmes have been developed to assist leaders to become effective mentors, participants would benefit the opportunity to experience both roles in a mentoring relationship - the mentor and the protege.

The following formats would be appropriate for an effective leadership development programme:

- University courses
- On-line learning
  - Participation in discussion groups such as the Change Agency
  - Internet publication of positional papers, policy analyses or literature and web site reviews
  - Web site development with an educational leadership focus
- Professional apprenticeships, internships and mentorships
- Summer institutes, conferences and seminars
- Credit travel study units
  - Courses, site-visits, meetings, conferences, seminars and workshops
- Independent study
- Collaborative research projects
- Portfolio development.

Based on my experiences as a principal and on recommendations from a variety of print and electronic resources, I suggest the following format considerations:

- Programme facilitators and instructors would be selected for both their content specialisation and their commitment to active, collaborative and authentic learning.
- The programme would be designed to allow educational leaders to present a varied portfolio of learning experiences for programme credit.
- Compulsory face-to-face courses would create a supportive network environment for participants.
- The following content would be required:
  - Applying constructivist learning theory and adult learning theory
  - Negotiation, mediation and conflict resolution skills
  - Mentoring, supervision and evaluation skills
  - Group processes and facilitation skills
  - Using information technology in instruction and leadership
  - Creating school, community and business partnerships
  - Interpreting and conducting educational research
  - School law, finance and site-based management
- Traditional course credit structure would be reconsidered to allow recognition for shorter modules and alternate structures.
- Several supervised practica, apprenticeships or internships would be required, including an experience involving community or business partnerships.
- Evidence of the participant actively involved in mentoring another educator would be required.

- Virtual or on-line course participation would be considered valid for a portion of the programme.
- Transfer credit from other institutions would be evaluated for acceptance into the programme.
- To maximise format possibilities, it would be important to continue to develop formal and informal linkages that have already developed locally with Association for Supervision and Curriculum Development, Phi Delta Kappan, Leadership and Learning, Alberta Teachers' Association...
- Programme design would include the partners (University of Calgary, Calgary Board of Education...) creating a leadership profile as a context for programme development and a conceptual framework for participants.

THE CONTEXT FOR CONTEMPORARY EDUCATIONAL LEADERSHIP

AN END TO CLOSED INFORMATION SYSTEMS

In the autobiographies of principals, Brubaker (1995) identified a changing context for educational leaders and a movement away from the "arrogance of a closed information system", where information, or lack thereof, determined a person's power position in the educational hierarchy. These closed information systems were characterised by beliefs that staff did not need or could not handle information other than that given to them by bureaucratic superiors. Because these educational leaders were more politicians than educators, they often told staff only what they thought staff wanted to hear. Although their rhetoric often centred on instruction, student learning and staff development actually received limited consideration. "Administrators were committed to preserving the status quo at all costs, and honesty was often replaced by rationalisation". It is my contention that such leaders resemble the dinosaurs who were not able to survive in their changing environment.

EDUCATION REFORM AND EDUCATIONAL LEADERSHIP

Recently legislators, the business community, professional organisations and parents have all demanded more access to information about schools and more input into educational decision making. In this context of education reform, a number of reports released in the United States during the mid-1980's underscored the role of school administrators in facilitating change. "The image of forceful principal leadership in curriculum and instruction became embedded in the minds of policy makers as a critical element of school reform". This perspective required a significant shift in role expectations for principals. Whereas principals had traditionally functioned primarily as managers of the status quo, they were publicly lauded as change agents. A growing body of literature also added credence to reformers by emphasising that change would not likely occur unless superintendents and principals were directly involved, committed to change, and served as transformative intellectuals. "As a result university educational administration programmes were also challenged to ensure that prospective principals would be able to work in restructured school contexts, learn new roles, mitigate the effect of bureaucratic controls that stifle the teaching and learning process, and serve as effective catalysts for change".

POLITICAL PRESSURES AND EDUCATIONAL LEADERSHIP

"In the 90's, superintendents and principals are expected to do it all". Education reform and calls for accountability are increasingly politicising the work of educational leaders at the same time as they have been told to take a larger role in curriculum and instruction and also to be supportive and humanistic with their students, staff and parents. Principals have indicated that current educational changes cause pressure for them because of a perceived need to do more, know more and be more accountable in an unstable environment. A common theme which has emerged is the lack of time to accomplish all that needs to be done and the difficulty in finding time to be the reflective practitioner which is expected. The frustration of always being the "person in the middle" is a major concern for many educational leaders.

Survey results have indicated that a number of principals are fairly solitary people, detached from staff, students and each other. Being a school leader may be lonely, stressful work, and often leaders cannot rely on their immediate peers for support because they may feel they are in competition. In a school district the superintendent sets the tone for principals, who in turn influence the lives of teachers. "The irony is that superintendents and principals who continue to view their role as primarily political diminish the importance of their own learning. They become walking contradictions - a confusing model that attracts others with a similar weakness".

TECHNOLOGY AND EDUCATIONAL LEADERSHIP

Technology is also influencing the context of educational leadership.

Technology...is destiny. Never before have schools faced such rapid rates of technological change. Never before has technology so directly affected teaching and learning. Never before have schools been so challenged by alternative information delivery systems. Never before have students experienced instantaneous world-wide communications in the classroom. Incorporating technology for instruction, evaluation and management requires that school cultures develop a new alertness and flexibility. Some technologies will prove beneficial, other less so. The discerning school will know the difference. The discerning school also will train for the skills required to be technologically competent. This information technology context creates considerable demands, as well as exceptional opportunities, for schools and their leaders. A better utilisation of resources, especially human talent and initiative, is required. Under these conditions, leaders must possess the skills to manage change and to create collaborative action. The challenge for educational leaders is to use local talent to identify and accomplish the missions of changing, globally-driven schools.

SOCIETAL TRANSFORMATIONS AND EDUCATIONAL LEADERSHIP

"We live in a world where pluralism, consumerism, increased mobility, fragmentation, democracy and increasing access to news and information is in; and where absolute truth, stability, traditionalism and simplicity are either questioned or simply passe". Educational leaders need to take an inclusive and collaborative approach in order to work effectively with contemporary families. Major trends and issues which affect society and, as a result, influence our schools include violence in the community, changing family structures, increasing diversity in our culture, advancing technological developments and an unstable economic and political environment. Given the paradoxes occurring in every facet of today's society, educational leaders must grapple with how to support and empower students and parents who live in our transformative world.

The chaotic pace of today's society is largely based on the value we place upon time-saving immediacy, the push for more and better, and our emphasis on what we do, rather than who we are. Family members are often faced with frantic, frequently conflicting schedules in which they struggle to maintain cohesiveness. It is important for educational leaders to understand that the critical difference between well-functioning and troubled families is not found in their form, but in the quality of their relationships and their adaptive processes. Students and families need to be viewed with an appreciation for their resourcefulness, rather than primarily focussing on deficiencies and problems. Regardless of the design for implementation, educational leaders need to create opportunities for families and communities to become part of the solutions. It seems clear that school systems neither can, nor should, be burdened with as much responsibility for rearing students as they have in the past few decades.

TRANSFORMATIONAL LEADERSHIP

Over the past decade, the role of the principal has evolved from instructional manager to instructional leader to transformational leader. Transformational leadership focuses on building a shared vision, improving communication and making decisions collaboratively. Begley (1994) presented a profile of school leadership in Canada for the 1990's and outlined five key leadership dimensions: manager, instructional leader/programme facilitator, school-community facilitator, visionary and problem solver. My recent work as a principal has included all of these dimensions.

This transformational view of leadership places special emphasis on the principal's role in leading other leaders, in school-based management and in acknowledging the changing relationships between the principal and the staff, parents and members of the community. Such leadership creates bonds among leaders and followers within a collaborative change process which results in a more responsive and innovative environment. The notion that transformational leadership behaviours come into their own in times of growth, reform and crisis has been typical of my recent experience.

Consistent with this perspective, the Indiana Principals' Leadership Academy, an American leadership development programme, has endeavoured to inculcate a transformational view of the principalship. The programme was designed to assist principals to function as "a leader of instructors as well as an efficient manager; a team player with strengthened communication and leadership skills; a role model of personal and professional improvement; and a key change agent in the improvement of school environment, curriculum and instruction".

SURVIVING IN EDUCATIONAL LEADERSHIP

School leadership involves "extensive face-to-face communication, is action oriented, is reactive, the presented problems are unpredictable, decisions frequently are made without accurate or complete information, the work occurs in a setting of immediacy, the pace is rapid, there are frequent interruptions, work episodes themselves tend to be of very brief duration, responses often cannot be put off until later, resolution of problems often involves multiple actors, and the work is characterised by a pervasive pressure to maintain a peaceful and smoothly running school in the face of a great deal of ambiguity and uncertainty". Even though many educational leaders have brought a strong sense of purpose and a personal resiliency to their work and the challenges are attractive to them, contemporary educational leadership definitely requires learning throughout their lives. It appears essential for educational leaders to place the highest priority on being both learners and teachers while also knowing how to take care of themselves in the political arena.

EDUCATIONAL LEADERSHIP DEVELOPMENT

GROWTH IN EDUCATIONAL LEADERSHIP DEVELOPMENT PROGRAMMING

During the 1980's the field of school leadership development became a growth industry in the North America, Europe, Australia and parts of Asia. Prior to this time, professional development for school leaders was generally one or more of three basic types: attendance at the national convention of the individual's professional association, enrolment in university graduate courses taken to earn an advanced degree or to gain salary increments, or participation in staff development offered in conjunction with government curricula or instructional programmes. None have proved to be powerful approaches for developing the leadership capabilities of school administrators. "They were not designed to enable administrators to thrive in the job, implement complex reforms or engage in ongoing, school-based improvement".

Under the leadership of Roland Barth, the Harvard Principals' Center was developed to meet needs expressed by principals for ongoing professional growth and development. This centre cultivated experiences and activities that were consistent with the problems, pressures and demands experienced by principals in their schools. Because of positive responses from participants, variations of the Harvard model were adopted by emerging leadership development centres in a variety of countries. These principal-led centres were characterised by high levels of client involvement in the identification of needs and goals, in formal governance, and in the design and delivery of training.

At the same time, administrative training also represented a potential solution for educational policy makers under siege. Research regarding organisational change was unequivocal concerning the critical initiation and support roles played by educational leaders. Policy makers came to view administrative training as an instrument for implementing education reforms, and they also began to initiate leadership academies in various states. In these state-initiated and funded academies, organisational needs rather than individual needs were the primary basis for programme development.

The United States federal government invested over 30 million dollars in school leadership development between 1986 and 1990; by 1990 over 150 principals' centres, school leadership development units or state leadership academies had emerged. Programmes were also being sponsored by school districts, research and development laboratories, universities, professional associations and private agencies. Similar growth was shown in other countries. Along with the growth in the number of service providers was an increased variation in programme design and delivery. "Market pressure for instructional improvement led programmes to focus on school improvement, instructional leadership, effective schools, and instructional supervision". Programmes evolved away from a didactic model of instruction and were oriented towards the work of administrators.

LEADERSHIP DEVELOPMENT PROGRAMME EVALUATION

If skill development and implementation are the main goals of leadership development programmes, then a particular form of summative evaluation is needed. If normative change and personal and professional renewal represent primary goals then quite a different evaluation is warranted. Questions which need to be addressed by all leadership development programmes include: "how training interventions influence the development of school leadership, how that leadership is subsequently exercised in the workplace, and what is the impact of that leadership on the school".

Despite the growth in leadership development programming, little systematic research has been conducted on either the operation or outcomes of these programmes. Policy makers have concentrated available resources for services to clients rather than on the evaluation of programmes. Generally, the effectiveness of these new approaches to school leadership development cannot be confirmed, despite their broadly-based support among practitioners and policy makers.

Researchers have described the issues and dilemmas that evaluators face in the field of educational leadership. They have cited the difficulties in isolating the effects of leadership training on the local organisations in which principals work. "Evaluation of impact is even more problematic during a period of shifting priorities in the school's policy environment. Given the implementation of multiple policies and programmes during this same period of time, it is possible that factors other than participation in the training programme may better explain eventual developments" (Ekholm, 1992, p. 383). Empirical evaluations of administrative training programmes, if undertaken at all, have generally been designed so that causal inferences concerning programme effects are speculative at best. "This shortcoming has forced policy makers and practitioners to rely on preconceptions and faith that leadership development was actually making a difference in the lives of school administrators and their schools" (Hallinger, 1992, p. 300).

Considering the lucrative business perspective involved with educational leadership development, there may also be other reasons for limited evaluation. "In a field where there have been few documented cases of demonstrable performance improvement and accountability is low, there is no reason to expect service providers to seek formal feedback" (Wallace, 1992, p. 348).

RESTRUCTURING EDUCATIONAL ADMINISTRATOR TRAINING PROGRAMMES

According to some perspectives "a number of educational administration curricula have remained relatively unchanged for decades because these university departments are by nature conservative and inherently resistant to change". Scholarship in educational administration has tended to accept theories developed in non-school contexts as appropriate for the study of school leadership (Greenfield, 1995). Although many of those ideas were useful, they were often very abstract and were not context sensitive. Common concerns related to traditional models of administrator training appear to transcend both national boundaries and the type of training approach used. Bjork and Ginsberg (1995) enumerated issues of concern:

the problem of matching training with practitioner needs; the lack of evaluation of individuals holding administrative positions; the success of training as measured by the satisfaction of the participants; the tension between academic versus practice-oriented content and materials; the lack of school experience of academics; the disparate quality of the curriculum; the lack of research in school administration outside of the United States, Canada and Australia; the tenuous assumption that good and effective administrators are good teachers of school management; the lack of a specification of qualifications and definition of duties of the principal.

Studies regarding traditional patterns of administrator training have found that innovations are needed in both the content and the process of the training.

Recently the professional preparation of aspiring principals has begun to reflect an increased responsiveness to the work that they are expected to perform. There appears to be a movement away from the managerial, authoritarian and top-down leadership styles that were typically associated with the science of educational administration. "The transition towards collegial and empowering forms of leadership has been catalysed by a reconceptualization of the principal's role, debates about the congruence between theory and practice, and efforts to link training experiences with school-based practice". Both theoretical and empirical evidence also have indicated the need for increasing the use of appropriate alternative instructional strategies, including simulations, case studies, practice-based and problem-based models, more complete integration of field-based activities and more student-centred rather than professor-centred instructional approaches in developing educational leaders (Bjork and Ginsberg, 1995). There is also a serious interest in establishing more formal relationships with school districts (Bjork and Ginsberg, 1995).

A number of researchers have shifted their attention to theories of human cognition as a better way of explaining the nature of educational leadership. Some professors of educational administration are experimenting with problem-based instructional approaches as one response to the challenge of situating administrative learning experiences within relevant contexts. Problem-based learning has been used as a cognitive apprenticeship in the educational administrator preparation programme at the University of Connecticut (Cordeiro and Campbell, 1995). An extended apprenticeship with at least one practising expert administrator has been a key programme component. "Other components include a reflective practicum, cohort learning involving research teams, and the integration of both simulated and authentic problem-based learning projects". Recent efforts to align training and actual practice are being reflected by an emphasis on the development of group processing skills, collaborative leadership styles and communication skills, participatory decision making, consensus building, reflective thinking and mentoring (Behar-Horenstein, 1995). These changes are consistent with reforms in other professional preparation programmes including medicine, business, law, architecture and pharmacy (Leithwood and Steinbach, 1992; Novak, 1992).

In the United States, a group of universities have founded the National Alliance for Restructuring Graduate Education Administration Programmes to focus on changing programmes of principal preparation, assessing the applicability of the NASSP training material, and disseminating their findings among other universities to encourage departments to consider revising their programmes (Behar-Horenstein, 1995). Newly reconstituted departments have been renamed departments of educational leadership, and redesigned programmes have been formulated to promote an holistic approach. "Their vision for preparing prospective principals attempts to include a carefully conceived balance of knowledge and interpersonal skills that will enable leaders to effectively guide change, explore innovative ways to cope with the challenges posed by our changing society, and support individuals who are reluctant to move towards less traditional models of schooling".

PERSONAL REFLECTIONS ON LEADERSHIP DEVELOPMENT

In my tenure as an elementary and middle school principal, several experiences have been key to my own leadership development. My reflections on these experiences may also provide some assistance in programme design. In one experience, I was given the task of closing an existing elementary school, overseeing renovations to the building, and organising a new middle school which was also being developed as a technology project site for our province. An advisory committee was organised to guide project development with membership from the provincial university communities, teachers' and trustees' organisations, corporate partners, local and provincial government, parents and the local school district. My experiences during the six years of involvement with this project prompted me to reexamine my perceptions of the role of the principal, the nature of effective staff development, and the competencies required of educational leaders.

The aspects of this leadership development experience which had most impact on my professional growth included:

- Our regularly scheduled advisory committee meetings with various stakeholders which modelled the collaborative processes that we attempted to transfer to the daily operation of the school,
- Our advisory committee meetings, our presentations at conferences, our technology mini-conferences, our visits to other technology projects, and the visitors to our school which provided a refreshing

perspective on the technology developments in our school and on the possibilities for technology which appeared outside our educational sphere,

- Being part of action research regarding our project which was organised by a professor from the University of Regina,
- The sense of accountability and urgency which the project created, (or "being in a fishbowl" as our staff described it), with regards to implementing various aspects of middle school philosophy and to technology integration into curriculum and instruction,
- Being involved in a mentoring relationship with both the research professor and our director of education who asked challenging questions, provided intriguing reading material, but allowed me the flexibility to pursue issues about which I was passionate.

In another instance, I was required to become part of an instructional improvement and employee assistance plan for a staff member. This situation required considerable investment by the teacher, a colleague of the teacher, a Saskatchewan Teachers' Federation executive assistant, our director of education and me in restructuring beliefs about teaching and student learning, in changing personal organisational and planning processes, and in redesigning instruction and evaluation strategies. While the improvement plan involved a variety of other elements, I participated in approximately five hours of observation and conferencing each week with the teacher for an entire year. In addition there were many other meetings with the teacher, the colleague, the executive assistant and the director. At the end of year, I was required to write a report documenting our work, describing the instructional improvement of the teacher and making recommendations for the future placement of the teacher.

The aspects of this leadership development experience which had most impact on my professional growth included:

- Being involved in a mentoring relationship with both the executive assistant and our director of education who provided expertise in staff development and created a heightened sense of accountability for my work with the teacher,
- Revisiting counselling theory and its application to integrate a much wider variety of staff development and supervisory strategies than I was accustomed to using,
- Being responsible for mentoring a staff member required reflection on the validity of my beliefs, organisational techniques and instructional strategies,
- Grappling with the ethics of working on a real, but exceptionally complex and confidential, issue using a collaborative approach.

In a third situation, I became part of reviewing school system policy regarding teacher supervision, evaluation and employee assistance at the same time as developing system policy for administrator supervision, evaluation and employee assistance. Considering it an opportunity to learn something and to also improve present practice, I volunteered to chair the committee reviewing the teacher professional growth policy. This committee included teachers, consultants and both school-based and central office administrators. We were constrained only by school board regulations for policy review. Because of what seemed to be obvious connections with teacher professional growth and because I had not received any sort of comprehensive, written assessment of my ten years of work as principal, I also volunteered to be a member of the committee to develop system policy for administrative appraisal. In creating the administrative appraisal policy, our committee developed a local profile for leadership using the process described by Begley (1995).

The aspects of this leadership development experience which had most impact on my professional growth included:

- The opportunity to do action research on a topic of personal interest which would have immediate impact on professional practice,
- Working collaboratively with a group of experienced, knowledgeable staff who came from diverse perspectives.

In the fourth experience, I began searching for technical assistance related to computer networks and in the process developed an informal partnership with a family who eventually provided invaluable assistance to our entire school system.

Because of a suggestion from a staff member, I invited a parent from one of our feeder schools, who also happened to be one of the network managers for a local telecommunications company, to visit our school. I asked for his suggestions, and he volunteered to show me his company's network system. His interest in computers and in the technology opportunities his children would have in our system was combined with my need for practical, inexpensive solutions to computer access for students and staff. I also was very curious about how technology was being used in business.

During the course of this 4-year partnership, he (with the assistance of his wife and daughters) planned our network restructuring, helped install nearly 50 new computers, created an intranet web site for our school, provided inservice to our staff, organised a computer club for our students, and was an on-call technology trouble shooter for our school. Most of this assistance happened on a volunteer basis in the evenings and on weekends where we worked together with one or two other staff members.

In return he learned about technology in an educational setting, had a reason to learn HTML programming, developed skills as technology trainer for teachers, and a gained a reputation of technology guru. As a result of his work with our school, he was hired for a short term as a consultant to upgrade the networks in our system and to provide some training. Now, he is currently employed by our school district as the system technology coordinator and also coordinates the community Internet access for our city.

The aspects of this leadership development experience which had most impact on my professional growth included:

- Searching for creative, inexpensive solutions to educational issues by working with community resources,
- Working collaboratively with a group of experienced, knowledgeable individuals who came from very diverse perspectives,
- Being involved in a mentoring relationship with individuals who provided expertise in technology and at the same time being a mentor to those same individuals regarding education systems and instructional strategies.

These were all active, authentic, collaborative, supervised learning experiences in an environment which promoted creative thought and risk-taking behaviours. There were a variety of perspectives presented and norms to support openness of information and sharing of expertise. There was also considerable coaching or mentoring involved. Each of these experiences required that I be reflective and present my findings in a written format, but the learning was accomplished through intense, face-to-face interpersonal interactions.

4

Strategy of Effective Leadership Development

The most important thing to understand about great leadership development is that it is not a programme. Great leadership development is a strategy and culture. As part of Brandon Hall's Analyst Insight programme, it received a recent member question concerning leadership development. The member wanted to know the benefits or disadvantages of creating a GE-style leadership programme that takes recent MBA graduates and rotates them through the organization for a year or more with a focus on learning an organization's culture and succession planning. The idea sounds great—but what works for GE may very well be a disaster for a smaller, less global organization. The real value of looking at case studies or industry examples is not simply for imitation purposes, but rather to identify those nuggets of brilliance that are relevant to your specific organizations situation and context.

Warren G. Bennis, the founding chairman of The Leadership Institute at the University of Southern California, said, "The most dangerous leadership myth is that leaders are born—that there is a genetic factor to leadership. This myth asserts that people simply either have certain charismatic qualities or not. That's non-sense; in fact, the opposite is true. Leaders are made rather than born." Although research doesn't prove the effectiveness of specific programmes, many organizations do have leadership development strategies.

If leaders are truly made rather than born, how are you creating new leaders in your organization? Every organization understands the value of leadership, and any employee being led can tell you whether or not their company has effective leadership. The most important thing to understand about great leadership development is that it is not a programme. Great leadership development is a strategy and culture. A leadership development strategy defines the goals and expectations for leaders in your organization. It also defines the key capabilities, competencies, and experiences of a successful leader in your organization. Those definitions drive leadership selection, rewards, and the various supporting development programmes. Managed in this strategic way, leadership development becomes more than simple lip service for your organization. When an organization has defined the strategy and culture for leadership development, then requirements for the supporting development programmes become easier to recognize.

These requirements generally include:

- Target audiences
- Selection processes
- Prerequisites
- Programme levels
- Learning methodologies
- Key success indicators
- Support
- Communication needs

The first step for a company considering a leadership development programme is to focus on its target audience. Do you want to create a GE-style programme that takes recent MBA graduates and rotates them through the organization for a year or more with a focus on learning an organization's culture and succession planning? Or do you want to develop a programme for your current employees to build their leadership skills in their current positions in a programme available to everyone? Review the talent needs of your organization and determine how you find, encourage, and promote successful leaders, then focus on developing those individuals.

Once you determine your audience, create your goals and determine the best way to achieve them. There are many options for delivering leadership programmes. Do you want a blended programme with online modules, coursework, and videos? Will a two-day, face-to-face workshop fit your needs? Do you want information that is specific to your organization and its culture or do you focus on timeless leadership exercises and ideas useful for anyone in any position at any organization? Even though you are excited about your programmes and developing your chosen audience, don't forget the most important part for success. Successful programmes start with a strategy and business value. Your executive leadership team, HR department, and front-line leadership need to be on board and believe the vision and value.

WHAT IS AN EFFECTIVE LEADER?

If you Google the word leader, you get more than 300 million hits. On Amazon, there are 480,881 books today whose topics have to do with leaders. It doesn't help to go to Wikipedia to get a clearer definition because, right off the bat, 11 different types of leaders are named, from bureaucratic to transformational, to laissez-faire. In the field of leadership, there are as many opinions as there are writers, and there is also a lack of common language and tools.

So it's no wonder that if you ask any roomful of leaders or potential leaders what effective leaders need to be, know, or do, you get as many answers as there are people in the room. We believe that it is time to bring together decades of theorizing about leadership: we need to simplify and synthesize rather than generate more complexity and confusion.

From the body of interviews we conducted, we concluded that 60 to 70 per cent of leadership effectiveness would be revealed in a code—if we could crack it! Synthesizing the data, the interviews, and our own research and experience, we emerged with a framework that we simply call the Leadership Code made up of The Five Rules of Leadership. These make up leadership DNA.

THE FIVE RULES OF LEADERSHIP

1. Shape the future. This rule is embodied in the strategist dimension of the leader. Strategists answer the question, "Where are we going?" and they make sure that those around them understand the direction as well. They figure out where the organization needs to go to succeed; they test these ideas pragmatically against current resources (money, people, organizational capabilities); and they work with others to figure out how to get from the present to the desired future. Strategists have a vision about the future and are able to position their organizations to create and respond to that future. The rules for strategists are about creating, defining, and delivering principles of what can be.
2. Make things happen. Turn what you know into what you do. The executor dimension of the leader focuses on the question, "How will we make sure we get to where we are going?" Executors translate strategy into action and put the systems in place for others to do the same. Executors understand how to make change happy, assign accountability, know which key decisions to take and which to delegate, and make sure that teams work well together. They keep promises to multiple stakeholders. The rules for executors revolve around discipline for getting things done and the technical expertise to get the right things done right.
3. Engage today's talent. Leaders who optimize talent answer the question, "Who goes with us on our business journey?" Talent managers know how to identify, build, and engage talent to get results now. They identify what skills are required, draw talent to their organizations, engage these people, communicate extensively, and ensure that employees turn in their best efforts. Talent managers generate intense personal, professional, and organizational loyalty. The rules for talent managers center on resolutions that help people develop themselves for the good of the organization.

4. Build the next generation. Leaders who are human capital developers answer the question, "Who stays and sustains the organization for the next generation?" Talent managers ensure shorter-term results through people, while human capital developers ensure that the organization has the longerterm competencies required for future strategic success; they ensure that the organization will outlive any single individual. Just as good parents invest in helping their children succeed, human capital developers help future leaders be successful. Throughout the organization, they build a workforce plan focused on future talent, understand how to develop that talent, and help employees see their future careers within the company. Human capital developers install rules that demonstrate a pledge to building the next generation of talent.
5. Invest in yourself. At the heart of the Leadership Code—literally and figuratively—is personal proficiency. Effective leaders cannot be reduced to what they know or what they do. Who they are as human beings has everything to do with how much they can accomplish with and through other people.

Leaders are learners: from success, failure, assignments, books, classes, people, and life itself. Passionate about their beliefs and interests, they expend enormous personal energy on and give great attention to whatever matters to them. Effective leaders inspire loyalty and goodwill in others because they themselves act with integrity and trust. Decisive and impassioned, they are capable of bold and courageous moves. Confident in their ability to deal with situations as they arise, they can tolerate ambiguity. Over the last few years that we have worked with these five rules of leadership, we have come to some summary observations:

All leaders must excel at personal proficiency. Without the foundation of trust and credibility, you cannot ask others to follow you. While individuals may have different styles (introvert/extrovert, intuitive/sensing, etc.), an individual leader must be seen as having personal proficiency to engage followers. This is probably the toughest of the five domains to train and some individuals are naturally more capable than others.

All leaders must have one towering strength. Most successful leaders assume at least one of the four roles in which they excel and most are personally predisposed to one of the four areas. These are the signature strengths of your leaders. Each leader must be at least average in his or her "weaker" leadership domains. It is possible to train someone to learn how to be strategic, execute, manage talent, and develop future talent. There are behaviours and skills in each domain that can be identified, developed, and mastered. Leaders must be able to grow. The higher up the organization that the leader rises, the more he or she needs to develop excellence in more than one of the four domains.

BUILDING AN EFFECTIVE LEADERSHIP DEVELOPMENT PLAN

All organizations need strong leaders. And, as research continues to support, organizations with formal leadership development programmes in place are far more likely to have the highest calibre talent at the helm in the future. Other benefits of such programmes include higher retention rates, significant cost-savings and better financial outcomes. Nonetheless, broader industry data from Bersin by Deloitte, Aberdeen Research and the Center for Creative Leadership, among others, has revealed that many organizations still struggle in developing and executing leadership development programmes.

In fact, nearly half of those who participated in a recent newsletter survey on this very issue reported that a lack of a formal leadership development programme is the biggest challenge their organizations face to identifying and developing leaders.

In response, here are six elements that organizations can consider when building effective leadership development programmes:

1. Define what leadership looks like in your organization. The best place to start this evaluation is with your current "successful leaders." Determine the specific characteristics that make certain individuals stand-out in terms of their skills, behaviours and performance. Define a core set of competencies and determine what gaps may exist between the abilities you will need in a leader and what you currently have. Any subsequent leadership development programme needs to be built around the skills and behaviours related to those competencies.
2. Consider the company culture. Leadership is just as much about skill as it is about "fit." After all, one of the main reasons more than half of new CEOs don't make it to their fourth anniversary is poor organizational fit. Therefore, organizations with superior leadership development programmes dedicate as much time analyzing internal people and cultural dynamics as they do the external environment.
3. Build the infrastructure. Determine what tools, processes and people you will need in place to help identify, develop and retain future leadership talent. The use of psychological and behavioural assessments for instance, has been statistically linked to current and future success in leadership roles. Other considerations should include how development and training will be delivered (*e.g.* formal programmes, on-the-job "stretch" assignments, etc.) and the potential expenditures. Understand which existing leaders and decision-makers need to be involved in the process, and at what stages. Finally, set forth a plan for evaluating and measuring programme effectiveness.
4. Identify high potential talent inside the organization. Who

demonstrates the greatest potential for future organizational impact? Insight from performance management appraisals, behavioural assessment data and direct conversations with employees can help identify these individuals. Be sure to look at all levels of the organization. As a Bersin study notes, "leadership development is not about developing one leader at a time or even one leader level at a time. Rather, it is about looking across all leader levels and creating a strategy to build leadership capabilities across that population and often across multiple geographies."

5. Make leadership development the business imperative. Identifying and cultivating leaders, closing talent gaps and succession planning must be viewed as a corporate-wide initiative. Aberdeen's Leadership Study found that Best-in-Class organizations abide by a culture and mindset where the development of a strong leadership pipeline is the responsibility of everyone in the organization, not just something that HR must do in a vacuum. Without support at all levels, the foundation built to accelerate leadership development will collapse.
6. Make leadership levels a choice, but develop at all levels. The best leaders choose to lead, and individuals may find that their niche is at the individual level, managing others, or managing an entire enterprise. Regardless of whether you're developing leaders of others or the C-level, ensure that they have the coaching and training they need.

While most organizations recognize the importance of establishing a leadership development plan, those that take the necessary steps to create a formal process will benefit from a keen competitive advantage in the future marketplace.

DEVELOPING LEADERSHIP STRATEGY

ORGANIZATIONS HAVE TEACHABLE MOMENTS TOO.

Much has been written about the importance of providing developmental opportunities for individuals at the appropriate "teachable moment." There is ample evidence that managers benefit more from educational experiences that are "just in time" for them to use them rather than "just in case" they eventually need a new set of skills. These moments often occur when individuals have just been asked to change their identities-*i.e.*, become managers rather than individual contributors, managers of managers, or general managers with overall operational responsibility for a business unit. Similarly, organizations seem to have moments when the development and articulation of a leadership strategy are especially appropriate. In our research, it appears that these opportunities generally occur when there is a new CEO who wishes to align the organization around a new strategy, when two organizations have merged, or when there is a significant organizational crisis.

For example, when Jim Owens became CEO of Caterpillar in 2004, one of his early decisions was to empower the Leadership College of Caterpillar University to create a "Leadership Quest" programme for the firm's high potentials. This programme built on an earlier initiative that created the firm's "leadership framework" or competency model and was intended, according to Owens, to "give our next generation of leaders an infusion of 'yellow blood'." In 2002, Washington Group International (WGI) emerged from Chapter 11 with a four-person "Office of the Chairman" headed by Stephen Hanks as CEO and a new three-fold mission statement that identified "people" and their development as first priority. According to Hanks, "The company that develops talent the fastest will take the hill."cEach benchmark company used a key organizational transition to develop, articulate, and align a new leadership strategy with the strategic direction of the firm. These transitions became teachable moments for the organization and formed crucial starting points for achieving excellence in leader development.

LINKING CORPORATE STRATEGY AND LEADERSHIP DEVELOPMENT STRATEGY CREATES WINNERS

The direct link between a leadership development strategy and corporate strategy provides great benefit to an organization and its employees. Alignment with the corporate strategy is clearly a key concept for successful leadership development. Organizations that realize this establish a leader development philosophy that permeates all levels of the organization and is meaningful to all employees. At Caterpillar, alignment is achieved by receiving input from the executive office, business units, and process owners of the critical success factors. To further embed leadership development into the business strategy, metrics were established to connect leadership to the business. PwC links development activities to its strategy to become the "distinctive firm." Programmes that are successful are designed to reinforce corporate strategy, thus ensuring linkage and success. PepsiCo's leadership development strategy is grounded in the belief that strong leaders are needed for success in the marketplace. As these short examples show, each benchmark company worked hard to ensure that emerging leaders are prepared for the future and its realities and not bogged down with the past.

EXECUTIVES USE LEADERSHIP DEVELOPMENT AS A POWERFUL TOOL TO FORMULATE, TRANSLATE, AND COMMUNICATE STRATEGY

While education is a relatively small portion of the entire developmental process for leaders, carefully crafted learning initiatives can be important in providing input from throughout the organization, effectively communicating the reasons for and implications of corporate strategy to managers who will need to translate the strategy for employees throughout the organization so they understand their role in making it happen.

Various studies have concluded that 60 to 70 per cent of all strategies fail to be successfully implemented.[1] Our benchmark companies seem to have discovered that one way to beat these odds is to ensure that everyone in the organization understands the strategy, the reasons for it, and their role in making the strategy happen. These companies also understand that effective developmental activities can be an effective means of sharing the information and providing some of the tools for successful implementation.

LEAN COMPETENCY MODELS AND VALUES ARE THE FOUNDATIONS OF STRATEGIC LEADERSHIP DEVELOPMENT

A simple leadership model with a concise statement of values serves as an important point of focus in leadership development. None of the best practice partners had a "scientifically valid" competency model; most had created their own or adapted it from a set of competencies developed by an outside firm. The benchmark companies in our research kept their values and competencies simple and straightforward, understanding that competencies should apply at all levels within an organization and directly lead to better performance.

BUILDING AN INTEGRATED ARCHITECTURE FOR STRATEGIC LEADERSHIP DEVELOPMENT

STRATEGIC LEADERSHIP DEVELOPMENT IS A PARTNERSHIP BETWEEN SENIOR EXECUTIVES AND MULTIPLE HUMAN RESOURCE SYSTEMS

Senior executive support, usually starting with the CEO, is vital for success in strategic leadership development. Yet, even the most effective CEO cannot assure success without the involvement of the entire human resource system. Conversely, training and education professionals will not be successful unless they reach out and collaborate with their colleagues in line positions and in other human resource specialties. For example, within Cisco's HR function, the organization's Worldwide Leadership Education group works with leaders to identify candidates for its leadership development programmes. Executives then help to design the programmes, ensuring that the programme meets business needs and aligns with strategy.

At Washington Group International, corporate leadership and the business units share responsibility for leadership development. The development and strategy office is responsible for the design, development, implementation, and maintenance of the programmes while the office of the chairman reviews, approves, and provides feedback on moving forward with development. The 14-member senior executive leadership team meets regularly to discuss leadership development. As leadership development increases in importance in corporations, partnerships with executives and HR must continue to be strengthened in order for these efforts to succeed.

STRATEGIC HUMAN RESOURCE DEVELOPMENT (HRD) IS A KEY PART OF THE CORPORATE PLANNING CYCLE

Another test for determining if developing leaders is a strategic priority for a company is whether there is a HRD component to the planning cycle. The benchmark companies in this study make people planning something that every key executive is expected to address in concert with their human resource partners (usually including succession planning) and their immediate superior. In other words, it makes sense to consider what key players are expected to implement the strategy and what assistance they need to enhance the probability of success.

Washington Group International leverages its annual strategic and business planning sessions to discuss employee development and leadership development needs for the organization. Similarly PepsiCo's career growth model aligns with the organization's annual operating calendar. These last two findings lead to a strong conclusion that the successful development of leaders requires a strategic alignment of planning and all human resource systems.

HRD CAN WIN THE SUPPORT OF TOP MANAGEMENT BY INVOLVING THEM IN STRATEGIC LEARNING INITIATIVES AND BY KNOWING THE BUSINESS

Most of the exemplars in this study have a high degree of executive involvement in the delivery of key corporate programmes. Similarly, executive involvement in programmatic design can ensure that programme content addresses topics of genuine concern to this key constituency and can contribute to higher levels of support for the ongoing initiative. At Cisco Systems, each programme has an established cross-functional steering committee that ensures linkage between the programme and the business. The business leaders on the steering committees help drive the design of the programmes and recruit appropriate executives into the classrooms

A Board of Governors for Caterpillar University includes the CEO and senior executives who approve learning budgets and priorities as well as determine policy. An advisory board for each college includes senior leaders from business or "user" groups. This group has a geographic and subject matter mix and membership from most of CAT's business units. While it is important to involve line executives who have a deep understanding of the business challenges facing an organization, this is not enough to ensure programmatic success. Successful HRD partners must also understand the business as well as leading edge leadership concepts.

LEADERS WHO TEACH ARE MORE EFFECTIVE THAN THOSE WHO TELL

One of the surprising findings of this project was the degree to which senior executives practice the concept of "leading by teaching." At PepsiCo Paul Russell, Senior VP of Corporate Training and Development, speaks of "the magic of leaders developing leaders." According to Russell, the missing adult learning principle is that, "People learn best when they get to learn from someone they really want to learn from! At PepsiCo, the 'teachers' our executives want to learn from are our own senior leaders. They are world class, widely respected and have proven that they can do it HERE!" Senior executives are asked to share their personal perspectives, build participant confidence and skills while demonstrating support for their growth. Of equal importance, senior leaders get greater teamwork from participants and get to know key young leaders, while developing more loyalty, motivation, productivity, and better alignment around vision and key strategic initiatives.

CORPORATE LEARNING INITIATIVES TEND TO FOCUS ON HIGH POTENTIALS

Substantial organizational impact can be gained by involving small numbers of people with high potential who will return to their regular jobs and translate their learning for others in various operations. Similarly, many key corporate programmes can be adapted by business groups who wish to provide a similar experience for their key people that align with the corporate emphasis.

While PricewaterhouseCoopers designed its PwC University experience for 2000 U.S. partners, and Caterpillar involved all managers in their 2005 strategy rollout, most key corporate initiatives in our study were focused on high potentials. Caterpillar's Leadership Quest involves approximately 50 key mid-level leaders per year. PepsiCo's CEO programme involves approximately 40 high potentials each year. Washington Group International's Leadership Excellence and Performance (LEAP) project began in 2002 and had graduated 48 participants by mid-2006. Cisco's Executive Leader Programme focuses on the company's strategic intent and serves approximately 40 top leaders annually. This programme was designed for employees who are newly promoted to the vice-presidential level, or who are filling a vice-presidential role.

IMPLEMENTING SUCCESSFUL, STRATEGIC LEADERSHIP DEVELOPMENT

HRD OWNS THE PROCESS AND MAINTAINS STRATEGIC CONTROL

A somewhat surprising finding was the degree to which the exemplar firms maintained control of the design and delivery of their leadership development programmes while leveraging input from trusted outside partners or advisors. All had relatively small staffs for the HRD function, yet had delegated relatively little control to outsiders. Since PwC is a professional services firm, it has a greater involvement with outside professionals-it believes their partners' time can be better spent on helping their own clients than trying to become experts in HRD. PwC's Learning and Education Group has a very small group involved in leadership and partner development, which is totally involved in every aspect of their programmes but relies on external vendors for some design and most delivery. Caterpillar works closely with the Hay Group and Duke Corporate Education in key programmes, but leverages the input from outside specialists to provide the latest thinking in leadership initiatives while maintaining a specific business focus for both design and delivery.

HUMAN RESOURCES DEPARTMENTS LEVERAGE THEIR TALENTS WITH THE JUDICIOUS USE OF CONSULTANTS

While leadership development remains firmly under the control of the company, the lean corporate staffs in these benchmark companies leverage their time and talents with the judicious use of outside expertise. Because of the emphasis on knowing the business and on lead staffing, most of the benchmark companies involve outside firms or specialists in both the design and delivery of their learning initiatives. Yet, no matter how busy they are, they never completely turn over either challenge to others.

INTEGRATION OF LEADERSHIP DEVELOPMENT WITH OTHER TALENT MANAGEMENT SYSTEMS CREATES SYNERGIES

Organizations committed to leadership development understand its relationship with other talent management systems and practices. The best-practice partners incorporate their leadership development programmes with others, such as performance reviews, management development, and succession planning. Washington Group International is such a strong proponent of this mindset that they integrate every aspect of talent management. This process begins with establishing a vision of what positions will need to be filled and then forecasting, identifying, and preparing candidates for these positions. Subsequently, employee development plans are carefully crafted for each employee. An overall employee development strategic plan then feeds the succession planning process, which in turn is used in the leadership development programme.

Cisco uses executive coaches to accelerate development as part of its high potential programme. In this programme, high potentials are paired with an external executive coach for a year and even though the coach is an external resource, he or she is fully trained and knowledgeable in "the Cisco way" prior to the assignment.

EVALUATING SUCCESS

DEVELOPING PEOPLE IS A GROWING MEASURE OF EXECUTIVE SUCCESS

Best practice partners take the development of people very seriously. They seem to believe that financial results are a "lagging indicator" of organizational success, while people development is a "leading indicator." Consequently, people development is becoming an important part of the assessment of executive performance. PepsiCo has historically allocated one-third of incentive compensation for developing people with the remainder for results. In 2007, the company is moving to an equal allocation of incentive compensation for people development and results. Pepsi also utilizes the results from its semi-annual climate survey and 360 degree feedback as part of the performance review process.

Caterpillar found that their managers were superb at the "execution" portion of their leadership framework and satisfactory in the "vision" category, but needed to pay more attention to the "legacy" (developmental) set of behaviours. Consequently, they have begun to focus on this theme in learning programmes and in performance assessment.

RETURN ON LEARNING IS INCREASINGLY MEASURED BY CORPORATE SUCCESS RATHER THAN INDIVIDUAL PERFORMANCE

Among our best practice partners, Caterpillar was, perhaps, the most rigorous in attempting to measure the return on its learning investment. Since Caterpillar University was established during a recession, this may have forced them to establish the value proposition for learning early in their history. As part of this proposition, Caterpillar University created a document called the "Business of Learning" where each college developed a value proposition for key initiatives based on net benefits, ROI, and other standards. This later evolved into the enterprise learning plan, a 161-page document that discussed the state of learning at Caterpillar, articulated the value proposition for learning, and estimated the ROI for Caterpillar University at 50 per cent. Caterpillar does not repeat this process for all subsequent iterations of a programme and are beginning to speak about "Return on Learning" (ROL) rather than the more formalized process for ROI.

Cisco collects both quantitative and qualitative measures. Worldwide Leadership Education has a formal system for measuring the outcomes of leadership development strategy. Examples of metrics include "price range for a one week course," "customer satisfaction scores," "percentage of class graduates who have used learnings in their jobs and had a positive impact," and "percentage of learners who stay with the company."

SUCCESSFUL PROGRAMMES ARE A PROCESS RATHER THAN AN EVENT

At one time, corporate educational programmes were a disconnected series of independent events. Today, they are typically part of an integrated career development plan that is tied to strategic objectives with specific, actionable objectives. The Cisco Leadership Series operates in a three-phase structure that facilitates the employee's ability to put learning into action. It is an "events-to-process" model. Employees involved in the various programmes progress through each phase: preparation, programme, and application on the job. While the face-to-face portion of Cisco's programmes may only be five days, the participant is involved in the process for eight to ten months.

Caterpillar's core leadership programmes leverage key transition points in its leaders' careers and build on one another in a building-block fashion. These transitions take place as individuals move from supervisor (*i.e.*, frontline leader), to manager (leader of leaders), to department head, and finally to executive. A person's movement through these programmes and transitions is all part of his or her developmental journey at Caterpillar.

LEADERSHIP THEORIES

AN OVERVIEW IN EVERYDAY LANGUAGE

OK. Why a page on leadership theories? After all, I said that I would help you learn the easy way, and that I would make learning to be a leader a practical process. Yes, that's true. But it will help if you can refer to some of the key theories of leadership, and their assumptions and implications, as you learn the practical things.

My approach to leadership theory is to give you some pointers on this page, and then (as I develop the pages – please be patient) the chance to link into some more detail. If you want to learn more you can then read the original work and even buy the book (t-shirt, baseball hat, etc, if they are available).

The choice is yours. So, here we go.

Naturalistic Theories

Naturalistic theories of leadership were the first to develop. They were built on the idea that leaders were born, not made. The earliest naturalistic theory was not really a theory as such, just a set of beliefs and assumptions. Every so often a society or culture threw up a great person who provided outstanding leadership.

Just think of these examples:

- Jesus Christ, the Messiah promised to the Jews.
- King Arthur, a king who will unite Britain, defeat its foes and return when needed.

- William Wallace, the liberator of Scotland against the English.
- Abraham Lincoln, Who ended slavery in the USA.
- Ghandi, the peace maker who held together the fragile alliance in India at the time of independence.

At the time that people believed this explanation of leadership, in most societies the great leader was normally a man. One example of an exception was Boudicca, the queen of the Icene in ancient Britain. The belief or assumption was that such greatness could not have been learned but was inherent, part of their genetic make up. It was probably hereditary (or so it was believed)! This is one reason why ruling or aristocratic families emerged.

As the scientific method began to be applied to psychology, the study of human behaviour, a new naturalistic approach to leadership theories emerged – trait theory. The trait theory of leadership still assumes that leaders are born, not made. But it sought to identify those personality traits associated with the best leaders, to help understand leadership and to identify people who, ahving the same traits, could (it was assumend) make good leaders. Trait theory still has its adherents. Some psychometric instruments used in the recruitment of leaders were built on the idea of inherent or "built in" traits.

Functional Leadership Theories

Functional leadership theories are based on very different assumptions. They focus on what leaders actually do. That is, their actions or functions. One of the best known and most influential of functional theories of leadership, used in many leadership training programmes, is John Adair's"Action-Centred Leadership". From here it is a short leap to the belief that if one person can do something, then others can learn to do it. We are now in the world of leaders being made, not born. And we open up the possibility of leadership development and planned leadership training.

This question of whether leaders are born or made is part of the whole question of whether human behaviour is due to nature or nurture. Functional theories of leadership are developed by studying successful leaders and identifying the actions and behaviours they show. Large studies with lost of data make it possible to correlate the actions with the successful results.

Situational Leadership Theories

Functional leadership is all very well but it doesn't help us to deal with changes, different situations and the nature of the people being led. Situational theories of leadership were developed to find good ways of adapting leadership actions to meet the needs of different situations and circumstances. One classic situational model of leadership (Hersey and Blanchard) is concerned with identifying the ability (or competence) and willingness (commitment or motivation) of those being led, and then determining the best style of leadership to follow. Other approaches (eg, Lewin,Tannenbaum and Schmidt) suggest of continuums of leadership style.

Leadership style here refers to the broad approach adopted by a leader. A leader's style of leadership is often based on a leader's own beliefs, personality, experiences, working environment and the situation at the time. Some leaders work within one leadership style. Others are more flexible and can adapt their style of leadership to meet the needs of different situations.

Autocratic vs Participative Leadership Theories

These theories of leadership developed out of the concept of leadership style. However, they focus very much on the balance of power between the leader and the followers. Autocratic leaders tend to make decisions and impose them on others. They often believe that they are best placed to make the decisions, that others should accept their authority. Some such leaders have certain personality traits, such as a need to be in control of situations. Autocratic leadership is suited to certain situations, such as emergencies or time critical circumstances. But they don't tend to nurture other people or get the best results from followers who are capable and motivated.

Participative leaders consult others and involve them in the decision making process. They may make the final decision but in consulting others they are demonstrating consideration, respect for others and the ability to listen. The assumption behind this approach is that it tends to be appreciated by followers who return the favour by being loyal and committed. Participative leadership also develops other people and builds support for the overall direction, leading to a shared vision and common goals. Participative leaders often also adopt a facilitative leadership style. That is, they empower and encourage others to take make decisions, take action and act with authority, normally within defined boundaries.

Transactional vs Transformational Leadership Theories

Another way of looking at leadership approaches is to do with the type of work and the relationship between the leader and the follower. Transactional leadership theory is based on transactions or exchanges between the leader and the follower. It assumes that the working relationship is one where the leader issues the work, praises or criticises, rewards or punishes. The follower has little responsibility, other than doing as they are required, correctly. All works well if both leader and follower carry out their part in the transactions as expected. This approach is more often seen in low skilled jobs, where procedures are clearly defined or where there is little change.

Transformational leadership theory is all about change. Transformational leaders inspire others to follow a vision. They create opportunities for people to show flair and to take responsibility for new ideas. They are often very extravert, charismatic and strategic. They see the big picture rather than the detail. They inspire great loyalty, providing they succeed. If they fail, or are seen to be hypocritical, the followers may well become disillusioned or cynical. Transformational leadership is more appropriate in fast changing situations, where people have high levels of skill and where the leader can afford to get involved in the detail.

Moral leadership

Moral approaches to leadership emphasise the role of the leader in various moralistic positions, such as:

- Making the world a better place
- Treating people well
- Caring for the environment
- Religious beliefs
- Being true to, and acting consistently with, one's vision.

Various leadership writers have included moral elements in their work. They tend to suggest that leaders are more likely to be successful if they have a positive impact on others - rather than lead others just to benefit themselves. Politicians and religious leaders, in particular, are expected to be moral leaders, partly because they address the issues above or adopt a moralistic platform. Business leaders are perhaps expected to be less moralistic. However, when they do truly act for the good of others in general, and not just themselves and their shareholders, they tend to be highly regarded.

LEADERSHIP: CULTURAL CONSIDERATIONS AND ENVIRONMENTAL PRESSURES

Leadership may also be seen or understood in light of organizational cultures and the influences of outside or external pressures. Plentiful and widespread literature speaks to these important internal and external nuances and in several differing contexts. The following discussion touches on these subjects in hopes of providing a broader grasp of the meaning of leadership. First, the general distinction or dichotomy of organizations often cited in the literature should be mentioned. Two very different organizational typologies, first clearly identified in 1947 by Max Weber, are frequently denoted. These are 1) the traditional or hierarchical "bureaucracy" type, and 2) the informal or fluid organizational model.

The traditional model organization presents a rigid and structured organization where leadership is strictly oriented downward in a hierarchical and officious arrangement. The configuration here is departmentalized and strictly authoritarian in nature. On the other hand, the informal or fluid model is issue-oriented, flexible, adaptive, and inclusive where leadership is shared and non-linear. The fluid organization is "loose" or non-compartmentalized and encourages leader-follower shared-power arrangements conducive to self-motivation, autonomy, and collective action. Thus, in terms of the public sector, one model tackles public policy and problems in a strict, unbending, procedural way, and the other model addresses public issues and predicaments in a shared, mutual, and a freer or more accommodating way. Two sharply distinct organizational forms—two very different mindsets, values, processes, and actions.

It should be noted that while these two models are diametrically opposed to one another, still some experts agree that an organization can contain a "blend" of the two. In some large institutions, for instance, hierarchical arrangements exist but also pockets of shared- power structures exist as well. The U.S. Department of Defence generally is pointed out as a case in point of the blending of both models. In the DOD, for example, the armed forces command structure is tightly intact, but there also exists special departments that allow for creativity and informal leader-follower structures, such as those that deal with weapons design, strategic planning, and general research and development.

Having made this classic distinction in organizational theory, hierarchical and fluid or shared-power, a look at some of the thoughts contained in contemporary writings on the subject will be constructive at this stage. By way of illustration, Edgar Schein, in his book Organizational Culture and Leadership (1992), states that the term "culture" has over the past ten years come to refer also to the "climate and practices" of organizations. This includes also the "espoused credo and values of an organization." (Schein, Wren ed., 1995, p. 271). He therefore believes, that since this is so, it implies that organizational cultures can also be termed or described as the "right kind of culture," "a culture of quality," "an effective culture," and so on.

This is significant in that it allows for the critical analysis of organizational and leadership styles. Studying an organizational culture, feels Schein, allows for observing the shared "behavioural regularities of a group when they interact; the language used, the customs and traditions that develop, and the rituals that are carried out under certain circumstances". Like an anthropologist, an organizational researcher or consultant can, as such, decipher an organization or leadership style by looking carefully at group norms, values, philosophies, rules of the game (implicit rules for getting along), climate (the physical layout of the organization and lines of communication), and shared meanings (ideas or feelings that are shared). In the end, if these norms, values, behaviours, and rituals are effective ones, (or as Schein puts it, "if the organization and/or its leadership are 'functional' vis-à-vis 'dysfunctional'"), then a correct and useful cultural determination can be made.

Another interesting view of organizational culture and leadership is discussed by authors Terrance Deal and Alan Kennedy (1982). They attempt to describe what constitutes a "strong culture." Deal and Kennedy define organizations as human, living institutions. As they state in their book Corporate Cultures, organizations must be perceived not as "plush buildings, bottom lines, strategic analysis, or five-year plans". Rather, organizations must first be understood as persons, a group of human beings that coexist together in a culture of integrated values, ideas, and customs. A strong culture is one that allows for 1) "a system of informal rules that spells out how people are to behave most of the time, and 2) one that enables people to feel better about what they do, so they are more likely to work harder".

For Deal and Kennedy a strong organizational culture is additionally one that possesses the following characteristics:

- An environment where employees feel secure and are empowered to be creative and take calculated risks;
- An environment where employees "believe in something" (the organization's vision, mission, goals, etc.);
- A workplace where top management actively encourages training and learning experiences;
- An environment that maximizes communication, along lines both vertically and horizontally (*e.g.*, this includes an open door policy that gives employees access to everyone in the organization);
- An environment that regularly exercises ritual, ceremony, and play (*e.g.*, organization-wide celebrations, special recognition for performance excellence, employee team sports events, or informal get-togethers for socializing purposes); and,
- An atmosphere where management reinforces organizational values on a regular basis.

Stephen Harper (2001) affirms these views in his work and study of "visionary" organizations and leadership. He states that it is imperative that organizational strategies must place "a premium on its human resources". He continues by stating that successful organizational cultures are those that foster policies that "attract, motivate, and retain people who are energetic and innovative and who desire to be part of an organization, public or private, that strives to improve services and products and meet emerging needs." Harper highlights the notion of organizations that are sensitive to emerging customer needs. He asserts that visionary executives that look to future opportunities and invest resources in tomorrow's budding needs meet and sustain institutional viability. He observes that Peter Drucker says it is important for an organization and its leadership to be forward-thinking, that is, not only to invest resources in what comprises "today's breadwinners, but also what constitutes tomorrow's breadwinners.".

Finally, a few closing words on environmental pressures. All organizations and leaders face outside or external pressures. More particularly, public sector organizational leaders must be continuously attentive to constituent needs that, by law, are intended or authorized to be addressed. Public leaders must pursue, via the application of resources at their disposal, with the greatest efficiency and effectiveness possible, and with due reasonableness, the public's common good as it presents itself in all of its manifestations. In carrying out these public responsibilities, without fail, various social and economic pressures invariably come to bear and must be contended with in some appropriate manner. Leaders and their organizations must as a result meet these challenges through understanding, competence, and the powers and wherewithal they possess.

Burt Nanus (1992) states that a key to meeting environmental pressures is for leaders to think about the future. He asks essentially, "What are the future environmental threats and opportunities one should be strategically thinking about in order to be prepared to meet tomorrow's challenges?" Nanus declares in his narrative: To start thinking about the future, identify all the categories of relevant developments. For most organizations, these include future changes in the needs and wants served by the organization, in the major stakeholders, and in the economic and social, political, and technological environments. An additional category of "other" is sufficient to catch anything else of importance.

Nanus further offers a useful template of critical questions to ask regarding future and external "developments."

These include seven key questions as follows:

1. Generally speaking, what topmost changes are expected in the needs and desires served by the organization in the future?
2. What are, more specifically, the changes expected as relates to the organization's stakeholders?
3. What changes are expected in the upcoming economic environment?
4. What changes are expected in the social environments of the future?
5. What changes are expected in the shifting political environments?
6. What technologies are to be expected in the future?
7. What "other" major environmental changes are expected that may influence or exert pressures on the organization and its leadership?

LEADERSHIP APPROACHES

Beginning in the year c. 1910, leadership began to be studied or researched in more formal and varying ways. Since then, differing theories or approaches have emerged. According to the literature on leadership theories, many researchers and experts have typically focused on the "narrower aspects" of the concept of leadership and its practices and, as a result, have tended to represent leadership in a partial or limited way. Thus, leadership has frequently been defined and analyzed in a categorical or episodic sense. Gary Yukl, in Leadership in Organizations (3 Edition), identifies these categories (or periods) of leadership research in terms of basically four approaches: 1) the trait approach,

2) the behaviour approach, 3) the power-influence approach, and 4) the situational approach.

Additionally, Yukl recognizes that some researchers have mixed and matched some of these approaches into hybrid-forms of leadership theory and practice. He acknowledges, for example, that some of these "include participative leadership, charismatic leadership, and 'decision group' leadership". In the discussion which follows, these varying leadership approaches will be discussed as based on the works of several experts in leadership theories and their practical applications..

THE TRAIT APPROACH

The early part of the 20 century saw researchers in management studies begin to piece together a leadership theory that placed considerable emphasis on the personal traits or attributes of leaders. The underlying premise of the so-called "trait approach," is that leaders are different from other people in respect to the particular characteristics or traits that they possess. The trait approach states that certain individuals are leaders because they possess extraordinary attributes, such as energy, intellect, persuasiveness, and "uncanny foresight.". Gardner (1993), drawing on the works of Ralph Stogdill, Bernard Bass, and Edwin Hollander, among other experts, provides a taxonomy of attributes as follows: 1) physical vitality and stamina, 2) intelligence and judgement-in-action, 3) willingness (eagerness) to accept responsibilities, 4) task competence, 5) understanding of followers/constituents and their needs, 6) skill in dealing with people, 7) need to achieve, 8) capacity to motivate, 9) courage, resolution, steadiness, 10) capacity to win and hold trust, 11) capacity to manage, decide, set priorities, 12) confidence, 13) ascendance, dominance, assertiveness, and 14) adaptability, flexibility of approach. According to Gardner, it is additionally important to note that a leader is not necessarily one who possesses one or all of these traits, but rather a leader is—per "the trait theory generally applied"—one who comprises some acceptable proportion of the traits mentioned above.

Ralph Stogdill, in 1948, conducted a landmark and comprehensive study of more than 120 trait studies. His conclusion was that no "discernable reliability or coherent patterns existed". This conclusion convinced Stogdill that traits in-and-by themselves were not enough to adequately define and explain the concept of leadership. Resulting evidence and findings eventually affirmed among experts in leadership theory that it was wise to explore personal traits and attributes of leaders in light of other factors such as "behaviours and effectiveness".

THE BEHAVIOURAL APPROACH

In the late 1940s and early 1950s, the study of behaviourism in the fields of psychology and management science began to take hold. Leadership researchers began to identify a host of fairly consistent behavioural patterns among leaders. These included, for instance, styles that eventually took on designations as "autocratic," "democratic," and "laisscz-faire." Hersey and Blanchard (1979) and Chemers (1984) are mentionable researchers in the analysis and critique of the behavioural approach to leadership and these particular styles (autocratic, etc.). It is of interest to note that the autocratic style is, as the name implies, an authoritative and non-participatory approach to leading others. It is normally characterized as control-oriented and inflexible. Conversely, the democratic style is one that encourages participation and equalitarian principles of self-rule. The laissez-faire category is a more hands-off, self-determining, and tolerant approach to leading.

Yukl (1994) states that researchers and experts began to study the behaviour of leaders in two ways. First, they began to look more deliberately and systematically at how leaders actually performed their work. Specifically, leadership researchers evaluated carefully how managers or leaders used their time. This led to the conceptualizing of roles, functions, and duties. Activities of leaders such as planning, organizing, directing, staffing, communicating, etc. took on a new relevance. Second, researchers and experts began to compare these managerial-type functions among leaders to determine who were more or less effective in their jobs. Chemers (1984) states that the main tool for research here was the use of questionnaires, such as the Leader Behaviour Description Questionnaire or LBDQ. Again, similar to the narrow construct of the trait theory, continuing studies found problems with a single approach to explaining and understanding the multi-faceted notion and practice of leadership.

THE POWER-INFLUENCE APPROACH

The power-influence approach is an effort employed by researchers that came about to make sense of what leadership is and its various practices by methodically examining how power is used to sway others. This power-influence approach, especially as regards others, extends not only to subordinates as followers, but also to colleagues or peers, superiors and all other persons inside and outside of an organization (private or public). Thus, this approach "searches to explain leadership effectiveness in terms of the amount and kind of power possessed by the leader and how that power is exercised". Two differing perspectives are taken among researchers and experts utilizing the power-influence approach. The first view is one that encapsulates the proverbial cause and effect relationship, namely, "leaders act and followers react." This is exclusively a one-way relational phenomenon and fits neatly within the confines of behaviourism's autocratic style. The unidirectional equation for this power-influence view might look like this: L > F = FA (Leader influences follower and follower acts). The second view is more of a compatible two-way relationship where the leader and follower exert influence on one another. Hence power resides in both leaders and followers. This fits closely with the behaviourist view of an equalitarian or reciprocal leader-follower relationship.

THE SITUATIONAL-CONTINGENCY APPROACH

A. K. Korman, in 1966, reviewed more than 25 top management and leadership studies of his time. He found that no one leadership approach, by itself, could identify or predict leadership effectiveness because situations change. He concluded, therefore, "this suggests that since situations change, so must leadership styles and approaches". The situational approach to understanding leaders and their actions focuses on several factors. One such factor is the nature or kind of work an organization, or an organizational unit, does or performs. Another closely related factor is of course the particular circumstances and pressures, internal and/or external, which are occurring at any one particular time. A third factor would, according to the literature, involve the "characteristics of followers." In other words, the situational approach is thus a leadership hypothesis that states that leaders (incl., their attendant traits and behaviours) are unavoidably affected by situations that result from organizational cultures, circumstantial influences, and the characteristics (distinctiveness) of followers. A definition or understanding of leaders and their effectiveness, as such, requires the all-important placing of them (leaders) within a "situational" context. Also, Paul Hersey and Kenneth Blanchard have been time after time at the cutting-edge in their analysis and interpretation of the situational approach to leadership. In their view, Hersey and Blanchard place considerable emphasis on the relationship between the leader and his or her followers, while spotlighting the notion of follower "readiness." They define the leadership situational approach in the following way.

Situational Leadership® is an attempt to demonstrate the appropriate relationship between the leader's behaviour and a particular aspect of the situation—the readiness level exhibited by the followers. According to the model, the leader must remain sensitive to the follower's level of readiness. As personal problems arise, new tasks are assigned, or new goals are established, the level of readiness may change. The model prescribes that leaders should adjust their behaviour accordingly. Thus, situational leadership assumes a dynamic interaction where the readiness level of followers may change and where the leader's behaviour must change appropriately in order to maintain the performance of followers. Finally, a closing word on the "contingency" aspect of the situational leader approach. By this it is meant that many researchers use the term situational-contingency when referring to a leader's effectiveness as it relates to differing trait patterns and/or behaviours when they coincide with differing situations. Consequently, variable personal characteristics and behaviours are "optimal" or "more effective" in certain situations than others. This is contrasted with Yukl's more "universal theories" of situational leadership.

5

Better Management and Effective Leadership

IMPORTANT PERSONAL TRAITS OF EFFECTIVE LEADERS

Successful leaders come in a wide variety of personal characteristics such as their ability to make speeches in public or to relate to people in groups or individually. We have all met successful leaders that we wondered what enabled them to be effective. Some are smooth and some are rough. Some are charming and some..... It is impossible to find any one characteristic that all of them have and many non-leaders do not have.

Motivation is the most important characteristic (yes, it can be called a trait) of any leader. Even the shyest person may become a hard charger if something near and dear to them is threatened. I have seen numerous quiet people suddenly find their public voices when NIMBY (not-in-my-backyard) became real to them as some type of development became threatened their back yards. Talk to parents of school age children and many will step out of the quiet shells. After the threat or need passes, some of these people return to their non-public roles, but others find that they have some previously unknown or newly developed skills that can be used in other leadership activities. These will become the community and organizational leaders of the future.

Communications skills are the second most important. If you cannot communicate effectively, you cannot be an effective leader. But as I discuss below, communications is much more than being a good speaker. Despite the great diversity among leaders, there are some characteristics or traits which most successful leaders have. These are the "Traits" listed here. Very few leaders have all of them to the limit, but the most effective leaders will have most of them well developed. A few leaders will have only a few of these traits such persistence or the ability to get people to work together, but they are likely to have those few very well developed.

The fourteen traits described here are the "tools of the trade." Not all of them will be used in every leadership situation, but like other tools, they are available if needed. All of these characteristics can be developed or attained. None are genetic, although some of the traits may be the gifts of wise parents to some very fortunate young people. For many of us, they are the results of hard work over years of time (very slowly developed habits in most cases).

I have talked to many successful politicians, bankers, judges and leaders of many other types, almost to a person they have said that they have worked over the years to further improve their skills. Some have done it through formal classes or sessions with professionals, other through observation and practice; but all have worked at honing their abilities. After looking back over my own struggles to obtain more of these, I have come to strongly believe that almost any person can with sufficient motivation and work develop to a considerable degree all fourteen of the traits. I quickly not that today, I am not a skilled speaker or writer, but I can get my message across. One of favorite activities is selling - of ideas. Turn me lose with a small group and a good idea and I am in close to heaven.

PERSONALITY

1. An outgoing style - the ability and enjoyment of "working the crowd" is a very useful skill both for leadership and many other parts of life. I have a friend who whenever he is in a meeting or a party, makes sure that he shakes every hand and greets every person. Charisma is often thought of as a trait of many leaders. We are not quite sure what charisma is. It is probably the ability of a person to gain very quickly the attention, respect and trust of others. Famous leaders like Martin Luther King and John Kennedy is said to have had charisma. No question, it is an effective tool for leaders in certain situations, but it is difficult to learn.

Humor and warmth are effective in most leadership (and non-leadership) situations. If we are not fortunate enough to have them now, we can develop them. Start by developing agood smile and laugh. This will be hard for many males in our culture who have been acculturated to be stoic with a stone face. Women have a distinct advantage in being encouraged to smile and to show emotions. This will take a long period of consistent self-conscious efforts. My father was a wonderful, but stoic Missouri farmer who smiled little. I, of course, modeled myself after him. Thus, I have worked on my smile for years (still do). The ability to deliver one-liners and tell a few jokes helps also. Joke telling must be done with considerable care. The most effective humor concerns your self. Forgetful jokes work well for me. After all, professors are supposed to be forgetful. Don't tell jokes that put down any group - no ethnic, no mother-in-law jokes, etc. You will lose more than you will win with such jokes.

Another useful characteristic is the ability to remember personal characteristics such as names, items about the family, how many children they have, etc. People like to hear their names. It recognizes them as a unique individual. I suggest taking one or more courses in "acting" for helping to add traits to your personality. We all "play" many different roles every day. Every young person knows the "child" roles as well as parents know the "parenting" role. Learning acting helps us to focus on characteristics of our own personalities by learning to more formally play roles. Some people think of acting as "faking it." The line between "faking" it and real behaviour is thin and hard to define. We must always be sincere; people do not like "acting" in real life. The time to start the change in your personal skills is today.

PERSUASIVE

Communications skills - you must be able to speak effectively in public and in most cases, you must have good writing skills also. You must be able to communicate in the style or jargon of the group or organization. Your message must fit your audience. For example, large words and complex sentences will not work with people of limited formal education. Writing in technical terms may help in a few instances, but writing in clear simple terms helps in almost all cases. Well-educated people can understand simple clear information; but those with limited education cannot go the other way. The old KISS principle (keep it simple - stupid) has much utility.

Words are often not enough. Most people today get most of their information from TV and the most widely read newspaper is USA Today. TV news programmes and USA Today both use simple styles with lots of colour, pictures and graphs. Pictures and other visual aids are especially useful in helping people understand abstract ideas. I strongly encourage you to take every opportunity through courses or informal opportunities to improve your communications skills. These traits, truly, are the bottom line of leadership - with them, successful leadership (and many other types of success) is an open door - without them, success will be a struggle.

PERSISTENCE

Keep trying - most social changes, large and small, is and should be slow. Major changes in values and beliefs often occur between generations. It is unusual for major social changes to occur in less than a few years or even decades. Changes in the educational system often take several decades. If change occurs too fast, people become uncertain about what is "right," good or appropriate. They lose their sense of security. Something as simple as a small change in curriculum of the local school system may take years. But if the idea is good, the results may last decades and effect many people. Also realize that in historical perspective, the changes you are working towards are small and incremental.

Be prepared for an effort of several years when you start the process of bringing about change in your organization or community. A university employs me and universities are very slow to change. For example, we are still teaching using nineteenth century methods even though we are almost in the twenty-first century. The major change has been in some cases, the chairs. Most, but not all, have been changed, but the professor still uses a chalkboard and basically, lectures. Obviously, many people with excellent leadership skills have tried to change the teaching methods, but the rate of change is very slow. It takes about fifty years for a significant change to occur in education. Leadership in major projects will require a large among of stamina and perseverance.

PATIENCE

There are times when you will need to relax and wait for events or time to pass. Many new ideas will become accepted after people have had time to think about them. Most people who are angry or excited about a proposed change will cool down with time. Patience is a hard attribute for many young and not so young to learn. Most things, especially if they are worthwhile, do not happen quickly. Self-discipline is an essential trait for leadership. Patience and persistence are essential twins for getting things done. Always remember it takes time, time for leadership, and time for change. Patience and persistence are very difficult traits for the young. The American culture wants it now - not tomorrow. But the real world does not work that way.

PERCEPTIVE

You must be sensitive to other people's wants and needs and to changes in these wants and needs. Genuine interest in another person will often develop a sense of trust by that person. A gifted politician is one who can carefully always perceive the current mood of his constituents. The ability to listen is an essential skill of a good leader. You must stay in touch with your supporters. If the group is large or unorganized, this is very difficult to do because of the lack of accurate feedback.

As a public leader, I find it difficult to differentiate between isolated concerns about issues which effect only one or a few people and more general concerns. Most people will not take the time to make contact and discuss issues unless the issue becomes important to them. Public leaders also have to aware of organized campaigns by relatively small special interest groups. How large a group or how important an issue do these people really represent? They often have the intent of benefiting only themselves.

PROBITY

Honesty and trustworthy, you need to be honest both now and in the future. Most people will believe and follow someone they trust. Openness and candor are characteristics that most people appreciate. There are a few people who will take advantage of such traits, but the vast majority will appreciate them. The age-old Golden Rule: "Do unto others as you would have them do unto you" is a good standard to follow both today and tomorrow.

Leaders of today are under very careful public scrutiny from the press and the people. Formerly private actions and records are now public. Several potential political appointments have been turned down because of past "sins." You may not plan to be a leader in the future, but events and plans change and you may find yourself unexpectedly in a leadership position. Suddenly, all of your current qualifications and past actions are under scrutiny. How will your college activities or other youthful escapades look in the future when you are seeking the office of _____? President Clinton's problems of trying to explain his youthful marihuana smoking with his famous "but I didn't inhale" statement illustrates the difficulty of justifying past actions. It is very difficult to reclaim a reputation that has been tarnished with charges of dishonesty or other questionable behaviour. I cannot leave this topic without noting that honesty along with some other traits is often more admired than practiced. Indeed, a question can be raised here. People want honesty, but do they also want in the same measure of candor? My observation is that people will say they want to know, but actually prefer not to have details, especially if they may be somewhat disagreeable.

PRAISE GIVING

"Strokes" - almost all people like praise and compliments. Almost everyone likes to be recognized especially if they have worked hard on the project. It may be possible to give too many kind words, but it is very difficult to do so especially if they are given in a sincere manner. If you, a leader, are working with a committee or other team, make absolutely sure that everyone is given full public recognition. If you don't, your support the next time is likely to be much less. The folk saying: "praise in public and criticize in private" is very effective. But the praise should be deserved; a person can quickly develop a reputation as overly "smoothie." Mistakes and errors must be dealt with as quickly as possible. If the errors are part of the public record, then your responses should be public also. However, you should take the public blame. Do not point to some supporter or employee and say: "it was all their fault." If you do, your career as a leader will be short!

Another folk saying that comes to mind: "honey attracts more flies than vinegar." People are more attracted by praise than by criticism and will be willing to work on change if their contributions are acknowledged. I can not say it to strongly, it is very important that people be given recognition for their contributions. A self-effacing leader who gives the credit to his/her supporters will attract many more followers than one who brags on "my" accomplishments. A simple thank you is very effective especially when sincerely given and meant!

POSITIVE ORIENTATION

The future should always be seen as bright and optimistic. Tomorrow will be better than today. Norman Vincent Peale in his best selling book of fifty years ago, The Power of Positive Thinking, contributed to a deeply held American belief about what the future will be like. We as a culture have an aversion to the negative except, paradoxically, in the mass media where the only "news" is defined to be negative stories - what went wrong today - crimes, injures, death and destruction. We prefer the positive in our personal and everyday lives. We want to think that the future will be better than today, that things can and will improve. Problems can be solved by our actions. And we want our leaders to portray a positive optimistic attitude. Problems are not "problems", but opportunities. Simultaneously, we want our leaders to be honest and realistic. So in dismal situations, the statements of optimism must be tempered. If there are no easy answers, say so. You must be open and honest.

W. I. Thomas wrote many years ago about self-fulfilling prophecies. If a person or group believes a thing to be true and operates, as though it were true, often it becomes true. This has been proven often in education and other fields. If a leader takes a positive stance, it will be more popular and the desired action is more likely to occur. Always assume that someone will closely examine your stance on almost anything you say or do. A motto you might want to try: "Pessimism breeds negativity. Optimism breeds opportunity."

PEOPLE BASED

Leadership must be of, by and for the people. The only reason for leadership should be for the benefit of the people. The current tendency is to look for the benefits to an individual and not to the larger group. One reason why many so-called leaders are distrusted today is that they are seen as self-serving - primarily interested in their own benefits. Congress is seen as a "good old boys' club" with high salaries and super plush benefits; not at all like the citizen-legislators which the founding fathers had in mind. The rapidly passing term limits on politicians are an attempt to reduce the number of professional politicians. Professional leaders of any type are likely to be seen as suspect.

POSSIBLE

A leader must be realistic to determine the art of the possible. How much can realistically be accomplished in the time and resources available? How strong is the desire for change? Are the people willing to pay the price either in reduced services or higher taxes - what ever it takes? Very often people call for changes, but when they find out how difficult or expensive it will be to solve the problems, they will not support the proposed solutions. Determining which ideas in any organization or setting are politically and economically feasible and which are not is a vital asset for any leader. Do not jump into "solving" a problem until you have given very careful consideration to the process of solution. Will the other people support the proposed solution? A little caution is a good asset for a leader.Bold and swift action by the knight on the white horse occurs primarily in the movies. An old folk saying has considerable wisdom for leadership: "fools rush in where angels fear to tread."

PRACTICAL

A leader must realize that pleasing all of the people all of the time is not possible. A leader must be practical in decisions made catering to the majority, perceptive enough to realize when the majority is right and strong enough to take action without the support of the majority when the majority is wrong. At the same time you must be strong enough to stand by your convictions and accept the criticisms - valid and invalid - which are sure to come. Again, practical and possible are twins that have considerable interrelationships.

PROGRESSIVE

An effective leader will move the group forward. Incorporating new strategies in leadership and communications is important. Sometimes progress may mean maintaining the current situation. It depends upon the group's needs and desires. And you must be progressive in other things such as media usage. A person cannot be a successful candidate for president or most other public offices if he/she cannot make full use of the media. The Kennedy - Nixon debates proved that many years ago. Similarly, many CEOs of businesses have found themselves suddenly facing the media to answer questions about their organization.

PREPARED

A leader must be knowledgeable about his or her goals, the variety of means for reaching the goals, the needs necessary to meet the goals and about the people in the group. An effective leader must be both organized and prepared. Many leaders have opened their mouths and inserted their foot and suddenly found that they were no longer regarded as leaders. A more modern folk saying is that "you should not have your mouth in gear while your mind is in neutral."

POWER-BUILDING

Even the best leaders can not tackle most leadership jobs alone. They need to have and to motivate followers to become involved in getting the job done. They must trust other people to get a job done and they must be able to delegate. A similar trait is the ability to network - to build linkages of friends and acquaintances that may be able to provide needed assistance at some future time. A classic study by James Coleman many years ago showed that who you knew was one of the most important things that influenced life successes.

Close examination of all fourteen of these traits show that all are learned. Some are learned early in childhood and some later. However, the average person such as you or I can make major changes in any of these. I know that many of my characteristics have changed greatly from my early years. If I were the same person as then, I could not begin to do what I do today. Changes in personality are very possible, but for you, only you can do it. The first step is to want to do it.

DIFFERENCE BETWEEN EFFECTIVE MANAGEMENT AND EFFECTIVE LEADERSHIP

Effective leaders establish a clear direction for their organizations. They communicate a compelling vision in their writing, speaking and presenting. According to Randall Dunham and Jon Pierce's leadership process model, developed in 1989, successful leaders accurately assess a situation before taking an action to get a positive result. These leaders motivate and inspire subordinates to take action, and they enable transitions and transformations. Effective managers, on the other hand, control and direct people according to established policies and procedures. They ensure that day-to-day operations flow smoothly. Organizations need both functions to succeed.

VISION

Effective leaders define their vision and motivate subordinates to adopt this vision, often during meetings and training sessions or in newsletters. Leaders display integrity, empathy, assertiveness and good decision-making skills to lead others effectively. Once subordinates accept the plan for the future, it requires an effective manager to carry out the vision by assigning resources and completing tasks. Managers ensure that employees have the skills, knowledge and capability to get the job done.

CHANGE

When market conditions change, effective leaders recognize the need for adjusting standard business practices. By taking risks and promoting innovative strategies, they make it possible for companies to capitalize on strengths and opportunities and mitigate or eliminate risks and threats. Managers tend to excel at maintaining operations, not changing them. Effective managers ensure consistency once a direction has been set.

PARTICIPATION

Autocratic leaders operate by making decisions without consulting their subordinates. This tends to work well during a crisis, such as a natural or man-made disaster. Under these circumstances, people appreciate a decisive leader who can take charge. Generally speaking, however, employees resent autocratic managers because people who use this style adhere to strict rules and often fail to recognize employee value. An effective manager requires the participation of her subordinates to get work done. By asking for input on how work gets accomplished, she improves employee satisfaction, morale and retention.

PLANNING

Effective leaders set goals for their organizations. They establish a long-term strategy. These leaders review the work of managers and provide sponsorship for activities. Leaders approve the allocation of resources, allowing managers to recruit and hire employees and spend money. Then, effective managers initiate, plan, execute, monitor and close projects to achieve the strategic goals. Their tactical efforts ensure that quality products and services get to market on time and under budget. While leaders and managers perform different roles in the organization, each function enables a company to flourish in the long run.

HOW TO BECOME A BETTER PERSON

HOW TO BECOME A BETTER PERSON

There are many people who are interested in knowing how to become a better person in life. Though there are many people who can guide you for becoming a better person, you can become one only if you are eager enough to bring about a change in yourself. So, in short, whether you become a better person or not entirely depends on your commitment and hard work. Given below are some steps to becoming a better person.

SUGGESTIONS FOR BECOMING A BETTER PERSON IDENTIFY YOUR MISTAKES

If you wish to learn to become a better person, then you should first of all learn to identify your mistakes. Think of what are those things which you do in your day to day live and are not liked by other people around you. One of the most important tips to become a better person is to analyse the mistakes and try to avoid them as far as possible. Remember, this is not that easy, it requires a lot of patience and courage to change yourself.

APOLOGISE FOR YOUR PAST MISTAKES

For all those who wish to know how to become a better person in a relationship, the simple answer is, apologise for your past mistakes. By doing so, you can give an impression to the people close to you that you are trying to change. If you do not apologise, then you will always be ridiculed in the society for being a person who is egoistic and badly behaved. By apologising to those whom you have hurt, you can hope to get a second chance from. them to prove that you are as good as the others tion.

FORGET THE PAST, THINK OF THE PRESENT

Forgetting the past misbehaviour and thinking about the present and the future is one of the best ways to become a better person. This is because it is impossible for you to change the past. However, by doing good things in the present, you can definitely secure your future. So, start your life afresh and pledge to go on the path of honesty and sincerity. If you find it difficult to remember how to behave under particular circumstances, you can maintain a personal diary in which you can write the dos and don'ts for yourself. Read the diary before you go to sleep every day. More on positive thinking.

HAVE A ROLE MODEL

Having a role model is essential for becoming a better person. A role model is someone whom you respect or adore. You should study the thoughts and sayings of these great people and try to understand what they actually mean. Read informative books on these people and this will definitely change the way you think and look at things. If possible, read the autobiographies of these people. This can give you a lot of inspiration and motivation as you will come to know how these people became great even though they were ordinary people at the beginning of their lives. However, just reading about the great people will not help you. You will have to practically implement their thoughts to earn respect for yourself in the society. Another suggestion for becoming a better person would be to believe in God and follow his preachings.

You can learn from anyone other than yourself. Of course you can learn some things on your own through experience, but you will never know everything, and other people are the main source for knowledge, advice, examples, and new perspectives. Having an example to go by can certainly make life easier, but all too often, our examples fall short of the mark.

How many times has an imperfection been revealed about someone that disappointed all of those who looked up to them? Even the best people on Earth have made mistakes. To be human is to be imperfect. There is nothing wrong with admiring someone for their talent, personality, or for their contribution to society. It is important, however, to realise that when you idolise someone, you can become a lot like them and reflect even their flaws. You might not even realise the bad habits you have picked up from people you love and respect.

On the other hand, it is not fair to completely discredit all of the good that someone has done for a wrong that they have done. Ultimately there may be something that your idol will say or do that you will not like. You should pick and choose what you do like about a person, use that as your example, and ignore the rest. While it is a good thing to look to other people and learn from them, it is hardly beneficial to limit yourself to a single human being as an ultimate example for life. Therefore, it is important to expand your horizons and learn to follow after a number of people.

SELF AWARENESS AND THE EFFECTIVE LEADER

Organizations benefit more from leaders who take responsibility for what they don't know than from leaders who pretend to know it all. Although it is probably one of the least discussed leadership competencies, self-awareness is possibly one of the most valuable. Self-awareness is being conscious of what you're good at while acknowledging what you still have yet to learn. This includes admitting when you don't have the answer and owning up to mistakes.

In our highly competitive culture, this can seem counterintuitive. In fact, many of us operate on the belief that we must appear as though we know everything all the time or else people will question our abilities, diminishing our effectiveness as leaders. If you're honest with yourself, you'll admit that really the opposite is true. Because whether you acknowledge your weaknesses or not, everyone still sees them. So rather than conceal them, the person who tries to hide weaknesses actually highlights them, creating the perception of a lack of integrity and self-awareness.

THE BENEFITS OF SELF-AWARENESS

It's easy to see how pretending to know everything when you don't can create situations that can be problematic for your entire organization. On the other hand, when you take responsibility for what you don't know, you benefit both yourself and your organization. On an interpersonal level, self-awareness of your strengths and weaknesses can net you the trust of others and increase your credibility — both of which will increase your leadership effectiveness.

On an organizational level, the benefits are even greater. When you acknowledge what you have yet to learn, you're modeling that in your organization it's okay to admit you don't have all the answers, to make mistakes and most importantly, to ask for help. These are all characteristics of an organization that is constantly learning and springboards to innovation and agility — two hallmarks of high performing organizations.

KNOW WHEN STRENGTH MIGHT BE PLAYED OUT

Most likely, your strengths are what got you to this point in your career. As your role in your organization changes, you must be careful not to overplay a former strength to the point that it actually becomes a weakness. For example, let's say you're great with detail and have done good things for your organization as an individual contributor and get rewarded with a management role. Continuing to delve in the details once you're responsible for projects and people will cause you to lose ground with 1) your reports, who will feel unnecessary; and 2) your superiors, who may rethink your readiness for managerial responsibility.

Acknowledging the need to become better at anything is only the beginning, and it's often the most difficult step in the whole process. In many cases, individuals successfully come to the realization that something's not working but have no clue how to change it into something that works. This difficulty to see in yourself what others see so easily is what makes the path to self-awareness so challenging. One way to get started is by soliciting and listening to feedback from those who work with you.

SOLICIT FEEDBACK

There are several ways you can get feedback about your work performance. Formally, you can get it through 360 multi-rater assessments. In a 360, peers, superiors and reports anonymously provide feedback on all aspects of your behaviour. Informally, you can make time once a day to reflect on the day's events, *e.g.* how people reacted to you, how fluidly you were able to work with or manage others, etc. To do this effectively on your own requires a high degree of emotional intelligence. Emotional Intelligence, or EQ as it's often called, is defined as awareness of your own and others' emotions, and how they are impacted by situations. Some people are simply born with a high EQ but with diligent introspection it can be cultivated to a degree in everyone.

If you fall into the latter category, another more practical method that falls somewhere in between the formality of a 360 and the informality of quiet daily reflection is to get in the habit of doing regular post-mortems on every project in which you are involved. In order to do this effectively however, you must learn to do two things: ask good questions, and listen without justifying or defending your actions.

ASK GOOD QUESTIONS

The skill of asking good questions can be invaluable to you and your organization. When the question is about your own performance however, it can be harder to be objective about negative feedback. When you show that you are equally open to all types of feedback, you demonstrate self-awareness and the willingness to learn. Plus, asking questions models a solid, transparent approach to problem-solving and decision-making that benefits everyone in an organization. But perhaps most importantly, it models that it's okay not to know everything, which encourages everyone that it's okay to be constantly learning.

By modeling habits of good self-awareness you help to create a more self-aware organization. An organization that is self-aware is open to learning and better equipped to adjust quickly to changes as the marketplace dictates. This ability is the defining characteristic of a learning organization and possibly the most compelling reason all managers at all levels should include self-awareness in their development goals.

LISTEN WITHOUT JUSTIFYING

Once you've solicited feedback it's crucial that you listen without justifying your actions or people will stop giving you feedback. Moreover, when you are busy defending your actions, you miss what the person is trying to tell you. If on the other hand you listen and accept feedback without defending yourself, you're more likely to hear what you need to hear, increasing your credibility with the person giving you feedback and creating a trust bond that will enable them to continue providing useful feedback in the future.

So how Self-Aware are You?

No doubt most of us would answer with confidence that we are pretty darn self-aware. Before you take self-awareness off your development radar screen, consider this: According to research* on management styles, you're more likely to be unawareof your behaviour and how it impacts others if normally tend to operate at the extremes.

For example, at one extreme are the "Originators." Originators tend to be quick decision-makers who aren't afraid of confrontation or taking risks. On the other end of the spectrum you'll find "Conservers." Conservers are much more rule-bound and conflict- and change-averse. Most people fall somewhere in between these two extremes and are aptly labeled as "Pragmatists." Pragmatists don't either seek out or avoid confrontation. More practical and flexible, they tend to focus on issues in the order in which they need to be resolved. So if you identify more with the descriptions of the Originator or Conserver, this may be an indicator that you are not as self-aware as you think you are. No matter where you fall on the spectrum of management styles, the benefits of greater self-awareness should be incentive enough to consistently seek (and listen to) as much feedback as possible on your performance at work.

When you pretend to know it all and never admit mistakes, you model behaviour that can have negative consequences for yourself and your entire organization. Conversely, when you are self-aware enough to openly admit missteps and concede that you still have plenty to learn, you turn mistakes are learning opportunities and give people permission to be collaborative without fear of appearing unqualified. To begin to increase your self-awareness, seek feedback on your performance from others by asking good questions and listening without justifying or defending your actions. Remember, organizations benefit far more from leaders who take responsibility for what they don't know than from leaders who pretend to know it all.

LEADERSHIP VERSUS MANAGEMENT

My focus on Learn-to-be-a-Leader.com is on leadership versus management. But are these just different words that really mean the same thing? Some organisations seem to use the term leader as a more fashionable term for a manager. But there is a difference between the two roles, although please remember that many people combine both in one job.

I believe:

"A leader is someone whose direction and approach other people are willing to follow."

And therefore, I see leadership as:

"Influencing others to follow a given direction."

The body that was set up in the UK to define national standards for managers (the Management Charter Initiative, or MCI) defined the role of the manager as: "Helping the organisation to achieve its objectives and to continually improve its performance" Although the MCI no longer exists, its successor, the Management Standards Centre, has continued to use this definition.

Same Difference?

At the core of this definition management is about purpose, structure, disciplines, processes, delivery and the mechanics of an organisation. We can contrast this with leadership, which is about vision, direction, influence, communication and the aspirations of people.

ANCIENT ROMANS AND ANGLO SAXONS

One way of thinking about leadership versus management is to consider the differences between the Ancient Romans and the Anglo Saxons. The Ancient Romans were structured, well organised and disciplined. They were role models for management. The Anglo Saxons operated as small tribes, led by charismatic chieftains who ruled by the will of their people and based on loyalties to a territorial ideal. Their style exemplified leadership.

AUTHORITY AND POWER

Managers get their authority and power from being appointed to a position by more senior managers. Leaders get their authority and power from being able to influence and persuade others to follow them. This is why I often refer to leaders being recognised as such by their followers. In fact, they can't be leaders until they have people to follow them! This point about authority does raise the possibility of conflict between those appointed (ie, managers) and those anointed (ie, leaders). But thats a very different meaning of management versus leadership!

SHORT, MEDIUM OR LONG TERM VIEW

Another difference between leadership versus management is that managers, as disciplined organisers and deliverers, often have to focus on the short to medium term whereas leaders, who provide vision and direction, are primarily concerned with the medium to long term. Perhaps I am oversimplifying this distinction but it might help us to understand that leadership versus management are two different, if related, functions.

Things Right or Right Thing?

You might have heard the saying that "Managers do things right, leaders do the right thing." To put it another way, managers concentrate on tasks, rules and compliance (that is, doing things right) while leaders concentrate on people, principles and purpose (that is, doing the right thing).

Separate and Distinct, or Related?

These various distinctions between leadership versus management might come across as suggesting that leadership and management are completely separate. In reality, actual people don't do either one or the other. They probably do some of each. Strictly speaking its not leadership versus management. The two are not separate or bipolar. They overlap. You can think of them as on a continuum with many steps between the extremes.

Think of the distinctions as the two ends of a slider control that can be adjusted to emphasise one function or the other. Each leader/ manager will adopt an approach somewhere between the two extremes, reflecting their skills and preferred management or leadership style.

Skills and Qualities

Just as the role and functions of leaders and managers are different, so are the skills and qualities that people need to be good at each. I will examine the skills and qualities of a leader in detail elsewhere but just think what skills (things people can do) and qualities (things that people are) a good manager will need.

They might include:

- Understanding goals and objectives
- Well organised
- Able to prioritise and plan
- Good communicator
- Works with groups and individuals
- Decision maker
- Works to systems, processes and procedures
- Monitors, reviews and improves.

And so on. Looking at this list, you might put some (but probably not all) of these items on a similar list for leaders. The two roles have their distinctive features but do overlap! In practice many people are good managers as well as good leaders. But it is also true that many good managers are not so good at leadership and many good leaders are not so good at management!

An Example From the Television

As I was writing this page, my family were watching a programme on the television. It featured a businessman setting up a new hotel. His vision was for a different style of hotel, totally flexible to demanding and wealthy guests who expected all services at any hour of the day or night. He challenged conventional approaches, was flamboyant and his staff and suppliers had many difficulties working with him. When he interviewed candidates for the position of general manager, he realised that he needed someone with different skills to his own. He looked for someone who excelled at being disciplined, organised and customer focussed. To put it another way, he sought a "manager" to complement him as a "leader", who would concentrate on management versus leadership - the latter rather then the former seeming to be what he enjoyed doing!.

LEADER AND MANAGER PARTNERSHIPS

Many strong leaders rely on a very different person as their "number two". They choose someone who complements them in that they have a very different personality, skill set and ways of working. In short, someone who is an excellent manager. These partnerships can often become very inter-dependent with the two people concerned moving jobs from organisation to organisation together.

MANAGEMENT CONTROL AND STAFFING

Although there is a tendency to want a "bright line" to define businesses as small, medium-size or large, this guidance does not provide such definitions. It uses the term "smaller" rather than "small" business, suggesting there is a wide range of companies to which the guidance is directed.

The focus is on businesses that have many of the following characteristics:

- Fewer lines of business and fewer products within lines
- Concentration of marketing focus, by channel or geography
- Leadership by management with significant ownership interest or rights
- Fewer levels of management, with wider spans of control
- Less complex transaction processing systems and protocols
- Fewer personnel, many having a wider range of duties
- Limited ability to maintain deep resources in line as well as support staff positions such as legal, human resources, accounting and internal auditing.

None of these characteristics by themselves is definitive. Certainly, size by whatever measure - revenue, personnel, assets, or other - affects and is affected by these characteristics, and shapes our thinking about what constitutes "smaller."

COSTS AND BENEFITS

Management and other stakeholders of public companies, particularly smaller ones, have focused great attention on the cost of complying with Section 404, with less attention given to the associated benefits. Although it may be difficult to measure impacts associated with inaccurate financial reporting, market reactions to corporate misstatements clearly signal that the investment community does not readily tolerate inaccurate reporting, regardless of company size. In that respect and with other benefits described below, effective internal control adds significant value. Among the most significant benefits is the strengthened ability of companies to access the capital markets, providing capital which drives innovation and economic growth. Other benefits include reliable and timely information supporting management's decision-making, consistent mechanisms for processing transactions across an organization enhancing speed and reliability, and ability to accurately communicate business performance with partners and customers.

MEETING CHALLENGES IN ATTAINING COST-EFFECTIVE

Internal Control

The characteristics of smaller companies provide significant challenges for cost-effective internal control. This particularly is the case where managers view control as an administrative burden to be added onto existing business systems, rather than recognizing the business need and benefit for effective internal control that is integrated with core processes.

Among the challenges are:

- Obtaining sufficient resources to achieve adequate segregation of duties
- Management's ability to dominate activities, with significant opportunities for management override of control
- Recruiting individuals with requisite financial reporting and other expertise to serve effectively on the board of directors and audit committee
- Recruiting and retaining personnel with sufficient experience and skill in accounting and financial reporting
- Taking management attention from running the business in order to provide sufficient focus on accounting and financial reporting
- Maintaining appropriate control over computer information systems with limited technical resources.

While all companies incur incremental costs to design and report on internal control over financial reporting, costs can be proportionally higher for smaller companies. Yet despite resource constraints, smaller businesses usually can meet this challenge and succeed in attaining effective internal control in a reasonably cost-effective manner. This is accomplished in a variety of ways, outlined in this guidance, many of which already exist today in smaller companies and for which management can "take credit" in considering internal control effectiveness.

Wide and Direct Control from the Top

Many smaller businesses are dominated by the company's founder or other leader who exercises a great deal of discretion and provides personal direction to other personnel. While key to enabling the company to meet its growth and other objectives, this positioning also can contribute significantly to effective internal control over financial reporting. In-depth knowledge of different facets of the business - its operations, processes, array of contractual commitments and business risks - enables its leader to know what to expect in reports generated by the financial reporting system and to follow up as needed when unanticipated variances surface. A related downside in terms of ability to override established control procedures can be addressed with specified protocols.

Effective Boards of Directors

Smaller hotels typically have relatively straightforward business operations with less complex business structures, enabling directors to gain more in-depth knowledge of business activities. Directors may have been closely involved with the company during its evolution and have a strong historical perspective. Coupled with what often is exposure to and frequent communication with a wide range of managers, this assists the board and its audit committee in performing oversight responsibilities for financial reporting in a highly effective manner.

COMPENSATING FOR LIMITED SEGREGATION OF DUTIES

Resource constraints may limit the number of employees, sometimes resulting in concerns regarding segregation of duties. There are, however, actions management can take in order to compensate for potential inadequacy. These include managers reviewing system reports of detailed transactions; selecting transactions for review of supporting documents; overseeing periodic counts of physical inventory, equipment or other assets and comparing them with accounting records; and reviewing reconciliations of account balances or performing them independently. In many small companies managers already are performing these and other procedures supporting reliable reporting, and credit should be taken for their contribution to effective internal control.

INFORMATION TECHNOLOGY

The reality of limited internal information technology resources often can be dealt with through use of software developed and maintained by others. These packages still require controlled implementation and operation, but many of the risks associated with in-house developed systems are avoided. Typically there is a limited need for Programme change controls, inasmuch as changes are done exclusively by the developer company, and generally a smaller company's personnel lack technical expertise to make unauthorized modifications.

Such commercially available packages also bring advantages in the form of embedded facilities for controlling which employees can access or modify specified data, performing checks on data processing completeness and accuracy, and maintaining related documentation. Further advantage can be gained by utilizing software that comes with a variety of built-in application controls that can improve consistency of operation, automate reconciliations, facilitate reporting of exceptions for management review, and support proper segregation of duties. Smaller companies can take advantage of these capabilities, ensuring "flags" or "switches" are properly set to take advantage of the software's capabilities.

MONITORING ACTIVITIES

The monitoring component is an important part of the Framework, where a wide range of activities routinely performed by managers in running a business can provide feedback on the functioning of other components of the internal control system. Management of many smaller businesses regularly perform such procedures, but have not always taken sufficient "credit" for their contribution to internal control effectiveness. These activities, usually performed manually and sometimes supported by computer software, should be fully considered in designing and assessing internal control. From a different perspective, there is another way monitoring activities can promote efficiency.

After the first year of assessing and reporting on internal control, many companies repeated the assessment process in year two with little if any cost savings. A different approach, however, can be taken to promote efficiency. By focusing on monitoring activities already in place or that might be added with little additional effort, management can identify significant changes to the financial reporting system since the prior year, thereby gaining insight into where to target more detailed testing. While for effective internal control all five components must be in place and operating effectively and some testing of each component is necessary, highly effective monitoring activities can both offset certain shortcomings in other components and sharpen targeting of assessment work with resulting overall efficiency.

ACHIEVING FURTHER EFFICIENCIES

In addition to considering the above, companies can gain additional efficiencies in designing and implementing or assessing internal control by focusing on only those financial reporting objectives directly applicable to the company's activities and circumstances, taking a risk based approach to internal control, right sizing documentation, viewing internal control as an integrated process, and considering the totality of internal control. The COSO Framework recognizes that an entity must first have in place an appropriate set of financial reporting objectives.

At a high level, the objective of financial reporting is to prepare reliable financial statements, which involves attaining reasonable assurance that the financial statements are free from material misstatement. Flowing from this high level objective, management establishes supporting objectives related to the company's business activities and circumstances and their proper reflection in the company's financial statement accounts and related disclosures. These objectives may be influenced by regulatory requirements or by other factors that management may choose to incorporate when setting its objectives. Efficiencies are gained by focusing on only those objectives directly applicable to the business and related to its activities and circumstances that are material to the financial statements.

Experience shows that this can be most efficiently accomplished by beginning with a company's financial statements and identifying supporting objectives for those business activities, processes and events that can materially affect the financial statements. In this way, a basis is formed for giving attention only to what is truly relevant to the reliability of financial reporting for that company.

FOCUSING ON RISK

While management considers risks in several respects, its overarching consideration is the risks to key objectives, including the risks to reliable financial reporting. Risk-based means focusing on quantitative and qualitative factors that potentially affect the reliability of financial reporting, and identifying where in transaction processing or other activities related to financial statement preparation something could go wrong. By focusing on key objectives management can tailor the scope and depth of risk assessments needed. Often risk is considered in the context of initially designing and implementing internal control, where risks to objectives are identified and analyzed to form a basis for determining how the risks should be managed. Another is in the context of assessing whether internal control is effective in mitigating risks to objectives.

In the context of assessing internal control effectiveness, there sometimes is a tendency to consider internal control using generic lists of controls appropriate to a "typical" organization. While these tools in questionnaire or other form may be useful, an unintended result is that management sometimes focuses on "standard" or "typical" controls that simply are not relevant to the company's financial reporting objectives or risks associated with those objectives. A related problem encountered is starting assessments with the details of accounting systems and documenting them in extreme depth without recognizing whether the entirety of processes are truly relevant to achieving reliable financial reporting. This is not to say that such approaches cannot be useful, as they can be. However, whatever approach is followed, efficiencies are gained when attention is directed to the objectives management has established specific to the company's business activities and circumstances.

RIGHT-SIZING DOCUMENTATION

Documentation of business processes and procedures and other elements of internal control systems is developed and maintained by companies for a number of reasons. One is to promote consistency in adhering to desired practices in running the business. Effective documentation assists in communicating what is to be done, and how, and creates expectations of performance. Another purpose of documentation is to assist in training new personnel and as a refresher or reference tool for other employees. Documentation also provides evidence to support reporting on internal control effectiveness. The level and nature of documentation varies widely by company. Certainly, large companies usually have more operations to document, or greater complexity in financial reporting processes, and therefore find it necessary to have more extensive documentation than smaller ones.

Smaller companies often find less need for formal documentation, such as in-depth policy manuals, systems flowcharts of processes, organization charts, job descriptions, and the like. In smaller companies, typically there are fewer people and levels of management, closer working relationships and more frequent interaction, all of which promotes communication of what is expected and what is being done. A smaller business, for example, might document human resources, procurement or customer credit policies with memoranda and supplement the memoranda with guidance provided by management in meetings. A larger company will more likely have more detailed policies (or policy manuals) to guide their people in better implementing controls.

Questions arise as to the extent of documentation needed to deem internal control over financial reporting as effective. The answer is, of course, it depends on circumstances and needs. Some level of documentation is always necessary to assure management that its control processes are working, such as documentation to help assure management that all shipments are billed, or periodic reconciliations are performed. In a smaller business, however, management is often directly involved in performing control procedures and for those procedures there may be only minimal documentation because management can determine that controls are functioning effectively through direct observation. However, there must be information available to management that the accounting systems and related procedures, including actions taken in connection with preparation of reliable financial statements, are well designed, well understood, and carried out properly.

When management asserts to regulators, shareholders or other third parties on the design and operating effectiveness of internal control over financial reporting, management accepts a higher level of personal risk and typically will require documentation of major processes within the accounting systems and important control activities to support its assertions. Accordingly, management will review to determine whether its documentation is appropriate to support its assertion. In considering the amount of documentation needed, the nature and extent of the documentation may be influenced by the company 's regulatory requirements. This does not necessarily mean that documentation will or should be more formal, but it does mean that there needs to be evidence that the controls are designed and working properly.

In addition, when an external auditor will be attesting to the effectiveness of internal control, management will likely be expected to provide the auditor with support for its assertion. That support would include evidence that the controls are properly designed and are working effectively. In considering the nature and extent of documentation needed by the company, management should also consider that the documentation to support the assertion that controls are working properly will likely be used by the external auditor as part of his or her audit evidence.

There may still be instances where policies and procedures are informal and undocumented. This may be appropriate where management is able to obtain evidence captured through the normal conduct of the business that indicates personnel regularly performed those controls. However, it is important to keep in mind that control processes, such as risk assessment, cannot be performed entirely in the mind of the CEO or CFO without some documentation of the thought process and management's analysis. Many of the examples contained later in this guidance illustrate how management can capture evidence through the normal course of business. Documentation of internal control should meet business needs and be commensurate with circumstances. The extent of documentation supporting design and operating effectiveness of the five internal control components is a matter of judgement, and should be done with costeffectiveness in mind. Where practical, the creation and retention of evidence should be embedded with the various financial reporting processes.

VIEWING INTERNAL CONTROL AS AN INTEGRATED PROCESS

It is useful to view the Framework's five internal control components as comprising an integrated process, which indeed internal control is. A process perspective highlights the interrelationship of the components, and recognizes that management has flexibility in choosing controls to achieve its objectives and that an organization can adjust and improve its internal control over time. As noted, the internal control process begins with management setting financial reporting objectives relevant to the company's particular business activities and circumstances.

Once set, management identifies and assesses a variety of risks to those objectives, determines which risks could result in a material misstatement in financial reporting, and determines how the risks should be managed through a range of control activities. Management implements approaches to capture, process and communicate information needed for financial reporting and other components of the internal control system. All this is done in context of the company's control environment, which is shaped and refined as necessary to provide the appropriate tone at the top of the organization and related attributes. These components all are monitored to help ensure that controls continue to operate properly over time.

The Totality of Internal Control

Each of the five components of internal control set forth in the Framework is important to achieving the objective of reliable financial reporting. Determining whether a company's internal control over financial reporting is effective involves a judgement. Internal control has five components that work together to prevent or detect and correct material misstatements of financial reports.

When the five components are present and functioning, to the extent that management has reasonable assurance that financial statements are being prepared reliably, internal control can be deemed effective. While each component must be present and functioning, this does not mean, however, that each component should function identically or even at the same level in every company. Some trade- offs may exist between components. Accordingly, effective internal control does not necessarily mean a "gold standard" of control is built into every process. A deficiency in one component might be mitigated by other controls in that component or by controls in another component strong enough such that the totality of control is sufficient to reduce the risk of misstatement to an acceptable level.

POWER AND LEADERSHIP

Leadership is a form of social dominance, and leaders can exert powerful influences on the behaviours, ideals and feelings of the led. This chapter is concerned with rank and how, in humans, dominance expresses itself through the use of various forms of power. We will note that leaders can use their power in many different ways. They can use it to gain recognition, status and superiority for themselves and in so doing can act to suppress, intimidate, subordinate and structuralise the hierarchy and make sharper the boundaries between insider and outsider (the good and the bad). On the other hand leaders can act to relax, encourage and nurture subordinates, helping them to reduce their dependence on leaders, to de-structuralise the hierarchy and soften boundaries. To obtain a leadership position, obviously requires some type of power.

NOTES ON POWER

In evolutionary theory power is defined by reproductive success - for sociobiologist that is the ultimate in power. Mostly, however, social power is explored in the contexts of the relationships and motivations of people. When we explore the social origins of power, which followed the advent of agriculture, we can see this as a history of the changing forms of dominant-subordinate relationships, and the different social patterns of living it sporned. Feminists philosophers sociologists and psychologistshave been among the many to have placed power central to their explorations. Apart from the interpersonal theorists dominant-subordinate relationship have been in the background, not the foreground, of these explorations.

Power is usually defined as the ability to influence or 'make happen'. The concept of power can be use in a scientific non-social way as energy - an electric company calls itself powergen - clearly no social dimension here. In relationships, however, we might speak of constructive power (*e.g.*, to build, create, give life, save life and nurture) or destructive power (to tear down, destroy). Usually the former is slow working over time whereas destructive power can be quick and immediate. What might have taken years to build can be destroyed in seconds. The immediacy of destructive power can give a person a very strong sense of their influence and energy - even their aliveness. The child builds the tower of blocks and then smashes it - with a smile. In all of us there exists impulses to create and destroy. And these can share complex relationships. We might create armies and weapons of destruction in order to destroy - but they can also be used to protect.

TYPES OF POWER

Hollander and Offerman, suggest three types of power: Power over others, the power to make or entice others to do things a leader wants; Power to, involving the degree of freedom to do as one wishes, also called empowerment; and Power from; involving the ability/power to resist the wishes/demands of others. As they point out high status involves all three forms of power, whilst subordinates have at best one or two and sometimes practically no such powers at all.

When it comes to considering the forms of power psychologists have suggested five main forms are suggested. Reward power is the ability to provide something that others want and will work for (e.g controlling access to wages, food, love, approval etc.). Coercive/punishment power is the ability to control others through actual or threatened aversive outcomes (*e.g.*, to injury the other or remove/withhold something of value to others). Both these are fairly direct, used by animals, and require little psychological capacity. The other three however require more complex psychologies. Legitimate power is linked to rights and obligations which require understanding and recognition of rights and obligations. It is used as a basis of law and socially defined roles (*e.g.*, the power of the captain, teacher, president, etc.). Expert power relates to an awareness of the superiority of another's knowledge or skill and it linked with respect and at times admiration (*e.g.*, doctors, priests, scientists). Referent power refers more to attractiveness, liking and person's charm or charisma. Many forms of power and indeed leadership requircs that the dominant has access to and can control and the attention of subordinates.

The interpersonal theorists have argued that dominance-subordination is a vertical dimension of relating while love-hate is horizonal dimension. So, therefore, it is possible to have both loving and hating/aggressive forms of dominance. To my mind these are all helpful ways of explaining the complexities of power and leadership, but at times they can hide those complexities rather than reveal them.

LEADERSHIP

Lindholm notes, in his study of charisma, that we do not always behave in our own genetic self-interest when it comes to following leaders. There has been more than one leader who has taken us on a trip into mass destruction. In 1978 the world was shocked by the Jones Town suicide of men, women and children. Some, who were not present at the time, killed themselves later. And this was not the first, nor will it be the last, time that followers have killed others and themselves in devotion to a cause, manipulated by a leader. It is our rank psychology that courts so much craziness. So in this chapter we explore some facets of leadership.

Leaders vary in style and basic psychology (*e.g.*, in terms of their charisma, skills/knowledge, tendency to punish or reward). But they are also shaped and given access to leadership positions/roles via their cultures and social relationships. Some leaders are elected by those they will lead, others are imposed (as in the military) by superiors. Some leaders are encouraged to adopt certain styles and do certain things because of what is expected of (and projected onto) them. In the preceding chapter we noted how George Orwell had to shoot the elephant, not from any personal desire to do so, but because of the expectations of the crowd and his concern to maintain his image of himself and of his "white-man" group. In his book, `On the Psychology of Military Incompetence', Norman Dixon notes that preferred leadership style varies according to the context. For example, in low stress times soldiers prefer democratic leaders, but in stressful situations, like war, they prefer autocratic, strong leadership on whom they can depend. Thus, subordinate preferences for styles of leaders are effected by personal and social stresses and the potentially saving, protective qualities the leader seems to provide. Given this, some individuals are able to manipulate group values for their own ends and farm support. Authoritarian leaders can, for example, exaggerate threats, especially from outsiders and thus increase their appeal by offering themselves as strong, protective and decisive leaders. In low stress times leaders may rely more on their intelligence and less on experience but the reverse is the case in stressful times.Thus, there is a complex interaction between leadership behaviour, the psychology of followers, and social context which allows, encourages or even demands certain actions.

Leadership behaviours can be expressed in many contexts and at many different social positions. It involves various combinations of power such as directing the attention of others, and the ability/power to control, guide, influence, encourage or coerce the behaviour and values of others. Nearly all humans have the ability to adopt leadership behaviours. Even in simple two-some's one may be more the leader than the other, although they may swap roles from time to time. Thus, leadership behaviours can emerge in just about any social relationship; *e.g.*, playground, street gang, terrorist group, church fete society, local cricket team, the hospital ward, business organisation, and government. Leadership research also makes the distinction between task orientated leadership and person orientated leadership. The person orientated leader will attempt to manipulate the values and emotions of subordinates, getting them 'devoted to the cause' that they will lead.

Although leader-follower relationships are to some degree archetypal potentials (and this is what can give them their passion and emotion distorting qualities) we should note that our first experiences of 'leaders' are our parents.

The Family

Family structures are also authority, hierarchical structures. Human family relationships, however, are highly contextualised within their cultures. Cultures legitimise the use of power within the family. They may not only amplify gender differences in the power exercised within families (men as head of the household) but bestow rights. In many societies men are (more or less) bestowed the right of sexual access to their wives and even today there are issues around whether rape can occur inside marriage. In the middle ages, wife beating was allowed, provided the stick was no thicker than a thumb. In modern societies, noted for their highly segregated and privatised families, power is exercised by the limitation of freedom of choice and rights. Thus, for example, women and children who are locked into abusive relationships may lack the resources or opportunities to move away. Male dominance of the family is thus encased in socially bestowed privileges and values.

For all animals, parents are automatically positioned to control the behaviour of their offspring. Thus, the parent-child relationship is also a dominant-subordinate one. In childhood, the experience of being subordinate to one's parents is also associated with enormous needs for care and acceptance from them. This combination of care eliciting and care giving with subordination, has the effect of blending different archetypal potentials together. It is not surprising, therefore, that humans can learn and develop their attitudes and emotional sensitivity 'to authority' from the experiences they have with, and of, their parents. So parenting is, in many ways, a leadership role because it involves differences in power and demands for obedience. And our attitudes to leadership and authority (seeking it, subordinating ourselves to it, or hating it) can be shaped during our formative years.

Society bestows and accepts the rights of parents to behave in certain ways to their children. Children are automatically assumed to come under the power and control of their parents. The use of physical punishment (and types of punishment in general), religious indoctrination, diet, indeed the right to impose various forms of life style are seen as parental rights. The state may intervene at times, as with laws on education, and there can be conflicts over the exact limits of power that can be exercised with families, *e.g.*, the state intervenes in cases of sexual abuse or if parents refuse blood transfusions on religious grounds. Generally though, children are indoctrinated to adopt the prevailing attitudes and values of their group be these religious, political, or gender. Young children can be taken on political marches, made to read the Bible or Koran, to view history through a particular lens and so forth. If any of these practices are crazy then we can easily pass them on.

Leadership Roles

Once out of the family there are other groups and social relationships in which we must find our place. Leadership roles can be ascribed and defined by social groups and one passes some entrance test or exam to enter them (*e.g.*, lawyer, doctor) which legitimises the use of power. As we saw in chapter five, in some societies obtaining the recognition of manhood legitimises the use of certain types of power and authority (*e.g.*, over women). Historically, leaders could be given their roles 'as of right' (e.g. by an institutionalised class or caste system). In fact many leadership positions (Kings, Emperors, and so forth) were family determined. Even today the family of origin and the social rank of the family can significantly influence a person's chances and aspirations to leadership positions. Top leaders of social institutions are rarely those who have risen through the ranks, but usually begin their claims from class-bestowed privileged positions. But the importance of the rank of one's family is also noted in many non-human primates. Females especially, usually obtain their rank from their mother's and aunt's rank. As it has been for millions of years, we leave the family and emerge into the social world where rank is everywhere.

Exercising Power

People often seek out leadership positions from which to use power and once there, their personality will influence how that power and position is exercised. So even though a social group may legitimise the use of power, and select an individual(s) for leadership roles, the way power is exercised depends on complex interactions between the person exercising it and those on whom it is exercised. Some may become leaders even against their wishes, via their popularity or the personal values they express. John Lennon, for example, along with other pop groups of the time, had an enormous effect on the values of the young. However, he consistently denied that he wished to be seen as any kind of leader. He wanted fame for his music.

Psychotherapists note that the acts of being attended and looked to, or treated as a leader (saviour, guru etc.) can ignite leadership desires. Indeed, without caution one can be intoxicated by it, becoming grandiose and carried away by it. There is an inflation of the up-rank archetype. For example, therapists have to be very careful of the idealisations, admirations and needs projected onto them, so as to avoid getting inflated ideas about themselves. Whether one is a doctor, lawyer or psychotherapist, it is very easy to fall victim to inflations of one's own rank and power; one's own importance.

One may never know how a person is going to behave until they are given or find themselves in positions of power; when they put on the uniform. Some years ago Zimbardo and his colleagues took a group of students and arbitrarily divided them into guards and prisoners. Before the week was out the experiment had to be stopped because about a third of the guards had become vindictive and authoritarian, devising various punishments for disobedient prisoners. The simmerings of a gestapo mentality were not hard to see. This was a shock to the researchers. So positions of power can inflate and excite underlying tendencies in a person.

Secure and Insecure Dominance

Styles of leadership have been studied in animals as styles of dominance. In most non-human primate studies to date, subordinates show greater activation of stress hormones than dominant animals, especially higher levels of circulating cortisol. However, in unstable groups dominant animals can show almost as high levels as subordinates. The work of Sapolsky, who has studied free ranging baboon's in Africa, suggests that secure, dominant baboons in stable groups have: Low stress cortisol levels, they differentiate well between a threatening rival and other animals; when threatened they escalate fights and usually win; if they lose they displace aggression on to a third party; they have high levels of non-sexual interactions with infants and females and are generally relaxed and affiliative.

High ranking but insecure baboons (especially if the group is unstable) have: High levels of stress hormones, tend to be more aggressive (generally and sexually), are more likely to pick fights (rather than just respond to threats), appear more suspicious, and are generally less relaxed and less affiliative. While these differences in leadership/dominance style reflect the stability of the group they also reflect individual differences. Thus, we see that security of the position may be important for the kinds of behaviour that dominant's express. This leads us to the idea of differences between secure and insecure dominance. Some human leaders certainly seem to show forms of insecure dominance.

This insecurity is mediated through both thc social context and personality. It is possible that in humans insecurity may be, in part, a general personality trait (as it seems to be for baboons and chimpanzees). The combination of strong needs for power in humans (to control others) compensates, perhaps, for basic personal insecurities, quite possibly of an insecure, avoidant attachment style. In fact many researchers have argued that aggressive leaders have had disturbed backgrounds with low parental warmth. There is a basic view in psychotherapy that 'where love was not there shall be a power and fear.'

We noted many researchers draw distinctions between threat/aggression based dominance and affiliation based dominance styles. Insecure dominance, we can suggest, shows itself in the readiness to adopt threat based leadership styles; that is leadership is primarily organised via the defence system. In humans the interaction between threat and affiliation is complex because humans can be far more manipulative of their social-presentation and image, *i.e.*, presenting themselves as affiliative when in fact they are not. As we shall now see, insecure patterns of dominance show up quite commonly in leadership styles.

Personality

Although this book has tried to veer away from being overly focused on traits within individuals (and research on leadership suggests that personality is only one facet of leadership for it is always the interaction that is important), our exploration of leadership does require some consideration of personality.

It seems to be the case that some leaders are more likely to have particular traits and personality styles which reflect quite serious insecurities. These may include: Narcissistic, obsessional, autocratic, authoritarian, psychopathic and hypomanic (or manic-depressive). The definition of narcissistic, which underpins many of them, is captured by Adler (1986).

These patients tend to be extremely self-centred, often needing praise and constant recognition in order to feel momentarily good about themselves. Rather than feeling a sense of their own worth or value, they require repeated bolstering from the outside. In their relationships with people, they tend to be exploitative and insensitive to the feelings and needs of others. Their behaviour can be superficially charming on the one hand and arrogant on the other. They expect special privileges from those around them without giving anything in return, yet they can feel easily humiliated or shamed and respond with rage at what they perceive to be criticisms or failure of people to react in the way they wish..... Many can elaborate active fantasies about magnificent success in love, sex, beauty, wealth or power. They often devalue people they have previously idolised and tend to split, *i.e.* see people as either all good or all bad, or alternate between these extremes. Adler's description highlights status evaluative and powerhostility components, the use of others for selfvaluing purposes, exploitativeness and sense of entitlement, and a comparative lack of the more prosocial aspects of human nature such as empathy, moral thinking, and care giving. They can have the motto 'if you're not with us you're against us'. They can be strident in emphasising the importance of their own vision and truck little disagreement. They can be envious, grandiose and expect allegiance. They can maintain this allegiance by a mixture of threats, shaming and offering favours and prestige to allies and followers. Yet for all this at times their style may inspire devotion.

The psychopathic person has many narcissistic traits but in addition is generally more callous, sadistic, distrustful, amoral, exploitative, ruthless and easily activated into violent fights. Their compassion for others is notable by its absence. Autocratic and authoritarian personalities are similar to the narcissist but they are extremely ranked focused. Norman Dixonused psychoanalytic theory to argue that these personality styles are a defence against uncertainty and anxiety; *i.e.*, insecurity. They must know their place and can be incredibly deferential and submissive to those ranking above them and controlling of those ranking below. They have strong beliefs in the value of the ranked authority system, the importance of obeying orders and are not so keen on democracy.

The manic-depressive traits, from which some leaders suffer, are believed to relate more to a mood disorder. Winston Churchill was a classic example. This leads them to swing between grandiose ideas about their self-importance, have marked needs for power, low frustration tolerance but they have high energy, are charismatic, take risks and are creative. However, when depressed they are riddled with self-doubt and feelings of worthlessness, with a tendency to hide away and feel suicidal. They usually lack the sadistic and callousness of the psychopath but can be paranoid to some degree and are very sensitive to threats and challenges to their own (and their group's) status. People with narcissistic traits (and these can be present in any of the above types) may not have full blown manic-depressive illnesses, but nonetheless they can show marked swings of mood and confidence.

Although these are usually regarded as personality or mood disorders, it is quite wrong to think that having a disorder consigns one to the backstreets of history. Indeed, some are not satisfied with simply being psychopathic and narcissistic in their own limited social domains. Their drive for leadership and greatness marks them out from other less leadership focused personalities. In such a pursuit these traits can be a positive advantage in making it big. Unfortunately, in the past and to some degree still, these individuals can take hold of whole cultures, societies, groups and organisations with a terrible cost. More worryingly, once in power their poor emotional and/or physical health can have very serious consequences.

Anti-Social and Prosocial Leadership Style

Running along side explorations of personality have been many efforts to distinguish leadership styles using different constructs. For example, Maslow distinguished democratic from authoritarian leaders; McClelland distinguishes the affiliative from the power orientated; Eisler distinguishes dominator (masculine) from partnership (feminine) styles; Kalma et al., distinguish between sociable and aggressive leaders. And elsewhere I have distinguished the prosocial from the anti-social leader.

So there is no single system of understanding and all have their insights and limitations. Much may depend on where you look of course, *i.e.*, whether you focus on the tasks, results or on interpersonal style. The types of leaders we will note shortly may well get results, but they tend towards the authoritarian, dominator, aggressive, anti-social leadership style. I will refer to these collectively as anti-social because their style can have very negative effects on and for others.

Anti-social leaders tend to come from insecure backgrounds with a history of abusive, emotionally cold, rigid/authoritarian or neglectful parenting which leads them to develop various mixtures of the above mentioned traits. Judged through the lens of the last two chapters we could see these individuals as being highly shame prone, sensitive to humiliation, extraordinarily status conscious, and in need of defending against humiliation at all costs. The way this is done, as in the Hitler complex, is not just via defence of self but an active promotion of one's superiority - in other words heightened activity of a primitive up-rank, archetypal mentality. To be superior promises the power to defeat any who would make claims on one's status or position. Although one can certainly link such psychologies to reproductive strategies - and genes - these distal explanations do not always help us understand the complex of forces which bring these archetypes to such prominence within any one person at a point in history. Thus we should always consider family background and social context.

Anti-social leaders have particular philosophies, motives and tendencies which include: A perception of the world as competitive and the strongest wins; a belief in the superiority of one's social group, often with a fear, dislike or even contempt for outsiders; a belief in the importance of strength and pride; a belief in the importance of close ingroup loyalties as a protection against external badness (us against them); a need for control and power over others; a fear of losing status; a belief that their own way (vision) is superior; a simple right versus wrong moral system or no moral system at all; a tendency to use people to met their own ends; and often a lack of care for others.

Prosocial leaders tend to have very different backgrounds, coming from a secure and warm family life and have developed the archetypal abilities to empathise and care for others. This there are far more altruistic strategies in their styles. Compared to anti-social leaders they have different philosophies, motives and tendencies which include: A preference for cooperative over competitive behaviour; a preference for partnership and peaceful solutions to conflicts rather than winning; a belief in the importance of valuing and nurturing others as people rather than as means to an end; a complex moral system; an opening up of groups and dissolving boundaries (we are all the same under the skin); and a sardonic sense of the heroic.

These are dimensions rather than absolute categories. One could compare (say) Nelson Mandala with Hitler to get a feel of the differences. But, in general, it is probably preferable to think of style rather than 'the individual' because at times a person may show one face of leadership but at other times another. They may have mild tendencies towards either prosocial or anti-social styles or these styles may be marked and rigid. They may appear highly prosocial to ingroup members who show allegiance but anti-social to outsiders and defectors. They may be intuitively inclined towards (say) prosocial leadership but the social group (electorate) which supports them demands another style, and invalidates their prosocial efforts - telling them they need to be tough-minded. The ease (and degree) by which a leader will compromise their own values in order to get elected or chosen suggests that for some, gaining leadership roles is more important that pursuing personal principles. Personal principles can be too costly. On the other hand, the group might encourage an amplification of a preferred personal style. Some who are mildly aggressive become more so with being encouraged to go further and be more ruthless. As we noted above insecurity can effect style, but this insecurity may come from stresses in the environment.

People who are groomed for leadership by virtue of their families' social position, ie., they are placed in leadership positions, need not be socially skilled. However, some anti-social leaders are highly socially skilled, good orators and good at manipulating the values and (usually) needs for superiority, certainty, and strength in their followers.

Fear Based Patterns

Sometimes those with anti-social leadership styles can inspire devotion. At other times, as in China and the old USSR, they bring to life social patterns of fear and suspicion. Such regimes usually only survive with the support of a hidden class of 'secret police' who are ruthless and vicious and can create the fear of 'the knock on the door in the middle of the night'. Societies never seem to have had much problem in finding such folk and such 'police forces' can include a fair number of both narcissistic and sadistic personalities, who colour the whole police force. Anti-social leaders, protected by the young men of the secret police and other arms of enforcement, may slowly age and can in fact be quite old before they are deposed or simply die in post. China and the USSR were classic examples of this. For some supporters, appeasement and compliance is used to reduce the potential aggression of the leader(s) and/or his/her supporters. That is, the primary internal psychological organisation in both leaders and subordinates is defensive rather than relaxed and open. The fear based anti-social leadership style and its effects are the most easily detected. Even if the leader appears friendly, fear and apprehension can be common experiences. The psychology of subordinate, is to make sure they know where the threat might be (and for what), and avoiding it, or at least taking necessary steps to reduce it. Behaviourists would call this 'punishment' based control. The ethologist Michael Chance called this pattern of social behaviour agonic - meaning that the defensive aspects of fight/threaten (in the dominant) and appeasement/submit or flight/escape (in the subordinate) are primed. This leads to constrictions on the patterns of attention, reduces open exploration and may reduce the development of compassionate values.

If you watch members of a group interact when the leader is out of the room and compare this to when he/she is present you can sometimes have a feel for whether an anti-social style is operating. When an anti-social leader enters, the previous fun and jokey exchanges may cease, as does the free exploration of ideas. There is a switch in attention. Everyone watches their backs to ensure they are not the next to be attacked and they are preoccupied with the mood the leader is in. Bad moods signal hard times and times to watch yourself. Every thing is done to avoid putting the leader in a bad mood - even withholding important information about 'bad news' or mistakes. The poor folk who do put the leader in a bad mood can be blamed by other subordinates for causing them a hard time. At one meeting a subordinate said to another "why did you say that. You know what he's like. Now we are all going to suffer. Why couldn't just keep your mouth shut." My housemaster at school was very much like this and it was well known that the other masters (we called them master then not teachers) were wary, if not frightened, of him. He was a cane happy sod.

Of course, at times anti-social styles are unintended and reflect poor social skills, or stress, but at other times anti-social leaders enjoy the idea that others are apprehensive of them and believe this ensures them respect. Indeed, a belief in, and even admiration of, fear based respect probably marks the anti-social leader.

Industry is just beginning to recognise that some leadership styles are disastrous; that there is a dark side to charisma. Perhaps in our modern age there is a gradual fading in the valuing of tough leadership (but it is gradual and at times I doubt it). Those who do well at interview and present themselves with confidence, keenness and are socially skilled (often being male helps too) have often appeared the preferable people to place in positions of power and leadership. However, unless you observe them working with their team you have little idea how they will perform as leaders. Some turn out to be narcissistic, who value themselves but not others, are competitive with subordinates and shaming. They create such poor morale and inhibit other's creativity that they can cost an organisation dearly. Nearly all of us will have had some experience of having to work with these characters. So management training is all the vogue right now, teaching how to be socially rewarding and supportive, able to appreciate subordinate feedback and build a cooperative-friendly team spirit.

The thing to watch out for is those who can mimic such behaviours in 'training workshops' but do not really (privately) value these behaviours. So there can be slippage in their non-verbal behaviour and style. They may say 'the right things' but not feel or act friendly. At the slightest conflict they become aggressive/shaming, threatening to escalate conflict unless the other backs-down. Non-verbal behaviour is so important, I believe, because it taps right into the reptilian brain, and this, in interpersonal interactions, is what can set the emotional tone of the relationship(s). Indeed, we know that people monitor non-verbal communication at least as much as verbal. The way leaders deal with conflicts (of interest) both verbally and non-verbally is crucial to the skill of a leader. Good prosocial leaders have the ability to keep conflicts serious but also playful. People don't feel personally attacked; they play the ball not the player. Leaders like the Dalai Lama, Nelson Mandela and Gandhi are well known for such abilities.

Prosocial leaders are rarely feared. They encourage free exploration and affiliative styles. They are easy to approach and open to the opinions of others. Subordinates do not fear them because as leaders they do not use shame and humilation as a means of control. Generally, subordinates enjoy working with and for them and do not feel patronised or looked down on. Prosocials are concerned to see others mature, grow and pass on. They are not envious of others success. Their dark side is that they may not perform well in conflict situations - or at least can be very stressed by it and indecisive. Their needs for affiliation can interfere with tough decision making.

Leadership and Deception

As mentioned above a prosocial style can be superficial - it is a con and deception devised to be attractive to others. It is seen most commonly in cults, but not uncommonly in politics where self-presentation to win votes may hide a dark, scheming and manipulative style. That the prosocial style is a deception is revealed at times of conflicts of view, doubt, or if a member of the group desires to leave the group and defect. Everything changes for the potential defector. Where before they were wanted and esteemed now they are degraded (*e.g.*, called scab, traitor, heretic, weak, or made fun of etc.). They can be threatened with fear of permanent expulsion, loss of status and prestige, loss of support, or outright persecution from the previously supportive group and its leader. To put this another way when a subordinate looks for the exit they find they are trapped - it is hard to leave, or if they do, impossible to return. Many religions use this threat of course. No-one can love you like God can love you - if you leave the clan, the religion, you will put yourself beyond God and his love. Don't defect.

So the superficial prosocial leader knows how to play the game. They can stay prosocial as long as they receive sufficient subordinate, compliant, loving, or devotional signals. Jim Jones was almost certainly one of these types. They are among the most dangerous because of their skilful manipulation of needs for love, acceptance and conformity in subordinates, and their ability to create a sense of protection and belonging for ingroup members, with subtle (and sometimes not so subtle) undercurrents of fear.

Most of our history has not been shaped by leaders who have been on management training courses. It is alarming how much human history, not to mention our value systems, have been shaped by people who, at least from our position, seem rather crazy and certainly anti-social. Our civilization, culture and even our self-identities have been significantly shaped by our leaders and the mimicry of their values. Even now we don't take nearly enough care in choosing our leaders. But through most of our history we have not had that much choice.

AN HISTORICAL LEGACY OF ANTI-SOCIAL LEADERS

Gaius Julius Caesar was born around 100 BC. He was a man of extraordinary personal ambition. According to Grabsky's recent study of commanders, Caesar was a great commander. And well he might have been, but he was an archetypal, anti-social leader. From a very early age he was fixated on the desire for power and status in Rome. He, like many with anti-social leadership styles, was quite willing to take subordinate positions and ingratiate or grovel if it suited his purpose. He was known as a good orator and a ruthless manipulator. He also bore grudges. Once, when he was captured by pirates off the island of Rhodes, he joked with them that he would hunt them down and crucify them. When his ransom was paid and he was released he did exactly that.

Caesar worked out that the only way to gain power back in Rome was via developing his reputation as a military commander. His conquests had no other purpose as far as we can tell except to impress and give him power. For this he was prepared to wage wars that would kill and enslave very many thousands.

Among his many campaigns was the invasion of Gaul, which at the time was most of Northern Europe. He regarded the Gauls as semi-barbaric; a typical outgroup perception for the anti-social leader. There is no doubt that he was a courageous commander and gained the loyalty of his men by fighting with them, often shoulder to shoulder. Not all anti-social leaders are like this. But he also succeeded in stifling the growing culture and civilization that was emerging in Gaul and changing the course of western history for ever; all for personal ambition.

In fact Grabsky's book is full of descriptions of people who to can be described, a degree at least, as to have anti-social leadership styles. Of Lord Nelson he says "He was vain, ambitious... He made up his own rules and disobeyed orders." Nelson came to symbolize the best and worst traits of a leader. Devotion to country is also devotion to subdue outsiders and see enemies everywhere, and although sacrifice and courage are also represented in the character so is ambitiousness, status seeking and greed. Of Napoleon, Grabsky's narrative tells us of another ruthlessly ambitious man, who appeared to fear passing into history without trace. New looks at history suggest that Richard the Lionheart was actually a thug and the crusades pretty barbaric affairs. Francis Drake a plunderer and slaver - facts not commonly taught in our idealised history books.

Hitler is the most obvious, recent and extreme form of anti-social leader. He was moody and unpredictable and full of ideas of the need for conquest and the creation of the super-race. Unlike Caesar, who from the outset was interested in personal power, Hitler always linked his greatness and that of the German people together. Indeed, the rescuing hero type of leader is also potentially dangerous for he (it is usually a he) can inflame the insecurities of people, work on their grievances and offer himself as a saviour. As Lindholm notes, Hitler was devastated by the defeat of the first World War:

But Hitler did not disintegrate. His experiences had altered him, so that at this hopeless moment he received the call that reformulated his identity. Voices, like Joan of Arc, told him to rescue the motherland from the Jews. His blindness miraculously vanished as Hitler suddenly knew himself to be the saviour of his adopted nation. Henceforth, he and Germany were, he felt, mystically merged and he could act from his inner feelings with absolute certainty.

There is another fact that is not well known. According to Freeman Dr Morrell, the personal doctor to Hitler from 1936, was giving him large quantities of medication including sedatives, narcotics and amphetamine - often on demand. These may well have increased his tendency to psychosis and paranoia. Towards the end Hitler was not only showing the signs of syphilis but also Parkinson's disease, probably the consequence of such drug abuse.

Throughout history, the drives for power, dominance, saviourhood and rescuing heroes have been linked - and they can make a very unsavoury mixture. Indeed, one of the great tales of leadership, represented in many religions and cult groups, is of a leader's belief in saviourhood together with the subordinates need to feel saved, restored and reunited as a group. In Hitler the need for high dominance was obviously amplified as was a clear paranoid orientation to outsiders. The sheer scale of human suffering he brought to the world probably bears no equal. Like many effective leaders he was clever, manipulative, ruthless and a good orator, capable of arousing strong feelings of power, national pride and devotion to the cause. He was able to deceive Chamberlain that he was trustworthy. Like many he was a complex character, however, because, as Lindholm notes, he had strong needs to be loved and cared for. At the time he was persecuting Jews he passed a decree that lobsters should be given a painless death. He was also a vegetarian!

His contemporary, Stalin, was not much different. He cleverly out manoeuvred Trotsky after Lenin's death and hounded him into exile, where in Mexico in 1949, Trotsky was murdered with an ice pick in the head. Trotsky was not that pleasant himself and was quite able to shoot deserters, but he was a rival of Stalin's and possibly Lenin's preferred choice of successor. Stalin could not tolerate dissent, bore grudges and had no qualms in sending millions to the death camps. His will and vision were imposed with a terrible cost to the Russian people. Socialist ideals become a nightmare in his hands. Even now the power vacuum in this totalitarian state leaves room for new anti-social leaders to come through, peddling their paranoid messages and appeal to greatness to the oppressed.

It is a harrowing realisation that at the time of the second world war the main leaders of the conflict all had very serious problems. In Germany was a highly disturbed personality and drug addict, the leader of Italy not a lot better, Stalin was a clear psychopath, and as gifted as he was, Churchill suffered from manic-depression!

As we noted above, some individuals can appear to be prosocial leaders, even offering love and compassion, but such outward appearances actually hide, or over-lay a cauldron of hate and fear. This can be most deceptive - at least to some people. The Christian cult leader, Jim Jones gained his following by preaching a lot about love and offering saviourhood. He told his followers that no-one could love them like he could - all else was a pale shadow. He told people how much they could find love through him and he preached an idealistic and simplistic morality. Yet he was a loner who from an early age said: "I was ready to kill by the third grade. I mean I was so fucking aggressive and hostile, I was ready to kill. Nobody gave me any love, any understanding.... I'm standing there alone. Alone. Always alone..." (Quote in Lindholm, p. 140).

Moreover, like some anti-social leaders he focused sexuality and sexual values on himself. David Koersch was the same. For Jones:

Those who showed an interest in the opposite sex - and where therefore "compensating" for their homosexuality- were humiliated, or sometimes sodomised by Jones to prove their homosexuality.... Jones' sexual contact with men generated tremendous sexual conflict within some of them. He made his lessons in buggery all the more humiliating by always assuming the dominant position. As he conquered his partners, he told them again and again that it was for their own good. He derived no pleasure at all from the act, he told them, but made sure they did.

We shall look at 'followership' and ponder why these kinds of people get the attention they do. Hitler and similar others can only get power because there are many others willing to support them. It is far too easy to see the Hitlers of this world as bad and mad, who's personal rule is what does the damage. It is far more complex than this. Such leaders must have followers and supporters. For Hitler these were vast numbers in the military, police, academia, businesses right through to the clerks on the shop floor. Unless we understand the social, economic and political conditions that allow these individual's to come through - with their messages of strong leadership, power and pride - then we will not understand how such terrors can be brought to life. It is comforting to think that they, and the people who follow them, are crazy in a psychiatric sense - and may be some are. But even though these are extremes anti-social style leaders have impacted on our history substantially.

Problematic in another way are those who have these styles to a mild degree, and by their commitment to dogmas and ideologies are impassioned for what they believe to be a moral crusade. As Dixon points out, unfortunately virtue and crusades can be highly destructive. We might hope that such leadership styles are unlikely in democracies and certainly the excesses are constrained, but not completely.

Autocracy and Democracy

Autocratic forms of leadership are represented at both extremes of political activity, by the right and left wing have different concerns in regard to rank. The right wing is concerned with competition and the emergence of ranks and differences, protecting privilege, and with gaining, maintaining or identifying with a superior position. The left dislike competition and any form of ranks (at least that is what they say publicly, but we know about Animal Farm). They identify themselves with the low(er) ranks - the workers. The two wings can see themselves in complete opposition although the leadership styles can be similar. Many noted similarities of interpersonal style between Scargill and Thatcher at the time of the miners strike in 1984.

In many ways various leaders arise because they seem to offer solutions to the various social tensions inherent is our modern institutional life styles. We explored what these tensions, with recourse to the ideas of Eisenstadt. A potential threat to society comes from a failure to tackle these social tensions and find compassionate solutions for those who feel outsiders and are disadvantaged. The left has been labelled as a party of envy, fighting for the subordinates, the underdog, and is identified by the rich as a potentially inhibiting and grasping party concerned more with the distribution of wealth rather than its creation. The right is derived from a sense of superiority and fear of subordinate attack. Both, in different ways, can reflect authoritarian rather than compassionate values; both support the politics of conflict rather than consensus; and both think in terms of strong government to impose their own system of values (which are seen as threatening either to one or other ends of the hierarchy).

Do we really only have a choice between the politics of greed and fragmentation versus the politics of envy and corporatism? Without a clear psychological understanding of the dynamics of rank these polarised conflicts will continue, and although winners and losers may change places, overall nothing changes. Within the friction between competing groups one or other may gain the ascendency. But as Milgram noted:

Some dismiss the Nazi example because we live in a democracy and not an authoritarian state. But, in reality, this does not eliminate the problem. For the problem is not "authoritarianism" as a mode of political organisation or a set of psychological attitudes but authority itself. Authoritarianism may give way to democratic practice, but authority cannot be eliminated as long as society is to continue in the form we know. (p 179).

As I write this it is the fiftieth anniversary of the liberation of the Nazi concentration camps. For all the television programmes that there have been, all the stories sadly told, there was not one programme that I saw which had any in-depth analysis of the social-psychological forces that brought the Nazi state to life. The superficiality was, to my mind, frightening.

Recent Leaders

Although we now live in a democracy, it is in the very nature of the manipulation of power that democracy often fails to provide prosocial leaders. Hugh Freeman, who was president of the Royal College of Psychiatrists, has given a powerful and frightening review of how psychological and physical health problems have plagued many of our recent leaders in Europe and America. His review highlights many concerns, some of which are noted here. Woodrow Wilson suffered a number of mini-strokes that led to a personality change.

In 1945, at the time of the Yalta conference Roosevelt was so terminally ill he may not have really understood what was going on. J.F. Kennedy used amphetamine and steroids, both of which could have affected his judgement. Lyndon Johnson has been described as highly narcissistic with feelings of insecurity and grandiosity. In 1966-67, when the Vietnam war was becoming preoccupied with carpet bombing and defoliation, Johnson viewed his critics as 'enemies and traitors'. Nixon was known to have many narcissistic traits, to be exploitative and untrustworthy. At the time of the Watergate scandal he was drinking to such an extent, "that his aids thought him incapable of dealing with any business - however urgent- at these times."(p. 24) Ronald Reagan, towards the end, was known to be suffering from dementia, now sadly well advanced. Yet it was believed that if he could have stood again he would have won. It is true of course that the personalities of leaders do not exclude them from bringing social advances. Johnson did introduce important polices of social reform and a "new deal." But the pressures of modern leadership can still play havoc with a person and while they may be helpful to insiders they can be highly destructive to outsiders.

In Britain, Anthony Eden, at the time of the Suez crisis, was abusing drugs and alcohol and was described by some to be, "quite simply mad". As the history books are written on Margaret Thatcher and the up-surgence of the right in the 1980's, we get clear evidence of the autocratic leadership style. Ian Gilmour's book `Dancing with Dogma' leaves little doubt that at least some of the elements that go to making an autocrat were present in Thatcher's style. For example, Gilmour (who was one of her ministers in the early years) writes:

Mrs Thatcher regarded her first cabinet (and, I suspect, also her other cabinets) not as an aid to good government but as an obstacle to be surmounted. Her belief that dialogue was a waste of time rather than a means of arriving at an agreed course of action was a part of her rejection of consensus politics. Consensus, the Prime Minster later proclaimed, was achieved only by 'abandoning all beliefs, principles and values. Whoever won a battle,' she asked, 'under the banner of, "I stand for consensus"?' In her mind, of course, 'conviction' was diametrically opposed to consensus." (P 4-5)

As the years passed and more and more cabinet colleagues defected, speaking of her autocratic treatment of them, we began to get more insight into the psychology that controlled her. Rank and dominance and the need for greatness were written everywhere. And for whom was this greatness desired? Not for the poor who became poorer still, but for an elite; for an ideal of being British. Her obsession with enemies was revealed clearly when she said at the timc of thc miners strike in 1984, "We had to fight the enemy without in the Falklands.

We always have to be aware of the enemy within, which is more difficult to fight and more dangerous to liberty." (Quoted by Gilmour). So the miners were not just ordinary people fighting, often violently, for their jobs (manipulated by their own leader to a degree) but were potential enemies of the cause. This was a time when a Prime Minister openly talked about ninnies and wimps, and efforts at shaming. It was a time that ideology and causes matter more than people. It was a time when there was no such thing as society only a collection of individuals, until that is, Brussels threatened British interests, then the idea of Britishness made a come back.

When her end came it was shabby, marred by back-stabbing and retribution for the failures in the courage and loyalty of her subordinates (colleagues). Such an old story and somewhat typical of a person who has little ability to reflect on the self and see the sources of her difficulties as coming from within. To be fair to Thatcher though, it is less clear how much she was motivated by a personal ambition to be great, or more to rescue an identity for family and country. Certainly, her stated intent was to free people from government control, although in this quango-ised state of ours even this is doubtful. It is now estimated there are 7,700 quangos of various sorts, often staffed by conservative appointees and costly the state £54 billion. She was certainly a strong leader and enjoyed the title the 'Iron Lady'. We must leave it to the historians to decide. She changed Britain significantly. Who knows what we may now be like without her. But it is her style that marks her as being the autocratic type.

So we can see that anti-social leaders have a number of qualities. A need for power; a belief in their own way, a focus on the importance of strength, a tendency to talk in terms of fighting, conquering, pride and becoming great, a need to stress the importance of being more powerful than competitors, paranoid or contemptuous attitudes to those who are not ingroup members, a preparedness to subdue subordinates not with argument but with fear or shame - the language of wimps and ninnies.

In whatever context leadership arises, the lack of compassion for followers and subordinates can lead to appalling abuses of power; the first world war being a most tragic example. As Dixon makes clear, at times military leaders have seen their subordinates as no more than cannon-fodder. But even democratically elected leaders can show a complete lack of interest in certain sections of the groups they lead, except to keep them in check. Many leaders in the West appear to have a view of the "workers" as manoeuvrable production units whose value depends on whether they can be fitted in with wealth creating - *i.e.*, production fodder. Rebellion can be ruthlessly put down (e.g, the miners strike of 1984).

If we are becoming increasing cynical about our leaders, religious and political, and even democracy, we might remember our history and what has gone before. There is no way to avoid leadership. Sure, some will try to manipulate us to get our vote and sure they will have the various human failings, like sexual ones, but we can still insist on compassionate values once we sort out in our own minds the issue of how we want the world to look for our grandchildren. Do we want them to live in a polluted, highly competitive, 'dump the losers', world?

As Freeman makes clear some of our problems with leadership arise because our jerry built brains were never designed to cope with the leadership of the mega-groups we now live within, nor the mass of information leaders have to cope with, nor the uncertainties of positions that can change rapidly, nor the complexity of the competing interests of all the subgroups that exist within the modern state, nor indeed with the grandiosity and scale of power that is so much part of a modern nation state. To say that political leadership, with its hands on nuclear buttons and the arms trade, is in crisis, is an understatement.

LEADERSHIP AND ALLIANCES

Our animal-primate psychology is revealed in other ways when it come to leadership and flaws in democracy. One of the most serious problems facing us is that both primate and human leadership/dominance are always derived from alliances. So indeed, over many centuries human leaders have built around themselves a system of alliances (reaching back to simple surfdoms and chiefdoms) that ensure a continuation of elitist values and institutions. Because leaders need support they have to build in a potential reward system for followers and supporters, enabling them to gain power in the higher echelons of the group and protect their privileges. Thus, there is always a complex interaction between leaders and alliances. The use of favouritism and patronage to alliances is as powerful a mechanism in humans as it is in non-human primates. No chimpanzee can make it to the top without offering favours to alliances.

As Huttonpoints out this has been achieved in Britain via the continuance of an old system of favours and mutual supports, operated through the institutionalisation of the peerage, honour and patronage system.

.... the incapacity of the constitution to offer any check to discretionary executive government has even corrupted the Conservative Party, with the contagion spreading to the state. Honours are routinely awarded to party contributors; funds are accepted from foreign donors of questionable character and motive in return for undeclared favours; defence contracts and flotation of privatised utilities are awarded to government supporters in industry and city. What has been constructed in Britain, using the ancient and unfettered state, is a form of conservatives hegemony in the literal meaning of that word: a system of supremacy over others.

And moreover,

The Lord Chancellor, a member of the cabinet appoints the judgers who come from the same milieu as his party colleagues while the government's chief officer, the Attorney General is also drawn form the ranks of the governing party..... Judges appoint other judges in their own image, while the criminal justice system is increasingly involved in maintaining order. In whatever social milieu we explore, be it of the feminist critique of patriarchy, or the establishment of academic and scientific hegemonies, or the political institutions we inhabit, or even the rise of tyrants like Hitler, we see that leaders and alliances are wrapped around each other to protect their own interests and shape the values and pursuits of privilege - supremacy. Barkow's recognition of the rolc of status and prestige in forming and maintaining human ranks, is, in current human society the primate mind advanced by its skilful manipulation of favours.

Until these psychological aspects of our minds are addressed and confronted, as they work themselves out in our traditions, values and institutions, it is unlikely that we will be free from creating a certain craziness in our social spaces.

SELF-INTEREST ON THE WORLD STAGE

So it seems clear that many positions of power rely on forming alliances and various trades of favours to support mutual self-interest. Internationally this has had many tragic consequences. In the first place the growth of the arms trade and the power of western armies has led many western governments to support foreign groups and governments that were not far short of barbaric. And they did so from pure self-interest and xenophobia but clothed in the language of moral crusades and freedom. Chomsky's recent book Deterring Democracy leaves no doubt that the West has been involved in a fairly systematic process of propping up many two-bit dictators provided they leave open the door to western influence, (access to their resources) with tragic consequences for the people. In the history of modern wars we can see time after time the meddling hand of the West. Not only do they arm one, and at times both sides, but the conflicts of the lands fought over are often due to western influence. Much of Africa is split up into unrealistic nation states disrespectful of tribal boundaries with arbitrary borders due to the legacy of colonialism.

Time after time the desire to support alliances rather than stick to moral principles has been to our shame. The history of Vietnam is a history of broken promises. Ho Chi-Minh had helped the Americans against the Japanese and were promised that the Americans would do what they could to keep the French (whose colony it was before the war) out. In the six months of 1945 when they briefly had independence Mo Chi-Minh actually quoted from the American constitution. In the end though the alliance to the France was stronger than that to Vietnam and the French recolonised the South, creating a new rebel group in the north. Understandably the sense of anger and betrayal was immense. The rest, as they say is history. Turning a blind eye to our own and our allies immoral behaviour has been the source of much suffering.

Democracies then do not liberate us from pursuing self-interest and exploitation. We just do it in different ways, hiding our historical immoral behaviours and using appeals to national pride and self-interest with a little Xenophobia thrown in for good measure. This gets votes. As we shall see in our chapter on economics, once a society beings to loosen the restraints on self-interest, and anything goes in the pursuit of profit and wealth accumulations, societies begin to fragment and we end up with the worst economic and social depravities. A civilised society becomes civilised by the restraints it imposes on self-interest and exploitation.

Leading Change?

It is, of course, true that western societies, indeed the world, is undergoing rapid change. We need leaders who are managers of this change. These managers and leaders are going to have to address themselves to the increasing conflicts and tensions of competing groups. If our psychological health both nationally and internationally were put more on the agenda as a salient concern in managing this change then I suspect we might have a very different orientation to how we go about things. But sadly we don't. The pursuit of wealth and self-interest rule to day. At home the creation of short-term employment contracts, and increasing part-time work (which has far fewer rights than full-time) and the increasing insecurities gradually proliferating, as our cultures and communities fragment, suggests times of increasing violence, depression and various stress related conditions. Styles of leadership, from the reaches of government right down to the managers of industry and (what used to be) the nationalised services are caught in the whirlwind of these changes. If the stories of my patients are to be believed, as they lose their jobs or have wages cut, managers are veering towards increasingly, competitive anti-social styles.

Over and over again evolutionary psychologists (along with many others) will tell us that we cannot just create any social climate and think that humans will behave decently. Our minds are constantly monitoring the social domain, they are highly attuned to it and if the social domains provides cues for poverty, envy betrayal etc. we will react accordingly. Although many like to think that moral behaviour is about individuals, this is a cosy illusion. Moral behaviour grows from moral institutions and moral social structures that promote social fairness and the recognition of the needs of others, not just self-interest. Social policy matters. It is as much a top down as a bottom up process.

6

Effective Leadership Skills and Communication Development

AN INTRODUCTION TO LEADERSHIP STYLES

Leadership styles refers to the broad approach adopted by a leader. All leaders (at least all those leaders who already have followers) have one. If you are already a leader, that includes you. You just might not know what it is yet. But your followers do! Style is often based on a leader's own beliefs, personality, experiences, working environment and their assessment of the situation at the time. Some leaders work within one style. Others are more flexible and can adapt their style to meet the needs of different situations. So, what determines a leader's preferred leadership style?

DECISION MAKING

A very powerful part of your style of leadership is your need to make decisions. All leaders (including you and me) approach decision making based upon their own beliefs about their responsibility for decisions, as well as their followers' capacity to make decisions. A number of researchers have developed leadership style models based around decision making (eg,Lewin, Tannenbaum and Schmidt, Hersey and Blanchard). Each of these models look at a range of styles - from ones in which the leader makes all the decisions (and imposes them on the followers - what we would call an autocratic leadership style) to ones in which the followers are allowed to make decisions on their own (what we would call a facilitative leadership style).

A key element in each of these models is the assessment of which style is most appropriate at a given point, and whether the followers are able and willing to make decisions themselves. If the leader miscalculates, the followers are not likely to respond the way the leader would hope! Imagine - you are a capable and experienced person, motivated and wishing to get on (does that sound familiar?). But your leader keeps all decisions to themselves, barks orders and doesn't respond to requests for help. If it sounds implausible, let me assure you - that is exactly what many people experience from leaders who have not learned to be a leader! Another element here is that the more flexible you are as a leader - and the more able you are to judge the needs of the situation - the more likely you are to adopt a style that will work.

PERSONALITY

Personality can be interpreted as the typical ways in which a person behaves. Personality develops as we mature and is normally fairly consistent (or stable) by the time we reach adulthood. As a result we can predict how someone might well behave in different situations, although of course the person concerned always has choice and free will.

Some personality factors do influence our leadership style. For example:

- Outgoing and sociable leaders are more likely to connect with people and communicate with them.
- Tense leaders are more likely to be anxious about issues and communicate their worries to their followers.
- Leaders with a high need to be in control are more likely to keep decisions to themselves and to dictate them to others.

Leaders who are self-aware, who understand how their personality impacts upon others, are better placed to make good choices and adjust their style when needed. Various personality assessment questionnaires can be used to help leaders learn about the effect they have on others. That along with being willing to listen to feedback!

WORKING ENVIRONMENT

The working environment can have a big impact on the leadership style you might adopt. The two main influences here are:

- The demands of the organisation, its market, systems and processes
- The culture of the organisation.

Organisations that deal with safety critical products or services, that carry high risk, require fast responses or are coming under attack or criticism are more likely to foster aggressive styles of leadership. Those organisations that encourage continuous improvement and innovation, or which are keen to develop customers, staff and suppliers, are more likely to foster participative styles of leadership. Organisational culture refers to "the way things are done around here". It is the colective version of individual personality and determines how the organisation's leadership communicate and make decisions. An organisation's culture tends to reinforce compatible styles of leadership in its junior leaders.

ACTIVE LISTENING

In our active world of communication one cannot afford to exclude the art of listening. As a leader, you must listen to your constituents in order to be effective. You need to listen and correctly understand all messages from group members.

Active Listening differs from hearing. Hearing is the act of perceiving audible sounds with the ear and is a passive act. Listening, on the other hand, is the active pursuit of understanding what the other person is saying and feeling. In active listening, the receiver tries to understand what the sender is feeling and what the message means. The listener puts his/her understanding into his/her own words and feeds it back to the speaker for verification. It is important to feed back only what the listener feels the speaker's message meant, nothing more, nothing less. This creates an atmosphere of acceptance and understanding in which the speaker can explore the problem and determine a solution. To listen actively and to understand is not a passive or simple activity.

The following are important characteristics of a "good listener".

BE THERE

Be present in heart, mind and spirit with the person. You need to hear what he/she has to say. If you don't have the time, or don't want to listen, wait until you do.

ACCEPT

Accept the person as she/he is without judgement or reservation or putting the person in a mental box or category, even though she/he may be very different from you.

TRUST

Trust the person's ability to handle his/her own feelings, work through them, and find solutions to his/her own problems.

LISTEN

Don't plan what you are going to say. Don't think of how you can interrupt. Don't think of how to solve the problem, how to admonish, how to console or what the person "should" do. DON'T THINK TO STRUGGLE OR REACT...LISTEN!

KEEP OUT OF IT

Keep yourself removed. Be objective. Don't intrude physically, verbally, mentally. Keep Quiet. Listen. It maybe hard to be passive.

STAY WITH THE OTHER PERSON

Put yourself in the other's shoes. Don't become that person, but understand what he/she is feeling, saying and thinking. Stay separate enough to be objective, but involved enough to help.

DEVELOPING LEADERSHIP SKILLS

Leadership skills can be learned, and leadership development benefits individuals and organizations. Leadership development refers to any activity that enhances the capability of an individual to assume leadership roles and responsibilities. Examples include degree programmes in management, executive education, seminars and workshops, and even internships. These types of learning opportunities focus on developing knowledge, skills, self-awareness, and abilities needed to lead effectively.

Just as not all people are born with the ability or desire to play soccer like Zinedine Zidane or sing like Luciano Pavarotti, not all people are born with the ability to lead. Personal traits and behavioural dispositions can help or hinder a person's leadership effectiveness. While these are difficult to change, leadership is a set of behaviours and practices that can be learned through effort and experience.

Cognitive Capacities	Dispositional Attributes	Motives/ Values	Social Capacities	Problem Solving Skills	Expertise & Knowledge
- General Intelligence - Cognitive Complexity - Creativity	- Adaptability - Extroversion - Risk propensity - Openness	- Need for Socialized Power - Need for achievement - Motivation to lead	- Social intelligence - Emotional intelligence - Persuasion and negotiation skills	- Meta-cognition - Problem construction - Solution Generation - Self Regulation Skills	- Expertise and knowledge in specific areas

Leadership traits

A list of leader traits by trait category.

Successful leadership development is the result of three things:

1. Individual learner characteristics, including willingness and ability to learn
2. The quality and nature of the leadership development programme, including its structure and content
3. Opportunities to practice new skills and receive performance feedback

METHODS OF LEADERSHIP DEVELOPMENT

Leader development takes place through multiple mechanisms: formal instruction, developmental job assignments, 360-degree feedback, executive coaching, and self-directed learning. These approaches may occur independently but are more effective in combination.

FORMAL TRAINING

Organizations often offer formal training programmes to their leaders. Traditional styles provide leaders with required knowledge and skills in a particular area using coursework, practice, "overlearning" with rehearsals, and feedback. This traditional lecture-based classroom training is useful; however, its limitations include the question of a leader's ability to transfer the information from a trainingenvironment to a work setting.

DEVELOPMENTAL JOB ASSIGNMENT

Following formal training, organizations can assign leaders to developmental jobs that target the newly acquired skills. A job that is developmental is one in which leaders learn, undergo personal change, and gain leadership skills resulting from the roles, responsibilities, and tasks involved in that job. Developmental job assignments are one of the most effective forms of leader development. A "stretch" or developmental assignment challenges leaders' new skills and pushes them out of their comfort zone to operate in a more complex environment, one that involves new elements, problems, and dilemmas to resolve.

360-DEGREE FEEDBACK

The 360-degree feedback approach is a necessary component of leader development that allows leaders to maximize learning opportunities from their current assignment. It systematically provides leaders with perceptions of their performance from a full circle of viewpoints, including subordinates, peers, superiors, and the leader's own self-assessment. With information coming from so many different sources, the messages may be contradictory and difficult to interpret. However, when several different sources concur on a similar perspective, whether a strength or weakness, theclarity of the message increases. For this mechanism to be effective, the leader must accept feedback and be open and willing to make changes. Coaching is an effective way to facilitate 360-degree feedback and help effect change using open discussion.

COACHING

Leadership coaching focuses on enhancing the leader's effectiveness, along with the effectiveness of the team and organization. It involves an intense, one-on-one relationship aimed at imparting important lessons through assessment, challenge, and support. Although the goal of coaching is sometimes to correct a fault, it is used more and more to help already successful leaders move to the next level of increased responsibilities and new and complex challenges. Coaching aims to move leaders towards measurable goals that contribute to individual and organizational growth.

SELF-DIRECTED LEARNING

Using self-directed learning, individual leaders teach themselves new skills by selecting areas for development, choosing learning avenues, and identifying resources. This type of development is a self-paced process that aims not only to acquire new skills but also to gain a broader perspective on leadership responsibilities and what it takes to succeed as a leader.

LEADERSHIP DEVELOPMENT MODELS

McCauley, Van Veslor, and Ruderman (2010) described a two-part model for developing leaders. The first part identifies three elements that combine to make developmental experiences stronger: assessment, challenge, and support. Assessment lets leaders know where they stand in areas of strengths, current performance level, and developmental needs. Challenging experiences are ones that stretch leaders' ability to work outside of their comfort zone, develop new skills and abilities, and provide important opportunities to learn. Support—which comes in the form of bosses, co-workers, friends, family, coaches, and mentors—enables leaders to handle the struggle of developing.

The second part of the leader-development model illustrates that the development process involves a variety of developmental experiences and the ability to learn from them. These experiences and the ability to learn also have an impact on each other: leaders with a high ability to learn from experience will seek out developmental experiences, and through these experiences leaders increase their ability to learn.

The leader-development process is rooted in a particular leadership context, which includes elements such as age, culture, economic conditions, population gender, organizational purpose and mission, and business strategy. This environment molds the leader development process. Along with assessment, challenge and support, leadership contexts are important aspects of the leader-development model.

GENERAL ELECTRIC MODEL OF LEADERSHIP DEVELOPMENT

Another well-known model of leadership development is used by the General Electric Corporation. Managers with high potential are identified early in their careers. Their development is monitored and planned to include a variety of job placements to develop skills and experience, a rigorous performance-evaluation process, and formal training programmes at the corporate leadership center in Crotonville, New York. For top managers, the CEO leads some of the training; the CEO also reviews performance evaluations for high-potential managers during site visits to the various subsidiarydivisions.

IMPORTANCE OF DEVELOPING LEADERSHIP SKILLS

What makes a good leader? The answer varies widely depending on who you ask, with researchers disagreeing on the critical components that go into the most effective corporate chief. But there are traits they do agree on, including personality components and acquired skills. Some believe even the situation for leadership itself has a bearing on the effectiveness of the leader.

IMPORTANT LEADERSHIP SKILLS

- Commitment, resolve and perseverance – Driving every aspect of the organization towards a singular unified purpose.
- Risk-taking – breaking conventions and developing new products and services to establish marketplace dominance (and possibly even create a unique market).
- Planning – though a leader typically doesn't get too involved in the details, he or she must orchestrate a high-level plan that drives everyone towards the unified goal.
- Motivating – an effective leader must be able to encourage contributions from the entire organization, navigating the specific motivators of each individual or group to push the right buttons and inspire employees at every level to achieve not only their personal best but the best for the organization as a whole.
- Communication skills that rely on active listening – far more than just being able to speak and write persuasively, leadership communication skills incite others to work towards the stated goal in line with the path the leader has chosen.
- Possessing or obtaining the skills required to successfully achieve business goals – bringing a unique knowledge set to the table or acquiring it personally or through employees and other subordinates.

WHAT MAKES THESE INDIVIDUAL SKILLS SO IMPORTANT?

First, a distinction needs to be made: the difference between a leader and a manager. A leader is someone who does the right thing, whereas a manager does things right. Or to put it another way, management is an occupation, leadership is a calling.

As addressed in the list above, this calling demands a unique vision for success and the tools necessary to communicate and implement that vision. The leader must possess a set of clearly-defined convictions and the daring and skill to translate their vision into a reality. This is why many people believe, as seen in What Motivates True Leaders, that the most successful development of leadership skills takes place when the leader is geared towards the development of individuals or social constructs. This foundation creates a drive and a passion that many believe cannot be replicated or faked in situations where the leader is concerned solely with financial returns.

With effective leadership, all participants within the organization are confident someone they know is working towards the greater good, both on their behalf personally and that of the company, as well as the larger impact created by the specific product or service. And within this system, one of the most critical elements to success is a leader in whom they can place their trust. That's because true leadership is about taking people to places they would not or could not go on their own. And achieving that level of loyalty and dedication is next to impossible without the genuine allegiance inspired by true leadership skills.

IMPROVE YOUR LEADERSHIP SKILLS

Whether you consciously aware of it or not, on some level you are continually leading yourself and others – you don't necessarily have to have a large team reporting to you to be considered a leader and to need effective leadership skills. In one leadership study, qualities such as assertiveness, adaptability, intelligence and conscientiousness were cited as the most important leadership skills. Research clearly shows that transformational leaders – leaders who are positive, inspiring, and who empower and develop followers – are better leaders. They are more valued by followers and have higher performing teams.

As a result, it would only make sense that you strive to improve your leadership skills and get the most out of life for everyone in your sphere.

Consider these 11 tips for how to improve your leadership skills so to become a better leader and think about ways that you can implement these strategies in your daily life at work.

1. *Have a clear vision:* Take the time to share your vision, your mission and your goals with your team. Your job as a leader is to provide a clear path that your team can follow. Your team also must understand why the goals you have set are valuable to them. Take the time to explain to them, in detail, why and how your vision will not only improve the business, but how it will benefit them in return. Include your team in your strategic planning sessions, ask for feedback and get them to "buy into" your vision for the future of the company.
2. Know and utilize your strengths and gifts. You have unique gifts and natural leadership skills that you were born with and personal strengths you've developed over your lifetime. Realizing and utilizing these gifts and strengths will assist you in being a formidable leader.
3. *Be Passionate:* This is one of the most important leadership skills. Would you look to someone for guidance and leadership if they did not truly care about the goals of the group? Of course not! Great leaders are not just focused on getting group members to finish tasks; they have a genuine passion and enthusiasm for the projects they work on. Start by thinking of different ways that you can express your zeal. Let people know that you care about their progress. When one person shares something with the rest of the group, be sure to tell them how much you appreciate such contributions.
4. Live in accordance with your morals and values. Making choices and taking actions out of accordance with your morals and values leaves

you with a nagging "bad" feeling. This feeling seeping in from your subconscious mind hinders your success in your career and your relationships. On the other hand, making choices and taking actions aligned with your morals and values helps you succeed almost effortlessly as key leadership skills. People sense integrity and will naturally respect your opinion and leadership.

5. *Serve as a role model:* The best leaders walk the walk and talk the talk. As a result, group members admire these leaders and work to emulate these behaviours. If you want to become a better leader, work on modeling the qualities that you would like to see in your team members.
6. Set definitive goals and follow concrete action plans. You have to know where your destination is before you can map out a plan to get there. To improve your leadership skills, first set specific life goals with appropriate timelines. Design your goals by moving backwards from the end of your life to the present week. Then, formulate action plans you can commit to that will get you to where you want to be.
7. Maintain a positive attitude. No one respects a grumpy or negative person. With a positive attitude you are looking at the bright side of life. People are naturally attracted to you when you have a positive attitude. By being positive, you will lead a happier life, as well as be surrounded by other positive people. You will also magically attract exciting offers and possibilities.
8. Improve communication skills. Having great leadership skills includes your being able to clearly and specifically communicate your vision, goals, skills, intentions, and expectations to others. This also includes your ability to listen to what other people are consciously or unconsciously communicating. To become a great communicator, continually strive to improve your verbal, non-verbal, and listening skills.
9. Motivate others to greatness. The greatest leaders are those who include everyone in their sphere of influence by recognizing each person's greatest value. To be one of these leaders, look beyond the obvious and see others with insight and compassion. Many of history's greatest leaders have admitted that they rose to the top because another leader recognized and harnessed their potential.
10. Be willing to admit and learn from failures and weaknesses. Face it – No one is perfect, and everyone has made a mistake or two in their lives! The most successful leaders know that the key to success is not in avoiding falling or failing, but to learn from their mistakes. As a strong leader, you will also be able to communicate your weaknesses to your team, so that you and your team can appoint someone who excels at that particular task or activity.

11. Continue to educate and improve yourself. Great leaders demonstrate effective leadership skills, but most importantly, continue to improve themselves in every possible way. The person who thinks he is an expert, has a lot more to learn. Never stop learning. Be receptive to everyone's perceptions and information from around the world and beyond. Always grow and learn.

SKILLS FOR EFFECTIVE LEADERSHIP COMMUNICATION

- Making a connection with the audience is very important. Unless you are able to connect with your audience and vice-versa, there will be no depth in your words that will compel the audience to think. Connection here does not mean just superficial networking. You should emotionally connect with the audience to make an impact on them. Making the common man feel that they matter a lot has an enormous influence that will help them accept you as their leader.
- Communication is a two way process. Therefore, listening is as important as what you say. Listen carefully to what others say, and if required, make a note of it so that you can refer to it later. It will also help you to learn what others think about a particular subject.
- It is said that the first impression is the best impression, and the saying has a lot of truth in it. Making a great first impression has an enormous impact on the listener.
- Choosing the right words is a vital factor in leadership communication skills. Carefully chosen words can make a huge impact. Powerful words have the potential to charge up people and motivate them, while irresponsible comments can make the whole crowd turn against you. So always remember to choose your words carefully and cautiously.
- Developing leadership charisma is another quality of a leader. Learn to maintain authority while communicating.
- While communicating with your subordinates or co-workers; try to be transparent, open, and above all show trust and respect.
- Have a clear point of view. Unless you don't have a direction, it is not possible to guide and show others the path.
- Along with good communication skills, a leader should also have expressive body language and good eye contact. The ability to make the listener feel that you understand them is also equally important.
- Speech delivery is also important to leadership communication skills. How you modulate your voice, how you deliver the speech and your overall presentation are important to take hold of the audience so that they listen to you with interest.
- Practice is the key to great communication. A lot of practice can only

help you to master the art of great communication techniques. You may also take the help of a communication guide to learn the right body language while communi-cating in different circumstances.

DELEGATING RESPONSIBILITY

How can you help people in your organization prepare for future leadership roles and free up more time in your own schedule so you can do other things? DELEGATION. Delegation is the key to a successful organization. Sharing responsibilities keeps members interested and enthusiastic about the group. You may be reluctant to delegate because you want to make sure the job is done right (your way). They might take longer to accomplish the task than you doing it yourself. It will also help your health while improving the quality of the end project. But you can make members feel unimportant and become apathetic if you don't share the responsibility of making the organization a success.

REASONS TO DELEGATE

Group benefits:

- Members become more involved and committed
- More projects and activities are undertaken
- A greater chance that projects will be completed
- Increased opportunities for members to develop leadership skills
- Chance to fill leadership roles with qualified, experienced people
- The organization operates more effectively

Leader benefits:

- Not being spread too thin and therefore is less likely to burn out
- Gaining satisfaction from seeing members grow and develop
- Acquiring more experience in executive and administrative functions

An Appropriate Time To Delegate Is When:

- There is a lot of work
- A member has particular qualifications for or interest in a task
- Someone can benefit from the responsibility
- Routine matters need attention
- Details take up too much time and have to be divided

The Time Not To Delegate Is When:

- The task is something you would not want to do (menial work)
- Someone is under qualified or overqualified for the task
- The work is your own specified responsibility
- The area is big or is an unsolved problem, issue or matter dealing with the personal feelings of another or with confidentiality - the "hot potato"

Ways to Delegate:

- Ask for volunteers by a show of hands or pass a sign-up sheet for a particular project. (Interest is a great motivator!) However, this method can be impersonal and you could get "stuck" if none signs up.

- Appoint or suggest someone. Sometimes a member lacks self-confidence and won't volunteer; appointing him/her demonstrates your confidence in them.
- Assign through a committee. This takes the pressure off an individual and reinforces organizational structure.
- The "best fit" of person with the task is the most effective. Try to spread the enjoyable and responsible tasks around, giving more members status and value.

Guidelines for Effective Delegation:

1. Choose the appropriate people by interviewing and placing your members carefully. Consider his/her time, interest and capabilities. Specific responsibilities to be delegated to a particular person must be appropriate for the growth of that person at that time.
2. Explain why they were selected for this task.
3. Delegate segments that make sense; not bits and pieces of a task, but share the "big picture". People like to know how their segment will help the larger programme.
4. Discuss the task at hand. Discuss ideas; mutually set goals and objectives.
5. Whenever possible, give those who will be responsible for carrying out a programme a voice in the decision-making. Do not lower standards; don't insult your members!
6. Define clearly the responsibilities being delegated to each person. Explain what is expected of them and what the bounds of authority are. Be sure an agreement is reached on areas where the person can function freely. The end result is important, not the various steps. Everyone accomplishes tasks differently.
7. Find out how you will know when they need help. Make sure they understand you are willing to assist but must first be told when and how you can help. Give accurate and honest feedback. People want and deserve to know how they are doing. This is both an opportunity for giving satisfaction and encouraging growth. Allow for risk-taking and mistakes.
8. Support your officers and committee chairs by sharing information, knowledge and plans with them. It is incredible how many errors are made simply due to a lack of information. Share in their failures as well as their successes.
9. Delegate. Most responsible people do not appreciate someone looking over their shoulder, or taking back parts of their assignment before

they have a chance to do it. As a leader, it can be hard for you to "let go;" you like being in the driver's seat. Let them do the job! Delegating does not eliminate work, it simply changes it. As you delegate appropriately, a multiplier effect occurs.

10. Follow up. Check periodically to see if people have any questions regarding how a project is supposed to be done. This will also let you know how that individual is progressing on the task. There is a fine line between delegating and following-up.
11. Evaluate. You must not overlook the need to evaluate and measure the extent to which actions conformed to plans, if the plans went well or if the original plans were appropriate and worthwhile. Use appropriate feedback techniques. One of your most important roles as a leader is to help your members to learn and grow through both their successes and their failures! Your members are your greatest resource. Let them create and turn their creativity interaction!

EMPOWERMENT

ANONYMOUS

Anyone interested in the business field has probably run across an article or two on empowering employees. It seems leaders are truly realizing the benefits of training their subordinates how to handle situations and giving them the authority to do so. It may seem like a commonsense approach to success, so why haven't businesses picked up on this earlier? Well, like so many things in the world, it is not always as cut and dry as it may seem. Empowering others can take some creative work on the part of the leader. Some people like the idea of seeking approval for every minor step; that way if something goes wrong, they have someone to blame. Some people have not built up enough self-confidence to handle situations. Some leaders fear they will look unqualified, weak or indecisive if they seek input from other members. And sometimes leaders - for their own reasons - just don't feel comfortable relinquishing control to others no matter how much they trust them. If you are one of those leaders who cannot seem to let go - or you want to, but don't really know what this will entail - read on.

Following are the various roles a leader can take in empowering others to develop leadership abilities and even some self-confidence along the way.

DISCOVERER

It is important to note that there is no single "right way" to empower others. A leader's job consists of continually looking for new opportunities to accomplish the group mission. Are you always chairing the programme committees? Do you lead the meetings as well as write up the minutes? Maybe it is time to recommend someone else for these duties. Not only does this empower others, it adds to your free time as well. As a discoverer, it is important to be a visionary and be flexible to change.

ILLUSTRATOR

As a leader, it is extremely important to remember - and remind others - about the goals, values and mission of the group. You can set a path towards accomplishing goals so that others may follow suit. As an empowering leader, you can inspire goal commitment - but in a way that doesn't equal demanding compliance. If you are committed to the group goals, let it be known in the way you approach opportunities or deal with obstacles.

ENCOURAGER

In most organizations, the days of the leader's way being the only way are long gone. To empower others to take responsibility, be supportive: offer reassurance, recognize successes, believe in your members and take a vested interest in their achievements. You don't need to look the other way when failures occur, but dwelling on them accomplishes little. Acknowledge them, make improvements or suggestions for the future, highlight the successes and move on!

ENABLER

In some situations, enabling is viewed in a very negative light (*i.e.*, substance abuse). In empowering leadership, however, enabling others can be very positive. In this sense, enabling involves offering a helping hand to boost chances of success. You might consider yourself to be a coach or team builder in this position, which would be accurate labels for the roles you are playing here.

SMOOTHER

Finally, an empowering leader needs to facilitate accomplishments to the extent possible. This means smoothing the way for others by providing them with necessary information to complete a task, networking with outside contacts to build positive relationships and serving as a resource. This is a critical step in the empowerment process; people need to know they have the support and resources they need to help them accomplish goals.

The benefits to empowerment are numerous, not only to those being empowered, but to the leaders and overall organization as well. Aside from building self-confidence and increasing free time as mentioned earlier, take a look at some of the other potential benefits:

To the followers:

- Increased motivation

- Higher degree of learning
- Improved tolerance of stress

To the leaders:

- Increased organizational commitment
- Less role ambiguity
- Increased satisfaction with roles and the organization

To the organization:

- More flexibility
- Better sense of community
- Requests/problems handled with increased speed
- Group coordination and development

FACILITATION

We think facilitation is:

- Open discussion
- Challenging other participants and connecting with them
- Engaging in an open dialogue with diverse topics
- Safe environment for people's views
- Drawing out diverse views
- Being a devil's advocate
- About learning/expanding ideas
- Leading the group in the correct direction
- Developing group dynamics
- Encouraging people to step outside of their comfort zone
- Being inclusive, open-minded, understanding, tolerant
- Interjecting only when necessary, just observing and listening
- Having fun, getting everyone involved
- Encouragement of personal reflection

We do not think facilitation is:

- Imposing your own views on others
- Lecture
- Debate or confrontational
- About yourself, it's for the participants
- Ganging up on others or taking sides
- Just a few people discussing
- Forcing people to speak or giving answers
- An excuse to dominate, or yell
- Allowing personal attacks
- Getting emotional
- Asking one person to represent an entire social identity
- Making people conform

What do you do when someone makes an offensive comment?

- Give people an option to walk away
- Ask them a question to have them clarify comment, allows for re-evaluation
- Re-visit ground rules
- Facilitators take a more active role in discussion
- Break into smaller groups for further discussion
- Pose an alternative point of view
- Discuss assumptions and intentions of comment
- If all else fails, call a small break and the facilitator has a personal talk with the person
- If it's between two people, open the discussion up to entire group
- Don't get side tracked in a long discussion
- Ask the group to refrain from using offensive comments
- Be aware that people may react differently
- Be flexible and use your judgement to react

How do you create a safe environment?

- Create common guidelines for the group to follow
- *Icebreakers:* Finding commonalities
- Start with less sensitive topics to build trust
- Body language
- Diffuse tensions
- Drop your own reservations
- Give everyone a chance to speak, sit on the same level
- Anonymous question and comment cards
- Give people time for self reflection
- Silence is OK, give people an opportunity to pass
- Try to build a group bond, mix people together
- Identify reasons for people not participating
- Encourage different ideas
- Look happy, be enthusiastic
- Be mindful of diversity in the group and try to get to know everyone
- Be aggressive if you notice a potential problem

How do you get people involved to engage with each other?

- Icebreakers, find similarities, introductions
- Finding conflicting opinions
- "Go Around" exercises with option of passing
- Splitting into pairs, or smaller groups and changing groups
- Getting paper to write down thoughts, distribute thoughts and comments
- Asking individuals to state something they like about group, be supportive
- Exercises that require asking each other questions

- Bring different view together into focus
- Start with easier topics to help move into harder topics
- Make sure questions stimulate discussion, not one word answers
- Make questions neutral so they invite different answers

FOLLOWERSHIP

Followership: If you have never heard the term before or never thought twice about it, you are not alone. It usually appears as a "non-word" when documents are spellchecked on the computer. Is it a new concept? Not really; just one that is often overlooked or forgotten.

And just why followership is overlooked and forgotten is an intriguing question. Without followers, would there be leaders? Who would they lead? Who would become leaders if they were not first followers?

Leadership is an interactive activity: Leaders depend on followers and vice versa.

Team efforts are valued highly in today's workforce and such efforts require active followers. Followers set the levels of acceptance for leadership. And in many ways, it is more important for leaders to understand followers than for followers to understand leaders.

Followership can be defined as the willingness to cooperate in working towards the accomplishment of the group mission, to demonstrate a high degree of teamwork and to build cohesion among the group. Sounds pretty similar to leadership, doesn't it? Effective followership is an excellent building block to effective leadership. There are numerous sources to which one can turn to find helpful information on effective leadership, leadership practices and on becoming the best leader one can be. Fewer such sources exist on guiding one to be an effective follower, though there are some. *Take a look at the following behaviours, which have been identified as those comprising effective followership:*

- Volunteering to handle tasks or help accomplish goals
- Willingly accepting assignments
- Exhibiting loyalty to the group
- Voicing differences of opinions, but supporting the group's decisions
- Offering suggestions
- Maintaining a positive attitude, even in confusing or trying times
- Working effectively as a team member

As a follower, it is often easy to criticize the tactics, styles or ideas of a leader. This is especially true when one has been "beat out" for a leadership position and feels resentment, bitterness or jealousy. It is difficult to be an effective follower with such feelings lingering.

Sometimes it helps to critically evaluate our own views towards leadership, the organization and ourselves as followers in order to get a better understanding of the situation. Through this we can learn how to create change in ourselves, how to deal with difficulties and how to become productive and happy followers. We might also learn that being a leader is not as easy as it may sometimes appear!

Take some time to ask yourself the following questions - and don't be alarmed if some of them are a bit difficult to answer:

- Am I truly pursuing the mission and goals of the group while balancing my self-interests?
- What ideas, purpose or values do I share with the leader? The group?
- Should I be taking more initiative?
- What particular pressures and challenges does the leader face?
- If I and/or the group provided more support to the leader, might it improve her/his behaviour?
- The leader must have some redeeming skills, qualities and abilities that helped get her or him into this position of leadership. What are they? How can I help draw these out? How can I help change the environment so these skills and abilities can be demonstrated?

Although changing ourselves is usually not an easy task, most would agree it is easier than changing others. If you are experiencing frustrations or misunderstandings with your organization leader, take a step back and view the situation from the outside. Instead of asking how you can get the leader out of her or his position, ask how you can help her or him improve.

Even if you are perfectly satisfied with your leadership, it is necessary for you - just as it is for a leader - to evaluate your role as a follower/collaborator/group member to determine if you are performing in this role at the highest level possible. Remember, effective leadership requires effective followership. Do your best to make your group the best it can be!

GETTING STARTED AS AN OFFICER

Congratulations!! You've just been elected as a student leader; you're feeling great! And, at times, a bit scared, right? You've finally received the position that you've wanted for so long and perhaps you're experiencing a little bit of doubt. You want to give it your all, be the BEST officer your organization ever elected. You want everything perfect the first time - with no mistakes from anybody. Nice intentions, but as we all know, highly unrealistic. People are fallible; mistakes will inevitably be made. Here is some information that will start your thinking so you can avoid some of the common pitfalls and get a smooth start in your new position. So, relax, get comfortable and read on!

FUNDAMENTALS

IF: you are registered with the Associated Students of the University of Oregon
THEN: you may be eligible for or have access to:

- Mail file in ASUO office

- ASUO funding
- Fishbowl information tables
- Meeting space in EMU and around campus

IF: you want to learn more about effective leadership, leadership classes for credit, the leadership conferences, institutes and other programmes and services.

THEN: check out the Holden Leadership Center

IF: you want to utilize University facilities and services

THEN: you need an account with ASUO

IF: you have an ASUO account

THEN: stop by ASUO to make sure it is in order

IF: your organization has a treasurer

THEN: has he/she updated your financial books?

IF: your organization has a historian

THEN: have the old officers given a report to him or her?

IF: your organization has a secretary

THEN: does he/she have everything he/she needs from the previous secretary (meeting minutes, etc.)?

IF: you would like to have a smooth running organization

THEN: do the officers have written descriptions of their responsibilities from the old officers? Are the descriptions completely understood? Also, have officers create new responsibilities together as a team

IF: you want to reserve a room in a campus building or use other University services.

THEN: go to the ASUO office.

IF: you want to advertise on campus

THEN: check out the ASUO for advice and consultation or stop by the Oregon Daily Emerald (ODE) in the EMU

DECIDING ON A STYLE OF LEADERSHIP

The style of leadership that you choose will have a tremendous impact on your organization. You want to develop a style that you feel comfortable with and that will motivate the members of your organization to achieve the group's goals. What might prove helpful is to examine the styles of the previous officers. Write down what you like and dislike about the method in which goals were or were not achieved, and why. By doing so, you can discover what you believe is important to the organization.

For instance:

- Are you people-oriented (focusing mainly on how your members are doing)? Or are you task-oriented (focusing on what your members are doing)?
- Do you place fellowship (camaraderie) high in your priorities? Or is it more important to get the job done?

- Should all the other members decide? Or should just the Officers decide the organization's goals?
- Will you achieve goals by setting up different committees (*e.g.*, social committee, rush committee, blood drive committee)?
- What would you suggest the group goals to be? Ultimately, which style (*i.e.*, "tell and have done", participative, etc.) - in your judgement - would help the organization accomplish its goals most effectively in each situation?

Hopefully this has helped you to feel more prepared for your upcoming responsibilities. You can face your position as a student leader with anticipation and confidence! Remember that others elected you because they believed you possessed the ability to do well. Knowing that, should make believing in yourself easier. Emerson once said, "Self-trust is the first secret of success." And he is right. So, relax, be yourself, believe in yourself and enjoy the challenge!

GIVING EFFECTIVE FEEDBACK

One of a leader's responsibilities is to create and utilize a forum for open, constructive communication in which feedback is one important aspect. Feedback is communicating to a member or group(s) how their behaviour has affected us or other people. Effective feedback can (1) be heard by the receiver; (2) keep the relationship intact, open and healthy; and (3) validate the feedback process in future interactions.

Effective feedback, both positive and negative, is helpful to others. When you give feedback you are offering valuable information that will be useful to another person making decisions about how to behave. Feedback is not criticism. Criticism is evaluative; feedback is descriptive. It also allows us to build and maintain communication with others. Feedback provides the individual with information that can be used in performing personal evaluation.

Characteristics of Effective Feedback:

1. It is specific rather than general. To be told that one is "dominating" will probably not be as useful as to be told that "You were not listening to what the others said, I felt I had to agree with your arguments or face attack from you."
2. It is focused on behaviour rather than on the person. It is important that we refer to what a person does rather than to what we think or imagine he/she is.
3. It takes into account the needs of the receiver of the feedback. Feedback can be destructive when it serves only your own needs and fails to consider the needs of the person on the receiving end. It should be given to help, not to hurt. It is directed towards behaviour which the receiver can do something about.
4. It is solicited, rather than imposed. Feedback is most useful when

the receiver has formulated the kind of question which those observing can respond to.

5. It involves sharing of information rather than giving advice. By sharing information, we leave a person free to decide in accordance with goals, needs, etc. When we give advice we tell a person what to do and to some degree take away the person's freedom to decide for him/herself.
6. It is well-timed. In general, immediate feedback is most useful (depending of course, on the person's readiness to hear it, support available from others, etc.). The reception and use of feedback involves many possible emotional reactions. Excellent feedback presented at an inappropriate time may do more harm than good.
7. It involves the amount of information the receiver can use rather than the amount we would like to give. Overloading on feedback reduces the person's ability to effectively use your comments. When we give more than can be used, we are more often than not satisfying some need of our own rather than helping the other person.
8. It concerns what is said or done, or how it is said or done, not why. The "why" takes us from the observable to the inferred and involves assumptions regarding motive or intent. Telling a person what their motivations or intentions are more often than not tends to alienate the person and contributes to a climate of resentment, suspicion and distrust; it does not contribute to learning or development. It is dangerous to assume that we know why a person says or does something, or what they "really" mean, or what they are "really" trying to accomplish. If we are uncertain of the person's motives or intent, this uncertainty itself is feedback and should be revealed.
9. It is clear communication. One way of doing this is to have the receiver try to rephrase the feedback received to see if it corresponds to what the sender has in mind. No matter what the intent, feedback is often threatening and thus subject to considerable distortion or misinterpretation.
10. It allows time for the reviewer to ask more questions or to get better clarification. Along with the appropriate time, make sure to give effective feedback in the appropriate condition. This also depends on whether or not the feedback is individual group, etc.

LEADERSHIP CHARACTERISTICS

PROACTIVE VS. REACTIVE

The exceptional leader is always thinking three steps ahead. Working to master his/her own environment with the goal of avoiding problems before they arise.

FLEXIBLE/ADAPTABLE

How do you handle yourself in unexpected or uncomfortable situations? An effective leader will adapt to new surroundings and situations, doing his/her best to adjust.

A GOOD COMMUNICATOR

As a leader, one must listen...a lot! You must be willing to work to understand the needs and desires of others. A good leader asks many questions, considers all options, and leads in the right direction.

RESPECTFUL

Treating others with respect will ultimately earn respect.

QUIET CONFIDENCE

Be sure of yourself with humble intentions.

ENTHUSIASTIC

Excitement is contagious. When a leader is motivated and excited about the cause people will be more inclined to follow.

OPEN-MINDED

Work to consider all options when making decisions. A strong leader will evaluate the input from all interested parties and work for the betterment of the whole.

RESOURCEFUL

Utilize the resources available to you. If you don't know the answer to something find out by asking questions. A leader must create access to information.

REWARDING

An exceptional leader will recognize the efforts of others and reinforce those actions. We all enjoy being recognized for our actions!

WELL EDUCATED

Knowledge is power. Work to be well educated on community policies, procedures, organizational norms, etc. Further, your knowledge of issues and information will only increase your success in leading others.

OPEN TO CHANGE

A leader will take into account all points of view and will be willing to change a policy, programme, cultural tradition that is out-dated, or no longer beneficial to the group as a whole.

INTERESTED IN FEEDBACK

How do people feel about your leadership skill set? How can you improve? These are important questions that a leader needs to constantly ask the chapter. View feedback as a gift to improve.

EVALUATIVE

Evaluation of events and programmes is essential for an organization/group to improve and progress. An exceptional leader will constantly evaluate and change programmes and policies that are not working.

ORGANIZED

Are you prepared for meetings, presentations, events and confident that people around you are prepared and organized as well?

CONSISTENT

Confidence and respect cannot be attained without your leadership being consistent. People must have confidence that their opinions and thoughts will be heard and taken into consideration.

DELEGATOR

An exceptional leader realizes that he/she cannot accomplish everything on his own. A leader will know the talents and interests of people around him/her, thus delegating tasks accordingly.

INITIATIVE

A leader should work to be the motivator, an initiator. He/she must be a key element in the planning and implementing of new ideas, programmes, policies, events, etc.

LEADING A GROUP DEBRIEF

Debriefing can serve as an opportunity to reflect on an experience and make it meaningful by identifying what we learned about ourselves and others. The technique of debriefing is useful for group members following the completion of an activity or event. As a facilitator, your job is to lead a thought provoking, safe discussion by asking meaningful questions in a pre-planned sequence. A mature group will often lead their own discussion with little prompting from a facilitator. A debrief usually follows this sequence: rules, what, so what, now what.

RULES:

Rules can help to develop a supportive, caring climate for people to feel safe and free to express themselves. If time permits, rules for the group's interaction should be developed by the group, preferably before the service project ever takes place. Otherwise, a list of the rules should be posted and discussed with a hand-raise agreement by those who will abide by them before the debrief.

Suggested rules include:

- Honour confidentiality
- Give unconditional respect to self and others
- Participate as much as possible
- Speak only for myself, not others
- Be open and honest with group members
- Be silent if it feels right
- Stop the discussion if a rule is being broken and restate the rule

What?

This is the project report describing what happened during the entire project, who was involved, what was accomplished, what needs were met, etc.

Techniques for leading this part may include:

1. Sharing photographs,
2. A "go around"* where each person says one descriptive word or sentence about the project,
3. The "memory game"* where one person begins to recount the project but can be interrupted any time by someone saying, "Hold it!" if they thinks of something to add to that part of the story,
4. A group log/journal is kept where people sign in periodically to record date, time, events and ideas.

Questions to ask may include:

1. For the sake of refreshing our memories, will someone please describe (the project)?
2. We're going to go around the circle starting to my left. Would each person say one adjective to describe (the project) we just completed?
3. What were some things you noticed? Did any of these things surprise you?

So What?

The "what?" questions generally lead quickly into the "so what?" questions. This is where the participants identify what they think or feel about or learned from the experience. If you look back at the original reasons for volunteering and selecting the project, you will be able to ask evaluative questions to see if the volunteer's needs were met by doing the project. *Techniques for this section may include:*

1. "The whip" where you ask each person in the group to complete a sentence such as, "I'm glad that I...", or "When we were (doing

something) I felt...";2. "Partner dialogue" where you ask participants to discuss a question and have one of the partners summarize their discussion for the group afterwards;

2. Journalizing can be a single sheet of paper with questions to focus reflections on or blank paper for recording free-flowing thoughts; consider writing poems, drawing pictures or having a community journal;
3. "Fish bowl" where half the group sits inside a circle and discusses the project surrounded by the other half of the group who observes and summarizes the inside group's discussion; or
4. Quotations or readings that reflect the purpose of the activity can be read by the facilitator and participants can respond to them (the Leadership Library has several quote and readings books to choose from).

To ask about what was learned may include:

1. What do you know now that you didn't know before?
2. What attitudes and feelings do you have about the experience that you didn't have before?
3. Are you aware of any other changes that occurred in knowledge, skills, attitudes, or feelings as a direct result of this experience? If so, explain.
4. How did you actually learn what is most important to you?

To ask to evaluate the group may include:

1. What part of this project was most valuable for you?
2. How has this group been helpful to you?
3. How have you contributed to this group?
4. What are some things that would have made the group experience better for you?

Now What?

The "so what" questions should flow smoothly into the "now what" questions. These questions should take what was learned from the experience and apply that to future projects or interactions.

Questions to ask may include:

1. What do you think you will remember or retain in other ways after the experience?
2. Can you explain why this might be so?
3. What will you probably verbally share with or demonstrate to others in the future?
4. Would you make any personal changes in how you will contribute in the future?
5. What are some things you appreciate about the members of this group?

6. What changes would you suggest for future group experiences?
7. Where does the group go from here?

LEADING EFFECTIVE DISCUSSIONS

We all lead discussions: with family, with strangers, with friends. Thus discussion leading is a natural part of our lives. Yet many people are wary of trying to lead a discussion, as if it involves some sort of alien activity only experts can accomplish. This could not be further from the truth. The following ten tips are designed to help a novice discussion leader be successful from the beginning and thoroughly enjoy this basic human activity.

1. *Energetic Commitment to the Topic:* Your enthusiasm is contagious. If you think the topic is genuinely interesting, others will. Even if not everything about the topic sings to you, focus on the aspects that you find most intriguing. If nothing about topic grabs you, don't lead the discussion!
2. *Positive Atmosphere:* By keeping your group small (6-25), welcoming everyone, getting to know peoples' names, and getting people to know each other, you can help everyone feel at home and eager to share. Make your discussion group something people look forward to. Food never hurts.
3. *It's Not About You:* Many people feel self-conscious about leading a discussion—nervous about what others will think, afraid of failing. If you have followed the first tip, you need only remind yourself that this discussion is about the topic itself, not about you, or your discussion-leading ability. The more you think about the topic and the less you think about yourself, the better things will go.
4. *Be Prepared:* Of course the discussion leader should be prepared (by selecting potential readings, doing some homework, preparing discussion questions), but others who participate in a discussion group should also prepare in some way. For instance, group members should complete a reading, think about questions in advance, or prepare their own questions to discuss. Although "jam sessions" are valuable and often spontaneous, you should never rely on luck to create the conditions for good conversation.
5. *Don't Expect Perfection:* Discussion leading is a craft which is never perfected but improves with time. The best way to learn it is to do it and to pay attention to what works and what doesn't. Without being blind to your inevitable mistakes, focus on what clicks and build on that. Following the first four tips will increase the likelihood that even your first efforts will be surprisingly successful.
6. *Establish a Shared Frame of Reference for Discussion:* Usually a reading of some kind (distributed in advance) establishes a shared frame of

reference for discussion. Often the discussion leader needs to spend the first five minutes (not longer) reviewing key points about the reading and getting the group to focus in on the topic of the day. Be careful not to read your notes here. Just pick one or two ideas to summarize conversationally. Often there is discussion at this point, clarifying key concepts—perhaps even reading a sentence from the article and seeing what people think it means. It is important that if people are asked to read something in advance, it be interesting, and they actually wind up talking about it. Otherwise they will stop doing the reading.

7. *Prepare Discussion Questions that Call for Judgement:* We are often at a loss for what to say to get others talking. Something as simple as, "What do you think about the upcoming election?" might do the trick. You might luck into such a talkative group that "What would you like to talk about?" would suffice. More likely, your group will respond to a question which calls for judgement—some choice which decent people could disagree about. For example, if the topic is "U.S. Democracy" and the group has read a short article on this topic, one might ask "Do you think democracy in the U.S. is stronger or weaker since 9/11?"
8. *Establish Shared Standards of Value for what is Persuasive:* When a question calls for judgement, people will naturally disagree. At this point it is essential that no one feels personally threatened, slighted, or devalued. Thus it is important to establish evidence and logic as the keys to persuasion. Evidence may come in the form of references to the text under discussion, or other forms. The important thing to emphasize is that no idea is out of bounds, as long as it is not insulting to anyone present, as long as there is evidence and logic to support or challenge it, and as long as everyone gets a chance to contribute.
9. *Establish Positive Ways to Disagree:* Disagreeing with a person requires listening to them first. When I disagree with you I need to really listen to what you are saying, then try to repeat back your main idea: "Do I understand you to be saying that democracy is stronger since 9/11, because people feel more strongly about the value of democracy?" When I repeat our idea, you have a chance to say, "Yes, that's right," or "No, what I meant was...," and so on until you are satisfied I understand you. Chances are this process will allow both of us to modify our views and communicate better.
10. *Share Responsibility and Build Continuity:* Chances are other people will want to lead discussions and to choose readings to discuss. Encourage them to do this, and help them succeed by being a good participant when they lead. In the last five minutes of each discussion

encourage the group to identify the key pints that were most important and the ideals that they would most like to follow up on. Use these ideas to help shape future discussions.

These tips are not meant to be an exhaustive guide to discussion-leading, but rather helpful advice for those embarking on this project for the first time. I say nothing here about how to get quiet people to speak up or how to get dominators to hold back. These and many other unforeseeable personality issues require improvisation, which makes a good discussion like chamber music, a product of creative cooperation, present only for the hour that it happens, yet indelible, sometimes, in its effects.

MANAGING CONFLICT

Conflict is inevitable in any interpersonal relationship and can be a very positive experience, if managed properly. Why do we shy away from dealing with conflict? Many of us were raised to believe that conflict is something to be avoided, and is an experience of failure. However, conflict doesn't have to lead to failure, defeat, separation or termination of individual relationships. We all come to see the world in different ways, and we have different ideas about what's best for us and what's best for our group. It is actually a signal that change is needed and possible. The ability to manage conflict is probably one of the most important social skills an individual can possess. This information is designed to help you acquire this skill.

Specifically, it will offer information about:

- The different ways in which people deal with conflict.
- Increasing awareness of your own style of conflict management.
- A constructive method of conflict management which will not only lead to greater satisfaction of both parties involved, but also promote growth and development of your group.

COMPETING

An individual pursues his/her own concerns at the other person's expense. This is a power-oriented mode, in which one uses whatever power seems appropriate to win one's own position. Competing might mean "standing up for your rights," defending a position which you believe correct, or simply trying to influence others.

ACCOMMODATING

The opposite of competing. When accommodating, an individual neglects his/her own concerns to satisfy the concerns of the other person; there is an element of self-sacrifice in this mode. Accommodating might take the form of selfless generosity or charity, obeying another person's order when one would prefer not to, or yielding to another's point of view.

AVOIDING

The individual does not immediately pursue his/her own concerns or those of the other person if he/she does not address the conflict. Avoiding might take the form of diplomatically sidestepping an issue, postponing an issue until a better time or simply withdrawing from a threatening situation.

COMPROMISING

The objective is to find some expedient, mutually acceptable solution which partially satisfies both parties. It falls on a middle ground between competing and accommodating. Compromising gives up more than competing but less than accommodating. Likewise, it addresses an issue more directly than avoiding, but doesn't explore it in as much depth as collaborating. Compromising might mean splitting the difference, exchanging concessions, or seeking a quick middle-ground position.

COLLABORATING

The opposite of avoiding, collaborating involves an attempt to work with the other person to find some solution which fully satisfies the concerns of both. It means digging into an issue to identify the underlying concerns of the two individuals and to find a solution which meets both sets of concerns. This is clearly the most effective approach of conflict management. *Specifically it will produce the following results:*

1. Both sides' needs are met
2. Satisfaction
3. Mutual respect
4. Both parties feel enriched rather than belittled
5. Continuing effort of both parties to work together

How to Use the Collaborating Approach (Win-Win Negotiation) To Deal with Conflicts in Student Organizations

Diagnosis is the starting point - determining the nature of the conflict.

1. Is the issue a value conflict? It is extremely difficult to negotiate when the conflict is regarding a personal value. An example: a dispute over whether alcohol should be prohibited at a fundraising dance.
2. Is the issue a difference of expectations of each other? Understanding this type of conflict lies in the fact that each of us have different expectations which grow out of our experiences with the organization. When we interact with others whose expectations have grown out of their own unique experiences with the organization, conflict arises.

Initiation is the second step.

1. The most effective way to confront another in a conflict situation is to state the tangible effect the conflict has on you.
2. *Example:* "We have a concern in our committee. Although your

position on keeping a low budget for the officer training retreat is understandable it restricts us from having the retreat off campus, which is the desire of most members."

Active Listening is the third step - negotiators must be capable of hearing the other's point of view.

1. While listening, do not think about what to reply in order to persuade.
2. Argument-provoking replies should be avoided.
3. Active listening involves paraphrasing or restating what the other says. Idea or content should be considered as well as feeling.

Problem Solving is the final step.

1. Clarify the problem. After the above steps, each party should have a clear idea about what is the tangible issue.
2. Talk about what's needed/wanted (be clear on facts and information).
3. Generate a list of possible solutions. While doing this, let go of the solutions that you thought you had. Be creative! The best negotiator makes the other side feel good. Start by thinking "how can I make the other side happy?"
4. Decide together on the best solution acceptable to all parties, use consensus decision making skills. Don't try to persuade or coerce.
5. Plan the implementation of the solution. Make assignments of who, what, where, when and how. Plan an evaluation or review of the solution after a specified period of time.

All five styles of conflict management obviously have advantages and disadvantages. When dealing with conflict in personal relationships, any of these types may be useful in certain situations. The last style, collaboration, however, is highly recommended for dealing with conflict in student organizations. It results in something satisfactory to both parties. People often feel proud of themselves and feel a sense of personal power when they use this method. It's a sign of integrity and self-confidence when one is able to use this method with patience regardless of how difficult the situation may be.

TWO ISSUES WHICH YOU MIGHT HAVE TO DEAL WITH WHEN CONFRONTING A CONFLICT:

People Who won't Negotiate

Some people refuse to negotiate because they want to protect their special interests or privileges. Here are a few steps to take in dealing with such people.

1. Start to negotiate anyway.
2. Explain why it is in their interest to negotiate, why it is worthwhile to deal with the problems existing between you.
3. Talk about problcms and how thc collaboration will help them solve their problems or others' problems. Share the problem. For example,

bring to their attention the joint image that you're two sub-groups for the organization.

When Trust is an Issue

Here are a few suggestions for this problem.

1. Be trustworthy. Do what you said you would do.
2. Find a higher value that you both agree on. For example, you both want to project a positive image.
3. Listen.
4. Make an agreement in such a way that you know when it is carried out.
5. Start small.
6. There are people who simply can't/won't trust you, but do your best anyway.

MOTIVATING YOUR MEMBERS

The basic motivational philosophy of any organization towards its members should be to help them get what they want. Group members measure the quality of their organization through the trust, commitment and love its leaders show towards them. A leader will foster motivation within an organization by helping his/her group members develop a good healthy self image. If group members are to develop this healthy self image within an organization a leader must follow five basic rules: Do what's right, Do the best you can, Treat others as you'd like to be treated, Exhibit a positive attitude, and Expect the best at all times. Group members tend not only to look up to their leaders, but also tend to live up to their leader's expectations - good, bad or indifferent. Therefore, expect the best at all times and you'll increase your chances of getting it.

The word motivation comes from the Latin word movers which means to move forward satisfying a need. Since each person's motivation comes from within then we truly cannot motivate other people. However, if we know what personal motives or needs regulate a person's internal energy flow then we can still stimulate them into action. As a leader, it is important that you assess and understand your own motives as well as those of your group members. Are people participating in your organization to become knowledgeable about a specific academic or professional field? Is their participation a recreational or entertainment outlet? Is their participation a relief from the rigors of studying or are they involved to meet people? Whatever their reasons for joining your organization it is important to note that there are four major forces that motivate people: accomplishment/achievement, recognition, power and affiliation.

ACCOMPLISHMENT/ACHIEVEMENT

Achievers are people who want interesting work or the opportunity to achieve something significant. They thrive in situations in which they can take personal responsibility and calculated risks, set goals and solve problems. Achievers need constant and concrete feedback, especially the impact that their contributions have had on the greater whole. It is important to them that their contributions actually make a difference beyond their own immediate personal gain.

RECOGNITION

Certain people want to be appreciated for what they actually do in an organization and derive personal satisfaction from that direct involvement. They expect special benefits and privileges as a result of their participation and thrive on recognition from others, especially positive recognition.

POWER

Other people also want the opportunity to compete for responsibility and authority within an organization. They like to influence others directly and tend to manage groups well without being manipulative. They thrive on being involved in programme production and planning and also like the opportunity to apply new skills in the proper contexts.

AFFILIATION

People involved withing the group need to feel that they belong and are accepted by the group members. They like cooperating and being in on things, meeting and/or knowing many people, and enjoy having fun. Since members need to feel welcome then they must be kept informed at all times. They also care about their feelings and the feelings of others and derive satisfaction for a job well done, especially if it involves serving others.

If you can determine the source of an individual's motivation, you can begin to unleash his or her energies and ideas and maximize that member's potential within the organization. It is important that you allow them the opportunity to use their individual talents to the benefit of the organization. For example, if someone is an advertising major, ask them to coordinate your publicity campaigns. A leader must set goals that will help meet group member's wants and your organization's needs at the same time. Keep focused on the goals, talk about them often, and praise progress towards those goals.

Give your members an accurate view of the situation. Be honest. Listen and respond to the questions they raise. Most importantly, create an environment in which they feel free to raise questions. Be positive and appreciative of suggestions made by committee members. If you seem indifferent to members' opinions, your committee may lose interest.

Learn to look beyond a person's current abilities and identify any potential that needs developing. In doing so, you will increase the group member's satisfaction by allowing them the opportunity to achieve within the organization.

Group members need to be given some control over the job tasks, an opportunity to exercise responsibility, and a reason to feel they are learning and growing. Start delegating small tasks to your members. As they are successful in carrying out these tasks, give them more responsibility. Encourage them to make their needs known to you.

You can increase a person's motivation by:

1. Increasing the rewards he or she anticipates receiving or the individual's satisfaction level with the organization, and/or reducing the psychological time or resource costs he or she anticipates incurring.
2. Skillful leaders learn to use motivation selectively like a dash of pepper in food. As with so much in leadership development, common sense and simple approaches are usually the most effective ones.

The following methods of motivation tend to have "universal" application in most groups:

- Use people's names often. Make it a point to learn the names and connect the faces of the people in your organization.
- Actively listen to others. Demonstrate good, open body language. Be courteous/respectful.
- Be fair, honest and consistent — show no favoritism. Observe with equal care so you can determine which group members find joy in getting work done, which want praise for a job well done, which need leadership opportunities and which want to be part of a team.
- Keep members informed — what they're not up on, they're likely to be down on. Survey your membership to see what group members want or need and provide avenues for recognition.
- Build prestige into jobs by giving titles and appropriate authority.
- Give individual attention and demonstrate that you understand members and accept their strengths and weaknesses. Assess the chemistry among those who work together and make the necessary changes to make that chemistry more effective. Create various mentoring relationships within the organization by teaming up experienced members with newer members.
- Provide honest feedback — praise their successes publicly and privately give constructive criticism to help them learn from their mistakes.
- Involve members in goal setting and decision making and clarify your expectations of members and their expectations of you.
- Use ice breakers or team building activities in newly formed leadership teams or committees to energize the group members and strengthen the organization.
- Occasionally serve food at your meetings or have social events outside of work.

- Since motivation stems from inner needs, drives and goals, the leader's task in motivating others is to tap into these to supply a channel for their fulfillment. The individual members must still do the rest.

PUBLIC SPEAKING

Everyone has the potential to be an effective public speaker. There is no magic formula for success, in fact, the beauty of public speaking is that everyone is unique and has different strengths. All we have to do is prepare, cultivate our best habits, avoid pitfalls and let nature takes its course. The following ten tips are designed to help you do just that.

1. *Commit to the Topic:* Your enthusiasm is contagious. If you think your topic is genuinely interesting, others will. Even if not everything about it sings to you, focus on the aspects that intrigue you most. If nothing about the topic grabs you, don't speak about it.
2. *It's not About You:* Many people feel self-conscious about speaking, nervous about what others will think or afraid of failing. If you have followed the first tip, you need only remind yourself that this speech is about the topic itself, not about you or your abilities. The more you think about the topic and the less you think about yourself, the better things will go.
3. *Be Prepared:* Few people speak effectively without some kind of preparation, whether that involves research, or just thinking, organizing and practicing your delivery to a friend. The quickest way to bring on a sense of panic is to stand before a group without preparing anything to say. Conversely, the better prepared you are, the more you will relax. Yet being prepared is not merely a function of time spent. It involves focusing on what you want to say.
4. *Focus:* Greek and Roman orators knew that listeners would remember one point well made. You can imitate this sense of focus by putting your main idea in one sentence and trying it out on someone. If the response is a puzzled look, you will know to clarify or find a good example that captures the imagination of a listener. Once you know your focus, try to organize your speech organically, so that one idea grows from another and always in relationship to this focus.
5. *Find the perfect example:* The best ideas come alive with a good example, often from personal experience, with vivid details that allow the audience to envision each moment as it is shared. A good speech might have only one such example, but it will stick with the audience.
6. *Minimize notes:* Many people write out or memorize a speech or they make a long list of notes that they methodically plow through. These approaches undercut your natural ability to communicate, because

they take you out of the moment and turn you from a speaker into a reader. Be familiar with your speech and comfortable enough to make changes if necessary.

7. *Be Present at Your Own Speech:* Once you minimize notes to a few points, a quote, a key word—whatever you need—you will free your mind to actually think about what you are saying as you say it. This ability to be "present" minimizes self-consciousness by keeping the focus on your message rather than you. It also helps you think on your feet and reach you audience.
8. *Connect With Your Audience:* A speech is a dialogue in which you do all the talking. This does not mean that you monopolize the conversation, you become "partners in conversation" with your audience. Body language cues such as smiles, fidgeting and confused looks are all ways in which your audience communicates with you. The silent dialogue is essential to effective speaking, because it allows you to adjust to what the audience needs. Novices are usually "deaf" to this silent conversation, unable to pry their eyes from their notes. Experienced speakers make significant eye contact with specific listeners throughout a room. Make sure to practice your speech in front of people so that you become comfortable.
9. *Learn From the Questions:* If your speech is followed by a question period, and you have a chance to view it later on video, observe the differences between your presentation during your speech and you manner during the question period. Notice how you naturally interact with questioners, the spontaneous and appropriate energy in your voice and gestures, the sense of responding to someone, the ability to be specific and focused. The interchanges during the questioning can give you clues about your own greatest strengths as a speaker, and you can incorporate them in your next speech.
10. *Don't Expect Perfection:* Public speaking is a craft which is never perfected but improves with time. The best way to learn it is to do it and to pay attention to what works and what doesn't. Without being blind to your inevitable mistakes, focus on what clicks and build on that. Following the first four tips will increase the likelihood that even your first efforts will be surprisingly successful.

These tips are not meant to be an exhaustive guide to public speaking, but rather helpful advice for a novice.

Perhaps the most important thing to remember is that we are all public speakers from a young age, and the rewards for cultivating this necessary aspect of life go far beyond the classroom to help us shape the very fabric of our lives among others.

RUNNING EFFECTIVE MEETINGS

Do you dread attending meetings because they are dull, unproductive, disorganized and too long? With proper planning and preparation, any meeting can be effective and enjoyable. Meetings have several functions. They give members a chance to discuss and evaluate goals and objectives, keep updated on current events, provide a chance to communicate and keep the group cohesive. But most of all, meetings allow groups to pull resources together for decision making. If the facilitator starts with a careful plan and finishes with a thorough follow-up, the meeting will "run smooth."

The following are some tips to help you make your next meeting successful, productive and even fun.

Before The Meeting

1. Define the purpose of the meeting.
2. Develop an agenda with the officers and advisor.
3. Distribute the agenda and circulate background material, lengthy documents or articles prior to the meeting so members will be prepared and feel involved and up-to-date.
4. Choose an appropriate meeting time. Set a time limit and stick to it, if possible. Remember, members have other commitments. They will be more likely to attend meetings if you make them productive, predictable and as short as possible.
5. If possible, arrange the room so that members face each other, *i.e.*, a circle or semi-circle. For large groups, try U-shaped rows.
6. Choose a location suitable to your group's size. Small rooms with too many people get stuffy and create tension. A larger room is more comfortable and encourages individual expression.
7. Use visual aids for interest (*e.g.*, posters, diagrams, etc.). Post a large agenda up front to which members can refer.
8. Vary meeting places if possible to accommodate different members. Be sure everyone knows where and when the next meeting will be held.

During the Meeting

1. Greet members and make them feel welcome, even late members when appropriate.
2. If possible, serve light refreshments; they are good icebreakers and make your members feel special and comfortable.
3. Start on time. End on time.
4. Review the agenda and set priorities for the meeting.
5. Stick to the agenda.
6. Encourage group discussion to get all points of view and ideas. You will have better quality decisions as well as highly motivated members; they will feel that attending meetings is worth their while.

7. Encourage feedback. Ideas, activities and commitment to the rganization improve when members see their impact on the decision making process.
8. Keep conversation focused on the topic. Feel free to ask for only constructive and non- repetitive comments. Tactfully end discussions when they are getting nowhere or becoming destructive or unproductive.
9. Keep minutes of the meeting for future reference in case a question or problem arises.
10. As a leader, be a role model by listening, showing interest, appreciation and confidence in members. Admit mistakes.
11. Summarize agreements reached and end the meeting on a unifying or positive note. For example, have members volunteer thoughts of things they feel have been good or successful or reiterate the organization's mission.
12. Set a date, time and place for the next meeting.

After the Meeting

1. Write up and distribute minutes within 3 or 4 days. Quick action reinforces importance of meeting and reduces errors of memory.
2. Discuss any problems during the meeting with other officers; come up with ways improvements can be made.
3. Follow-up on delegation decisions. See that all members understand and carry-out their responsibilities.
4. Give recognition and appreciation to excellent and timely progress.
5. Put unfinished business on the agenda for the next meeting.
6. Conduct a periodic evaluation of the meetings. Note any areas that can be analyzed and improved for more productive meetings. A sample meeting evaluation checklist is attached.

MEETING EVALUATION CHECKLIST

The meeting was well planned:

- Members were notified in advance
- There was a pre-arranged agenda
- Officers and committees were ready to report
- The meeting room was pre-arranged

The meeting was well organized:

- The meeting started on time
- Guests were introduced and welcomed
- Agendas were available for all members
- The purposes for the meeting were made clear
- There was a transition from the last meeting
- One topic was discussed at a time

- One person has the floor at a time
- Discussion was relevant
- The chairperson summarized the main points of the discussion
- The meeting moved along at a workable pace
- Committee assignments were complete and clear
- Plans for the next meeting were announced
- All that was planned for the meeting was covered

Participation in the meeting:

- Members participated in discussion and voting
- The chairperson made good use of questions
- The pros and cons of all issues were considered
- Members gave suggestions to committees
- Responsibilities were evenly distributed
- Members participated in planning the agenda for the next meeting

The value of the meeting:

- Progress was made towards goals
- Something was learned

Attitude of the meeting:

- Attendance was good
- Everyone present was on time
- Members knew one another
- There was a "warm up" period before the meeting
- There was some humor during the meeting
- Members and officers helped one another when needed
- There was an atmosphere of free expression

TIME MANAGEMENT

Have you ever asked yourself how some people are able to work so many different activities into their schedules while others barely seem to have the time to attend classes? Are they smarter? Doubtful. More organized? Probably. Better at managing time?

Likely. Time management is important to any person, but particularly to student organization members and leaders. Involvement in co-curricular activities means that in addition to classes, homework, meals, jobs and socializing, another significant amount of time is taken up with organizational obligations. This information is designed to provide you with some suggestions on how to more effectively manage your time.

It is important to note that time management is a personal skill; only you know your peak work hours, your attention span and your eating and sleeping needs, which must be planned for. Finding a time management strategy that best fits your needs is important. The following steps can help you determine your strategy.

THE BIG FIVE

The five steps to effective time management are:

1. Plan
2. Assess
3. Organize
4. Prioritize
5. Schedule

Plan

Research and personal experiences have shown that individuals who set personal goals have a greater chance of success. These individuals have determined and set on paper what they would like to achieve and how they would like to get there.

The goals are realistic, believable and achievable. People who set goals also evaluate their progress and make any necessary changes on a regular basis. So, if you want to better manage your time, your first step is to set the goals you would like to achieve, either for the semester, year or throughout your college career.

Assess

Your next step is to assess how you are currently using your time. You cannot make productive changes unless you know what areas need to be changed. Keep a time log for three days from the time you get up until the time that you go to bed. Describe your specific activities in 15 minute blocks. The activity should be detailed and can include comments. Prioritize your activities: A-important to you; B-important to others; and C-maintenance (basic human needs). Maintenance items may become A priority items. For example, exercising may be maintenance once it becomes a habit, but could be an A priority until then.

Next, analyze your time log. Answer the following questions:

1. Were there any surprises?
2. Would you judge this to be a typical week?
3. What patterns could you identify in your time wasters? Interruptions?
4. What part of the week would you consider most productive? Least productive?
5. What time of the day do you feel was most productive? Least productive?
6. What activities would you like to eliminate totally? What would be the cost of doing so? What is the cost of not eliminating them?
7. Which activities during the week do you deem most rewarding? Would you like to spend more time doing them in the future? What is your plan for doing so?

Have someone review your time log. An objective observer may be able to point out discrepancies or patterns that you did not see.

Organize

Ideally, you should make a list each morning of everything that you want or need to do for that day. Don't plan out every minute and don't even think about which task is most important, just write them all down. Some people find it more helpful to list their "things to do" in 5 to 7 day groupings. In this way, they can plan for longer projects and get a better sense of their week. Whichever method you choose, keep in mind that everyone has good and bad days. Don't worry if you don't accomplish everything, just include the uncompleted tasks to your next day's list and get them done.

Prioritize

After you have recorded these "things to do", go over the list and rewrite in priority order which things you need to do at the top and less important/ pressing tasks at the bottom. Keep in mind due dates, commitments you have made and whether or not these tasks involve other people. If the items are for class, it is important to consider how much of the final grade they are worth. How you choose to prioritize is a very personal matter. What is important is that you are responsible with your priorities. Review your personal goals and how these priorities fit with your goals?

Schedule

The last thing to do is to take this list and begin to work these "things to do" into your schedule. You can't plan every minute of your day. Remember to leave room for breaks, socializing and those unexpected things that pop up. There's no use making a schedule that is impossible to follow.

Many college students find it helpful to keep a schedule book for the year. At the beginning of the semester, write down your classes, assignment due dates and exams. Carry your planner with you if you write your "to do" list in it!

Try these suggestions, see what works for you best and then be sure to integrate them into your learning lifestyle. Learning effective time management now will help you throughout your personal life and professional career. Learn to say no. You will reach a point when there is only so much that you can do instead of burning yourself out or not doing quality work. Learn to balance how much you can do with what you need to do.

UNDERSTANDING GROUP PROCESS

Group process refers to how an organization's members work together to get things done. Typically, organizations spend a great deal of time and energy setting and striving to reach goals, but give little consideration to what is happening between and to the group's greatest resource - its members. While working hard to achieve results, it is critical that members' needs be addressed. Membership in an organization is as much an opportunity to develop self confidence, refine skills and make friends as it is to support a cause, fundraise or educate the campus community. All of these can be done simultaneously, but most likely will not just happen on their own.

Group process can occur from within the group, outside of the group and anytime of year. Effective organizations take a close look at how members work together, which roles they fill and whether members are contributing equally. Through group process, observation and analysis can help identify problems early, thus alleviating the need for a major overhaul as the year progresses. Your vantage point as a group member provides a great opportunity to regularly observe how things are going. Depending on the frequency of meetings and an understanding of what to look for, you can be instrumental in ensuring group and individual success.

Elements of an organization which typically influence group proceedings include communication, participation, decision making and role fulfillment. When observing these specific areas you will likely see several things happening simultaneously. This is to be expected, but it can also be rather confusing. Initially, you may want to isolate a single aspect of the group. As you become more adept at observation, you can gradually increase your areas of focus.

OBSERVATION

One of the easiest aspects of group process to observe is the pattern of communication:

- Who talks? For how long? How often?
- At whom do people look when they speak?
- Who talks after whom? Who interrupts whom?
- What style of communication is used (assertions, questions, tone of voice, gestures, etc.)?
- Who sits where? Do the same people always sit in the same place?

The kinds of observations we make give us clues to other important things which may be going on in the group (*e.g.*, such as who leads whom or who influences whom).

PARTICIPATION

One indication of involvement is verbal participation. Look for differences in the amount of participation among members.

- Who are the high participants? Who are the low participants?
- Do you see any shift in participation (*e.g.*, highs become quiet; lows suddenly become talkative)? What are possible reasons for this in the group's interaction?

- How are the silent people treated? How is their silence interpreted? Consent? Disagreement? Disinterest? Fear? Etc.?
- Who talks to whom? Do you see any reason for this in the group's interactions?
- Who keeps the ball rolling? Why? Do you see any reason for this in the group's interactions?

DECISION MAKING

Many kinds of decisions are made in groups without considering the effects that these decisions will have on other members. Some people try to impose their own decisions on the group, while others want all members to participate or share in the decision making process.

- Does anyone make a decision and carry it out without checking with other group members (self-authorized)? For example, one person decides on the topic to be discussed and immediately begins to talk about it. What effect does this have on other group members?
- Does the group drift from topic to topic? Who topic-jumps? Do you see any reason for this in the group's interactions?
- Who supports other members' suggestions or decisions? Does this support result in the two members deciding the topic or activity for the group? How does this affect the other group members?
- Is there any evidence of a majority pushing a decision through over other member's objections? Do they call for a vote (majority support)?
- Is there any attempt to get all members participating in a decision (consensus)? What effect does this seem to have on the group?
- Does anyone make any contributions which do not receive any kind of response or recognition? What effect does this have on the member?
- Does the exec board make all of the decisions or do all of the talking or do the members?

ORGANIZATIONAL ROLES

A variety of crucial roles need to be filled to ensure group goal accomplishment and success. Roles are distributed among three types:

Task

Primarily expressed through trying to accomplish group tasks. Examples: initiator, contributor, information seeker and giver, elaborator, energizer, recorder.

Maintenance

Oriented towards improving relationships among members. Examples: encourager, harmonizer, compromiser.

Self Oriented

Focuses on personal needs regardless of group concerns. Examples: aggressor, recognition seeker, dominator, blocker. Process observation requires patience and the ability to focus on everyone in the group. Paying attention to these questions and roles can help you to better understand how the group is affecting its member and vice versa.

SKILLS FOR EFFECTIVE LEADERSHIP COMMUNICATION

- Making a connection with the audience is very important. Unless you are able to connect with your audience and vice-versa, there will be no depth in your words that will compel the audience to think. Connection here does not mean just superficial networking. You should emotionally connect with the audience to make an impact on them. Making the common man feel that they matter a lot has an enormous influence that will help them accept you as their leader.
- Communication is a two way process. Therefore, listening is as important as what you say. Listen carefully to what others say, and if required, make a note of it so that you can refer to it later. It will also help you to learn what others think about a particular subject.
- It is said that the first impression is the best impression, and the saying has a lot of truth in it. Making a great first impression has an enormous impact on the listener.
- Choosing the right words is a vital factor in leadership communication skills. Carefully chosen words can make a huge impact. Powerful words have the potential to charge up people and motivate them, while irresponsible comments can make the whole crowd turn against you. So always remember to choose your words carefully and cautiously.
- Developing leadership charisma is another quality of a leader. Learn to maintain authority while communicating.
- While communicating with your subordinates or co-workers; try to be transparent, open, and above all show trust and respect.
- Have a clear point of view. Unless you don't have a direction, it is not possible to guide and show others the path.
- Along with good communication skills, a leader should also have expressive body language and good eye contact. The ability to make the listener feel that you understand them is also equally important.
- Speech delivery is also important to leadership communication skills. How you modulate your voice, how you deliver the speech and your overall presentation are important to take hold of the audience so that they listen to you with interest.
- Practice is the key to great communication. A lot of practice can only

help you to master the art of great communication techniques. You may also take the help of a communication guide to learn the right body language while communi-cating in different circumstances.

COMMUNICATION SKILLSCOMMUNICATION SKILLS

The meaning of the word "communication" is at once both clear and obscure. It is clear enough in conventional usage, but obscure when we seek to determine the limits of its application. To illustrate, if someone talks to another and common understanding results (indicated by mutually satisfactory action), we have no qualms about saying that communication has occurred.

If, however, misunderstanding results (indicated by mutually unsatisfactory action), we are uncertain whether we should say that there has been poor, or no, communication. Further, if someone does not talk to another and the latter as a result gains certain impressions of the former, has communication occurred? Would it make any difference whether the first person deliberately did not talk or unintentionally failed to talk? If someone eavesdrops on a conversation, is he receiving communication? If from the antics of my neighbour's children or from the condition of his house I draw certain conclusions about him, has there been a communication? If classify a group of objects before me, say, several pieces of lumber, on the basis of certain characteristics, is there communication?

The problem is familiar: It seems impossible to draw a line between those situations that we conventionally term "communication" and those we do not, short of a purely arbitrary distinction. And the many and varied definitions of "communication" appearing in the literature of various fields of study often appear, at first glance at least, to compound the difficulty. We who are teaching speech must be concerned about defining communication. Certainly our concept of this process determines to no small degree our approach to speech training, how broadly or narrowly we view our subject, how we relate it to other areas of study.

To put the problem of defining "communication" in clearer perspective, thus assisting in the selection of a more consistent and pedagogically helpful concept of communication. To accomplish, shall present a number of definitions of "communication" in a twofold classification and examine the application of these definitions to a series of situations in which human responses and interactions occur. Such classification and application should give us some insights into the problem of definition, into the relationship among existing definitions, and provide us with the perspective necessary to select the most basic, consistent, and useful definition of "communication," and to see its relationship to the process of speech.

Definitions of "communication" fall into two broad categories. In one category are those definitions which limit the process of communication to those stimulus-response situations in which one deliberately transmits stimuli to evoke response. In the other category are those definitions that include within the area of communication stimulus-response situations in which there need not be any intention of evoking response in the transmission of the stimuli. The second category obviously overlaps the first.

The definitions have grouped into these two categories. In the first group there is no particular sequence; I include the various definitions to provide a broad view of the definitions in this category. In the second group I present the definitions roughly in the order of their inclusiveness. Our everyday usage of the word "communication" fits in here. Standard dictionary definitions reflect it. "Communicate" is defined as "To impart, bestow, or convey. To make known; give by way of information. To have intercourse, or to be the means of intercourse; to hold or afford communication; to converse." "Communication" is defined as "The act or fact of communicating. Intercourse by words, letters or messages; interchange of thoughts or opinions, by conference or other means; converse; correspondence."

Wilbur Schramm gives what he terms the classical statement of the communication process as ". A communicates B through channel C to D with effect E. Each of these letters is to some extent an unknown, and the process can be solved for any one of them or any combination. " Similarly, Carl Hovland states that communication is "... the process by which an individual (the communicator) transmits stimuli (usually verbal symbols) to modify the behaviour of other individuals (communicatees)." Elaborating the process of communication more fully, Mapheus Smith states, Communication behaviour in its simplest reciprocal form is the use of some action by one person, whether or not accompanied by a material object, as a stimulus to another person in such a way that the second person can perceive the experience of the stimulating person. The overt action of the first person plays the role of a symbol whose reference or meaning is the same for the two participants, with the result that common experience is perceived by both participants.

Smith uses the term "communicative behaviour" because it focuses attention on the process of interbehaviour. Two other definitions are interesting additions to this category for the distinctions they draw between communication as interaction and other forms of interaction. Charles Morris writes: The term communication, when widely used, covers any instance of the establishment of a commonage, that is, the making common of some property to a number of things. In this sense a radiator "communicates" its heat to surrounding bodies, and whatever medium serves this process of making common is a means of communication (the air, a road, a telegraph system, a language). For our purposes "communication" will be limited to the use of signs to establish a commonage of signification; the establishment of a commonage other than that of signification—whether by signs or other means—will be called communization. Thus, as Morris points out, the anger of one person may make another person angry, and signs may not have established the commonage. This sort of situation he calls "communization." On the other hand, someone may signify anger, and, without becoming angry himself cause someone else to signify anger. An incident of this type he calls "communication." George Lundberg puts his definition this way: We shall use the word communication, then, to designate interaction by means of signs and symbols. The symbols may be gestural, pictorial, plastic, verbal, or any other which operate as stimuli to behaviour which would not be evoked by the symbol itself in the absence of special conditionings of the person who responds. Communication is, therefore, a subcategory under interaction, namely, the form of interaction which takes place through symbols.

Lundberg adds that this definition is subject to certain qualifications. It is important to distinguish between "... communication and mere contact, or interaction whether on the verbal level or otherwise." "True societal communication consists of temporarily identifying oneself symbolically with the other as regards the particular situation involved in the communication." True communication, he says, is the kind of interaction through signs and symbols that leads to tension reduction or understanding. Similar interaction that leads to increasing tension is also communication, but of a different degree. It involves a different degree of symbolic identification.

In the last two definitions above there is recognition of processes or areas of behaviour very closely related to communication—the "communization" of Morris and the "interaction without the use of signs and symbols" of Lundberg—but which, however, they carefully mark off from what is strictly called "communication." The excluded areas of behaviour, in the present classification, would be included among the definitions in category two. In this group are the definitions that include as communication situations those situations in which there is no intentional transmission of stimuli to evoke response.

Two concepts of communication in this category are suggestive of the Morris and Lundberg definitions, but instead of excluding the closely related areas of behaviour they include them as special kinds of communication. Edward Sapir, in defining communication, wrote of "explicit" and "implicit" communication. The former is communication in the conventional sense, the use of language to establish common understanding among people (a Category One definition); the latter is the "intuitive interpretation" of the "relatively unconscious symbolisms of gesture, and the unconscious assimilation of the ideas and behaviour of one's culture".

Baker Brownell used the terms "direct" and "indirect" communication. The latter is a "... process wherein something converted into symbols is carried over from one person to another." This is conventional usage (Category Onc again). The former, direct communication, is a function of the "... identification of people with one another." This is communication without a symbolic medium; it is an identification of experience.

Theodore Newcomb states that when someone gains certain impressions of someone else the latter is communicating something to the former. To use his example, the man who allows junk to accumulate in his front yard communicates something to his neighbour whether he knows it or not. An almost identical point of view is that of Jurgen Ruesch, who states that "... as used in our sense the concept of communication would include all those processes by which people influence one another." And in slightly different wording, Henry Lindgren expresses it, "Communication, viewed psychologically, is a process which is concerned with all situations involving meaning." Several years earlier Charles H. Cooley had foreshadowed this broad concept of communication:

By communication is here meant the mechanism through which human relations exist and develop—all the symbols of the mind, together with the means of conveying them through space and preserving them in time. There is no sharp line between the means of communication and the rest of the external world. In a sense all objects and actions are symbols of the mind, and nearly anything may be used as a sign.

Some writers conceive of the term "communication" broadly enough to include non-human interactions. S. S. Stevens, for instance, gives what he describes as a "... broad, operational, and behaviouristic" definition of communication.

He states: Communication is the discriminatory response of an organism to a stimulus. This definition says that communication occurs when some environmental disturbance (the stimulus) impinges on an organism and the organism does something about it (makes a discriminatory response). If the stimulus is ignored by the organism, there has been no communication.

The test is differential reaction of some sort. The message that gets no response is not a communication. Stevens adds that his definition includes the clucking of a mother hen that brings her chicks, as well as a treatise on the information theory of communication. In Warren Weaver's definition the ultimate step is taken, to include the interaction of machines:

The word communication will be used here in a very broad sense to include all of the procedures by which one mind may affect another. In some connection it may be desirable to use a still broader definition of communication, namely, one which would include the procedures by means of which one mechanism (say automatic equipment to track an airplane and to compute its probable future positions) affects another mechanism (say a guided missile chasing this airplane).

With the above classification of definitions in mind, let us turn to an application of these definitions. Let us picture an office in which several men are working at their desks. At midmorning the boss emerges from his private office and briefly talks with an employee. Let us assume that he gives the employee instructions to prepare a report, which the latter does, to the complete satisfaction of the boss. We can, without quibbling, say that in this case communication between the employer and the employee has occurred. We can also say that in this case communication has been successful. If the report had not been correct in every detail, because of some misunderstanding of the instructions, we would still say that communication had occurred, though not so successfully. Now suppose the boss had stepped into the room, briefly looked around, and then returned to his office without having said a word or made a gesture de signed to evoke a response. It seems reasonable to suppose that Some of the employees would nevertheless respond. They might have wondered, for instance, if the employer were checking to see that everyone was busy.

It seems apparent, moreover, that the responses of the employees might have been the same whether the boss had in fact been observing their work or not thinking about them at all. And yet again, if the employees had expected the boss to appear and had he not done so, his non-appearance would undoubtedly have evoked certain responses. Let us imagine, to carry the hypothetical incident further, that one of the employees is working on a large chart. His desk is inconveniently small for his work; lack of space reduces his efficiency and makes his job appreciably more difficult.

The employee might respond by feeling frustrated and angry. He might further begin to consider his small desk a threat to his prestige, and an indication of the small value the company places on his services. Still another employee might be finding his chair uncomfortable, and besides squirming around for an optimum adjustment to it, could well be thinking that the boss feels little concern for the welfare and dignity of his employees.

These commonplace office situations, a moment's reflection will show, correspond to most, if not all, of the communication situations. There was transmission of stimuli to evoke response; there was an interchange of ideas; the use of signs established a commonage of signification; people interacted through the use of signs and symbols; and impressions of certain people—intended or unintended—were evoked in the minds of others.

These doubtless were, in Sapir's terms, intuitive interpretations of gesture and unconscious assimilation of office culture. Also there may have been direct communication in Brownell's sense of the identification of people with one another, which perhaps could be illustrated by the common feelings towards the company. All were situations involving meaning. Moreover, we could class all as discriminatory responses to environmental stimuli. If we apply our definitions by categories, we find that in terms of the definitions in Category One, only the first of the office situations described has the characteristics of a communication situation, that is, the one in which the boss instructed an employee to make a report. In none of the others was there a deliberate use of signs or symbols to influence behaviour.

All of these situations could, however, with the addition of the element of purpose, involve communication in the sense of Category One. Had the boss when he made his wordless appearance done so intentionally to evoke response, or had he intentionally not appeared when he knew his employees expected him to (the absence of a stimulus object in a certain context can be as meaningful as its presence), the definitions would apply. If the too-small desk and the inadequate chair had been purposely given to the men in question (to let them know, for instance, that they were not so important as they might have felt themselves to be) these would have been communication situations in terms of definitions in Category One.

If we apply Category Two definitions, on the other hand, we find that all the office situations described involve communication. The definitions of Newcomb, Ruesch, Cooley, Lindgren, Stevens, and Weaver would quite plainly make of each of the office incidents a communication situation. The "split" definitions of Sapir and Brownell are more difficult to apply, but it seems apparent that their "implicit" and "explicit" concepts would include those situations that had meaning for the individuals involved although they were not intentionally structured to have such meaning. The relationships among them, and their relationships to the situations described? In the first place, the classification itself gives us a perspective on the problem of defining "communication" by revealing various attempts to conceptualize the process. The classification reveals attempts to delineate certain types of interaction as communication to the exclusion of other types; it reveals attempts to include as a special kind of communication certain interactional behaviour that does not fit the conventional concept of communication, and further, a disregard of such distinctions and the inclusion of all forms of human interaction, direct or indirect, as communication.

And still further, it reveals definitions so broad that certain animal responses, and even mechanical interactions, fall into the category of communication. Secondly, the importance and value of viewing communication as response become apparent. It is evident from the classification and application of the definitions that in the first category the concept of the process of communication is from the point of vie of the transmitter of stimuli, and in the second category, from the point of view of the person responding.

Looking at the process of communication from the transmitter's point of view provides the most obvious method of delimiting the area of behaviour to be treated as communication, and consequently simplifies the problem of definition. If someone is transmitting stimuli for the purpose of evoking response there is communication; otherwise there is none. This is certainly one basis for definition, but it leaves a large area of behaviour—often indistinguishable from "communication" by the responder or an observer—inadequately related to it, and in a sense unaccounted for. Only the transmitter can know whether or not he is transmitting stimuli for the purpose of influencing the behaviour of others. When the process of communication is viewed from the perspective of the person responding, the above problem of what to do with the closely related behaviour no longer exists. There seems to be no significant difference in the process of response whether or not it is to deliberately transmitted stimuli, and therefore no reason to classify the responses on this basis.

To use the office examples again, in the non-verbal situations, if the responders had known whether or not the situations were intentionally structured, it might have made a difference in the behaviour elicited, but this difference would have been the result of their having perceived the stimulus pattern differently. Had they assumed intentional structure, then whether or not there was in fact intentional structure would have made no difference to their response. There may appear to be a problem in viewing communication from the point of view of the responder when we proceed from people's influencing each other through words, actions, or man-made artifacts as communication to including as communication the individual's response to some object in the natural environment that human effort has in no way structured.

Take, for instance, someone's responses to the moon. Yet, here again, apart from the very basic response of awareness, his reactions, intellectual and emotional, and the meanings he "sees" in the moon are a function of the influence of other minds; he is interacting, though indirectly, with other people. Thirdly, we are able to select a basic and useful definition of "communication." The logical end result of accepting any of the definitions in Category Two is the acceptance of the broadest of the definitions, that of Stevens, which includes all instances of discriminatory response to environmental stimuli as communication (disregarding, of course, mechanical interaction as communication). As a basic definition this is the most satisfactory. It is inclusive of the other definitions, and it provides a perspective that permits us to see the relationships between the many other proposed definitions of communication.

Viewed from the perspective of this definition, the other definitions differ from each other on the basis of the range of response-evoking stimuli included in the communication situation. By the same token, this definition permits us systematically to delineate areas of communicative behaviour for purposes of study, while keeping these limited areas of behaviour in a consistent relationship to the total area of communicative behaviour of which they are a functionally inseparable part. We can delineate these areas for study by delimiting the range of response-evoking stimuli that is to be included in a given communication situation. Thus we might include as communication only those responses to words, objects, or actions deliberately structured to evoke response in a given situation. We might include only responses to written words designed to "communicate" at a particular time. We might include only spoken words and bodily actions, or only spoken words, or spoken words in a face-to-face situation, depending upon what aspect of the human interaction we happen to be primarily interested in.

There can, of course, be no sharp line of demarcation between the responses defined as communicative and those that are not. There is, as Cooley stated, no sharp line between the means of communication and the rest of the external world. Moreover, delimiting the communication situation by limiting the range of response-evoking stimuli included does not cancel the effects of other stimuli.

The individual is constantly making differential responses to a wide range of stimulus patterns, environmental and internal, responses which are often inextricably intermingled with the responses to the stimuli that would be, by definition in a given case, included within the area of communicative behaviour. The process of limitation suggested here, however, makes possible a systematic approach to the problem of limited definition, and makes us more clearly aware of what we are including and excluding for purposes of study and how these parts are related to each other.

The broad, basic definition adopted here points to the basic nature of communicative behaviour. While it may often serve our purpose to consider as communication situations only those in which people are responding to verbal stimuli, or rather, to consider primarily their responses to verbal stimuli, we must recognize the integral relationship between such responses and responses to other stimuli. The problem of defining "communication" is not unlike that of defining "education." In a sense, all learning experiences are educational (perhaps all experiences beyond reflex action), but to make learning more rapid and profitable we set up certain conditions of learning and in general limit the term "education" to an application to learning under such conditions. But to see what is conventionally termed "education" in the proper perspective we must see it in relationship to the vast number of other experiences of which it is a functionally inseparable part. And so, too, must we see communication, particularly that process of communication we call speech.

COMMUNICATION SKILL
TRAINING COMMUNICATION SKILLS

The ability to communicate is the primary factor that distinguishes human beings from animals. And it is the ability to communicate well that distinguishes one individual from another. The fact, is that apart from the basic necessities, one needs to be equipped with habits for good communication skills, as this is what will make them a happy and successful social being. In order to develop these habits, one needs to first acknowledge the fact that they need to improve communication skills from time to time. They need to take stock of the way they interact and the direction in which their work and personal relations are going. The only constant in life is change, and the more one accepts one's strengths and works towards dealing with their shortcomings, especially in the area of communication skills, the better will be their interactions and the more their social popularity.

The dominating question that comes here is: How to improve communication skills? Well, the answer is simple. One can find plenty of literature on this. There are also experts, who conduct workshops and seminars based on communication skills of men and women. In fact, a large number of companies are bringing in trainers to regularly conduct sessions on the subject, in order to help their workforce maintain better interpersonal work relations. Today, an effective communication skill has become a predominant factor even while recruiting employees. While interviewing candidates, most interviewers judge them on the basis of the way they communicate. They believe that skills can be improvised on the job; but ability to communicate well is important, as every employee becomes the representing face of the company.

There are trainers, who specialize in delivering custom-made programmes on the subject. Through the session they not only facilitate better skills in the department of communications, but also look into the problems that come in the way of being able to convey messages effectively. They discuss these issues with the management and then sought to design programmes accordingly. For instance, time mismanagement becomes a cause for stress and frustration, which then hampers the possibility of healthy communications at work. Then in weeks to come the company organizes a programme on time management. Thus, a workshop on communication skills helps the management t to deal with the finer employee nuances about which they lack awareness. Communication is generally classified into a couple of types.

The classifications include:

- Verbal and non-verbal
- Technological and non-technological
- Mediated and non-mediated
- Participatory and non-participatory

Training has become an important aspect of corporate development and progress. In fact, an increasing number of companies have been identifying various areas where training is required; and the leading among them has been communication skills.

Management across the various industries have realised that improving communication skills amongst their staff not only helps them in communicating and negotiating better with clients, but also helps in maintaining better interpersonal relations at the workplace, which in turn brings about a harmonious and productive working environment. While conducting communication skills training, a trainer usually covers the following topics through the programme. However, the number and type of topics do vary according to training needs and the level being trained...

Here is a comprehensive and exhaustive list of communication skills topics that are included in the various training programmes:

- What are communication skills
- Business communication skills
- How to improve English speaking
- Taking responsibility for what is being communicated
- Listening skills
- Adaptation to differences
- Asking and accepting feedback-praises and criticism
- Assertive communicating skills
- Attentive listening skills
- Being aware of all communicated messages
- Being gently repetitive to drive in important points and messages
- Addressing people appropriately
- Ability to handle cognitive complexity
- Ability to resolve conflicts with a compromise
- Using specific examples with concrete examples
- Ability to confront a situation without upsetting the apple cart
- Speaking using descriptive language without being boring
- Using details and examples
- Filtering irrational thoughts and emotions
- Being empathetic
- Supportive communication skills
- Accepting manipulative criticism, without revolting
- Giving effective and needed feedback without being judgemental and aggressive
- Showing genuine interest through body languages, gestures and facial expressions
- Initiating the communication process
- Managing an interaction
- Ability to interpret without being biased or judgemental
- Recognizing emotions and being sensitive to other's feelings and emotions
- Taking responsibility for one's own feelings and emotions
- Paraphrasing without distorting original message
- Perceiving without letting one's own judgements cloud the actual perception
- Understanding what is being communicated from various perspectives
- Being polite

- Praising without being superfluous
- Making provisional statements
- Putting forth appropriate questions
- Remembering and recalling
- Revealing vital self-information
- Making supportive statements
- Being versatile
- Conflict resolution—win-win problem solving ability.

Communication Skills Course Objectives:

- Understanding how communications work
- Gaining active listening and responding skills
- Seeing things from other points of view
- Managing your assumption more effectively
- Understanding your own strengths
- How others may see you
- Looking at body language
- Increasing confidence
- Difficult people or situations
- Filling up your communications tool kit

COMMUNICATION SKILLS COURSE PROGRAMME

The course content may include many of the exercises listed below, and any additional material that the trainers feel is relevant to the delegates on the day. Everything to be done is participative and interactive. There will be work in pairs, small group work, games, processes and exercises designed to stimulate, challenge and develop people's knowledge and skills. They are also fun!

What Else Would You Like Out of a Communications Skills Course?

A chance for delegates to add anything they would like from the programme. The Communication Skills Course will be adapted and changed as we go along to better fit their needs.

Communications Dynamic-how it Works

This is an introduction to the dynamics of face-to-face communication skills-looking at what affects the participants and how they might take more charge of situations. It gives an overview of how communication works at its best, identifying where it can go wrong. The day will be based around this key aim, with delegates being given the opportunity to practice and experience each section.

Vocal Tone and Communication

There are a range of exercises which experiment with the effects of variations of tone. Each person will have the chance to identify their usual default style and also consider how their tone affects the way that they may be perceived. From there we will practice ways to turn up and down different aspects of our natural communications style. In unpicking how to achieve the tone you choose, participants can see how they can do so consistently.

How Words Communicate

We have fun looking at ways to deliberately mangle our message and bury its meaning under waffle, padding and jargon. The premise being that if we know how to make our communications worse, we can also see how to make them clearer. From here, we may get to share one of our best communication skills exercises which offers everyone a failsafe way to deliver a clear key message.

Impact of Body Language on Communication

There are a variety of exercises to demonstrate the power and control the listener has, through body language and attitude. Making ourselves consciously aware of our options means that we can remain on a front foot when it comes to communicating effectively.

What does your History have to do with Communication Skills?

What makes us who we are inside and outside of work? What is our history or our form with particular sorts of people, particular subjects in particular scenarios?

How Head Stuff Affects Communication Skills

What makes us who we are inside and outside of work and how does that impact on the sense we make of others and they of us? When was the last time you got something wrong? When you were last misunderstood? Mis-communication seems to happen most when we base what we do on assumptions, perceptions and misconceptions rather than upon objective fact.

COMMUNICATION BY EYE CONTACT

One of our most vital communication skills is eye contact and its effect upon the communications dynamic. Back to assumptions again, but what do we make of those who avoid looking at us directly or else those who seem to hold our gaze too long?

What does the Environment Communicate?

Being aware that non-verbal factors may either help or hinder effective communication is vitally important. How far do those more subtle or not so subtle details swing things one way or the other? As well as the physical environment generally and the effect of rearranging the furniture or opening a window, we will consider those other things that can make a difference. How does a family photo, symbols of status or the provision of simple or expensive refreshments affect a meeting, an interview or a difficult interaction? In reality there may be things about the environment that we can't necessarily change, like the choice of space, the colour of the walls or the temperature. Of equal importance is the effect of breaking natural physical boundaries, we can investigate how they too affect our communication skills far more than we might realise.

Geography and Communication

What is the effect of being on your territory or theirs? We will look at how the familiarity of a place and where we are geographically can dictate who dances to whose tune. Certainly culture, in its widest sense, influences how our behaviour and words are perceived. Being attentive to what is likely to cause a ripple means that we can be deliberate in our intentions. Its obvious, but successful communicators are sensitive to the culture and geography of a place and can predict the effect of their words and behaviour. Working to your Communication Strengths Everyone will give a brief description of what they already do that they know works about them. They will then have chance to reflect upon how others see them through the feedback of others.

COMMUNICATION SKILLS COURSE SUPPORT

The final exercise of the Communication Skills Course is for each delegate to devise a personal Plan of Action, identifying their personal take-out of the programme, where they know they will practise and areas for their development. Finally there are people identify what will stop them putting this into practise and what support they need to help themselves put the communication skills course work into practise.

Presentation Skills Training Objectives:

- How Nervous Energy can be Harnessed
- Making the Best Use of Existing Strengths
- Freeing up Body Language
- Myths and Rules about Presenting
- What you Are and Are Not Allowed To Do
- Developing an Individual Presentation Style
- How to Stimulate Easy Interaction with an Audience
- Preparing for a Non-Linear Presentation
- Ways of Getting Ideas Across
- Call to Action (Closing a Sale)
- How to be Entertaining and Stimulating
- How to Create Effective Support Materials

Effective Presentation Skills

What might the most common Presentation Skills issue be?

The fact that for most people, even experienced presenters, getting up and presenting in front of an audience can be a terrifying and even phobic experience. Yes! The number one phobia that most people share is making a presentation; speaking in front of a group of other people: colleagues, strangers, it doesn't seem to matter-it's scary. You may have people who are new to the presentation 'game' and who need to understand just what happens to them when they have to stand and deliver and how they can become confident and effective presenters.

You may have people who have been around the presentation block and are in a rut, giving acceptable, but not brilliant presentations. You may have people who have to present detailed and technical information without putting their audience to sleep. Presenting detailed information may be important but if the presenter's audience aren't engaged then they've made their job of putting across information even harder. All of these people could benefit from confidence-building Presentation Skills programmes.

In addition, you may have individuals who have to:

- Give Key Note Speeches
- Make Presentations at Conference
- Pitch Crucial Clients Presentations
- Make Boardroom Presentations
- Pitch Ideas Internally
- Talk to the Public or Media
- Make Sales Presentations

Good Presentation Skills Training

Presentation Skills Training that concentrates on 'how to get it right' is available in all shapes and forms. However there is very little presentation skills training that really addresses the key issue of Working Your Audience. Many presenters have no idea of what can be achieved. Most of us know the power of an audience. It is often the rather unnerving experience of being on the receiving end of twenty pairs of eyes looking at us in polite silence as if to say "Yes?... So?" It is this energy that can be harnessed to make dynamic, lively, memorable and effective presentations. It takes a little courage, but the rewards are enormous. Our 'Working Your Audience' Presentation Skills Programme gives delegates clear insight into how the dynamic of a presenter and their audience works, enabling them to make really effective presentations. Tailored specifically to each group Working Your Audience is a Presentation Skills Training Course designed to develop delegates into powerful, persuasive presenters.

Tailored and in House Presentation Training

Tailored Advanced Presentation Training comes in many formats from one-to-one through to fully tailored company wide programmes. Many of us are now required to make presentations as a part of our job. Indeed for some people it will limit their career prospects if they are seen to be reluctant to make them. For the lucky few it doesn't seem to be a problem: they seem to have always been able to do it and thrive on it. For the rest of us, however, presentation skills are something we learn. Given that it can be a daunting and even frightening area of learning for most of us, it would seem sensible to use an approach that seeks to make it easy and enjoyable rather than one that makes it even more difficult.

The difficult presentation skills path is the one where you learn to get it right first time, to be flawless in your delivery and to make no mistakes. This is "how to" learning. Learning what to do and what not do.

The easier path is the one where you learn how presentation skills work and develop a style, which includes your idiosyncrasies and quirks (this way you don't have to learn to behave differently when you present). Let me give you an example of what I mean. Most presenters are concerned about their body language when presenting, and rightly so: what you do matters as much as what you say. So you have a choice. You can learn the rules for what you are not allowed to do and apply them. For instance, as a presenter you shouldn't cross your arms, put your hands in your pockets, touch your ear or nose (apparently this means you're lying), sway from side to side. The list is a long one and fortunately you don't need it. You can take the easy route.

EFFECTIVE COMMUNICATION SKILL

"Identification is one of the key ingredients of effective communication. In fact, unless your listeners can identify with what you are saying and with the way you are saying it, they are not likely to receive and understand your message." The quote above is the underlying factor that explains the importance of communication skills. In fact, there are other such quotes, which are as follows that explains the importance of effective communications skills: Good communication is as stimulating as black coffee, and just as hard to sleep after. the newest computer can merely compound, at speed, the oldest problem in the relations between human beings, and in the end the communicator will be confronted with the old problem, of what to say and how to say it.

The colossal misunderstanding of our times is the assumption that insight will work with people who are unmotivated to change. Communication does not depend on syntax, or eloquence, or rhetoric, or articulation; but on the emotional context in which the message is being heard.

People can only hear you when they are moving towards you, and they are not likely to when your words are pursuing them. Even the choicest words lose their power when they are used to overpower. Attitudes are the real figures of speech. When people talk, listen completely. Most people never listen. The problem with communication... is the illusion that is has been accomplished.

The right to be heard does not automatically include the right to be taken seriously. Argument is the worst sort of communication.

PROFESSIONAL SKILLS ARE PARTICULARLY IMPORTANT

After ten years, these same drivers-rapidly changing technology, particularly information technology, corporate downsizing, outsourcing, and globalization-that provided the impetus for the professional skills are, if anything, even more critical today. This is especially true as industry views an increasingly larger portion of the science and engineering labour pool more like a commodity then a profession.

Consequently, a growing number of less developed countries, with lower wage rates and an abundance of young, intellectual capital are competing for work that less than four years ago was performed by highly paid U.S. professionals, many of whom were then in short supply. While we do not know the extent of this shift in work from the United States (and other G-8 nations) to offshore locations, we do feel that the trend is, for the most part, permanent and irreversible.

Hence, a new issue confronting engineering educators today is how to best ensure that our graduates will continue to bring value to a marketplace in which their salary demands are three to five times greater than their international competitors. Oberst and Jones put the question succinctly: "It is no longer just whether engineers are being treated as commodities, but how engineers and other highly educated technical people shape and are shaped by the emerging realities of a truly global workforce.

Engineers as a professional group are thus the canaries in the mincshaft of the new world economy. Whether engineers manage the transition from local to international workplace environments will determine if the profession remains attractive".

They cite four major mega trends that affect the practice of engineering and necessitate the acquisition of more than technical skills:

- Changes forced by the fragile world economy;
- Student and professional mobility;
- Use of communications and instructional technology; and
- Increasingly loud voice of the social imperative.

To them, the so-called "soft skills" are much more than public speaking, management skills, and the ability to work well in teams. What is also needed is an understanding of how the growing social consciousness around the world is making it imperative that engineering students understand the implications of their work.

We propose that the mastery of these professional skills combined with an ability to innovate will add sufficient value to U.S. engineering graduates so that price does not become the primary determinant of who is hired in the global marketplace. From continuing skill development through lifelong learning that prevents technical obsolescence to the ability to do engineering within its global (and/or societal) context, the professional skills arc critical.

Hence, globalization, which now includes the globalization of the engineering profession, is forcing us to reconsider the role of future engineering graduates and the education required to meet that role. In 1994, Morrow (then National Academy Engineering president) in a farsighted consideration of the issues facing undergraduate engineering education noted that it is not a given that the U.S. engineering education system will always be globally pre-eminent. There is clear evidence that many U.S. corporations now seek their engineering talent wherever they can find it throughout the world. Engineering design quality, low-cost engineering services, and responsive engineering production capabilities are determinants of where engineering jobs will be. U.S. construction companies use civil engineers in Korea; automobile companies use design talents in Europe; software companies use software engineers in India.

A decade later, it is now evident that countries like China and India, with large, well-educated workforces, have learned how to move large segments of their populations into the advanced industrial economy in a manner similar to Japan, Korea, and Taiwan before them.

Further, like Korea and Taiwan, they are continuing to build universities to produce larger numbers of engineering and science talent and hence attract additional foreign direct investment, acquire advanced technology, and pursue export-led growth strategies. Further, another trend from the early '90s will continue to impact engineering education-an increasing number of engineeringgraduates may never practice engineering; rather, they choose to use their engineering education to enter a wide range of fields from business, medicine, law, and management among others.

Hcncc, as somc havc prcdictcd, an undcrgraduatc cnginccring cducation may become the liberal arts education of the twenty-first century. Certainly, the increasing number of engineering schools introducing general or interdiscip-linary degrees recognize this. Consistent with this trend, Purdue recently created the country's first Department of Engineering Education, followed a few months later by Virginia Tech's creation of the second department. Purdue's new department combines its existing freshman engineering and interdisciplinary engineering programmes.

In the future, it plans to offer graduate degrees for students studying the science of learning and other topics in engineering education. There also are plans to add an engineering teaching certification programme for high school teachers and to pursue accredited undergraduate degrees in engineering education and interdisciplinary engineering. Virginia Tech has similar plans for its programme. Further, six states-Massachusetts, Arkansas, New Hampshire,

Florida, Texas, and Maryland-have mandated engineering courscwork in high schools, a trend that is likely to spread to other states in the coming years.

PROCESS AND AWARENESS SKILLS

It is against this setting that we consider how to best teach and assess these professional skills. We believe that mastering these skills will be a major determinant of the future competitiveness of U.S. engineering graduates, enabling them to become highly innovative global "problem solvers," which, in fact, we propose is what much of engineering is all about. To best examine these skills we have divided them into two categories: process skills-communication, teamwork, and the ability to recognize and resolve ethical dilemmas (a more advanced formulation of criteria) and awareness skills-understanding the impact of global and social factors, knowledge of contemporary issues, and the ability to do lifelong learning.

We designate the first set as process skills because students learn a robust process to address each one. In contrast, the awareness skills arc so designated because students learn how to be aware of the importance of each one and to include them in their problem-solving activities. In reviewing these skills, we cite examples of how some institutions are able to successfully teach them.

PROCESS SKILLS

Communication: We note that communication is the one skill that can certainly be taught and assessed. Indeed, most universities have departments of communications. The proceedings of both the Frontiers in Education conferences and the annual conferences of the American Society of Engineering Education are replete with examples of ways to integrate communication into the fabric of under-graduate engineering education. We are particularly impressed with those institutions now combining communication with global and social and ethical issues as part of design projects. Two noteworthy examples are Union College and the University of Utah.

At Union College, Spinelli has developed a course that examines the history of electrical engineering by combining the study of technological development within American and European civilizations with a concentration on writing, oral communication, and ethics. Certainly, placing technological developments within a social and human context is one way of approaching ABET's engineering criteria for ethics, communications, and broad education, in a course with significant technical content.

In a similar spirit, faculty at the University of Utah are using funding from the Hewlett Foundation to bring together communication, leadership (team building), and ethics into the College of Engineering's eight programmes over the entire four-year curriculum. They are building upon a successful model communication programme in mechanical engineering, where teaching assistants from the humanities have been brought into the engineering classes so that communication skills can be taught as "situational" learning. A similar ethics component is to be added.

- Functioning on multidisciplinary teams: More and more engineering courses are being designed to give students the opportunity to experience teamwork firsthand. These range from short, decision-making exercises to project management or business simulations lasting the length of the course.

This team-based course design trend reflects industry practice, where teamwork has become the prevalent mode. Companies use teams as an integral part of their product development, process improvement, and manufacturing activities. Such management techniques as concurrent engineering, total quality management, and business process reengineering are founded upon the concept of people working effectively in teams. Engineering educators, recognizing these trends, are designing more and more courses around teams. Such programmes as Columbia's Gateway design course, MIT's undergraduate design course and its "New Products Programme", and Rowan University's Engineering Clinics Programme make extensive use of teams composed of students, faculty, and outside sponsors.

These project-driven classes provide students with the opportunity to experience team design work from idea conception to completion. When properly structured, such courses can teach students the skills necessary to work effectively in teams. However, too often educators incorporate student teams into their courses with little thought to their best use. Minimal guidance is provided to students on group development, soliciting member input, consensus building, resolving conflict, and team leadership. Evaluation oftentimes is subjective and little more than a piecemeal integration of individual and group-level performance. Consequently, instructors often fail to capitalize on much of the learning that can occur through group dynamics and behaviour.

However, there are several outstanding examples where engineering educators have integrated teamwork and team skill-building activities into the classroom. An increasing number of engineering educators now realise that students cannot be thrown into team projects without support.

One of the primary methods created to help integrate team learning into the engineering classroom is the development of formal curricular modules that can be used by various faculty planning to have students work on team projects. Of note is the Clark School of Engineering, University of Maryland modular team training programme-Building Engineering Student Team Effectiveness and Management Systems (BESTEAMS).

Supported by the National Science Foundation, the goal of this programme is to provide a team curriculum that can be easily adopted by engineering faculty from various schools and at different levels of the undergraduate curriculum. This well-structured programme allows faculty to select from various modules, depending on the nature of the course and the knowledge level of the students, its three modules-introductory, intermediate, and advanced-cut across three major team skill domains-personal, interpersonal, and project management. The engineering schools at both the University of Tennessee and the University of San Diego have adopted this modular approach to provide engineering faculty with the tools necessary to develop students' team skills. The underlying foundation of these training modules is based on learning style theory, enabling student problem solvers to apply newly acquired technical skills more effectively by improving interpersonal interactions.

All levels of undergraduates have used these modules, which can be customised based on developmental level and technical knowledge of the student. The modular nature of all three programmes makes them easily transportable in full or in parts, thus allowing faculty to customise based on class structure, project design, and course material. Another key component for teaching students team skills is the type of team project students will be exposed to in the classroom. Recent literature is replete with examples from structured, simulated team experiences to authentic design projects, where students work on real problems for actual clients. As discussed later in this paper, there is now an emerging interest in using projects with global and/or humanitarian dimensions. Several experiential activities can help students better understand the behaviours and skills needed to be an effective team member.

At one end of the spectrum, there are literally hundreds of "off-the-shelf" group exercises designed to give participants hands-on experience. On the other end, there are many elaborate game simulations designed to provide realistic conditions that allow students to experience teamwork. The choice of team task depends on the educational objectives. For example, if the objective is to have students experience a specific aspect of teaming such as brainstorming, specific group exercises in which students practice common methods of group brainstorming to generate new ideas can be used. However, if the objective is for students to experience a broad range of team processes and behaviours, then more complex activities are suitable. Two guiding principles should be followed in choosing activities: fidelity and complexity.

Fidelity is defined as the similarity of the training situation to the students' present and future working conditions. The higher the fidelity, the more superior the transfer of learning to the workplace. The fidelity of a particular activity can be increased by matching the conditions of the work environment as closely as possible. This may be difficult, especially when it comes to physical conditions, but many of the environmental conditions can be simulated. An example is "temporal environment," which involves such factors as time limits and deadlines the team may experience. Research has shown that time has a definite effect on team performance. Such conditions as actual time to complete the task or make decisions should be matched to real conditions where possible. "Social context" is another environmental condition that can be manipulated. Few teams work in a vacuum; instead, they typically co-exist with other teams that are working within a similar context. The more that inter-group activities can be designed into the team activity, the more a team can engage in real-world team behaviours such as inter-group communication, coordination, and conflict. Complexity is defined by two subfactors: task interdependence and cognitive effort. The more complex the activity, the more team skills are required by the participant. Activities also can range from high to low degrees of complexity. In general, the higher the fidelity and complexity of the activity, the better the transfer of team skills to the workplace.

For example, programmes like Purdue's EPICS provides highly realistic teaming activities, with all the complexities experienced by a product design team. Some computer-generated simulations also can be both highly realistic and very complex. An example is the Centre for Creative Leader-ship's COLAB simulation that places technology management students in cross-functional teams with a focus on making decisions on new polymer processes to be commercialized. Each competing team's objective is to get the new process to the market in a timely manner. Students make decisions on the allocation of research and development resources, manufacturing processes, and marketing activities. There are both advantages and disadvantages to each type of activity. Experiential activities categorized as high fidelity/high complexity most resemble real workplace" conditions, but typically are more difficult for the instructor to manage, resource intensive, and time consuming for the student.

Activities that are lower in fidelity are typically more structured and easier to administer, but may be perceived as less relevant by the student, resulting in the experience having less of a learning impact. Finally, team activities that are lower in complexity may not challenge the team nor provide the environment necessary for intense interaction among team members.

Understanding professional and ethical responsibilities: As part of their educational process, students should be sensitized to the potential ethical dilemmas they may confront in their professional life. If an engineer is able to recognize a developing ethical dilemma, he or she should be better able to first clearly frame it and then begin the process of resolution. Stephan, in questioning whether or not engineering ethics can be taught, quotes philosopher Michael Davis in giving four good things that can result if successful: students can become more aware of the ethical implications of their work, they can learn ethical standards, they can become better judges of ethical conduct, and they can become more willing to put their ethical knowledge into action.

To Stephan, the true test of engineering ethics education is how graduates behave in the workplace during their careers, certainly a difficult outcome to measure a priori. Much attention has focused on how engineers perceive, articulate, and resolve ethical dilemmas that arise when complex, advanced technologies are developed, such as the explosion of the Challenger, the Three Mile Island Nuclear Power Plant accident, Cherynobl, the DC-10 cargo door, or the Ford Pinto. In fact, an entire field, disaster ethics, has emerged from studying such events. While we believe that such lessons remain relevant to practicing engineers, of more importance may be how to recognize and then resolve those dilemmas that may arise in the routine practice of engineering. Engineers frequently work under cost and schedule pressures, situations that can lead to increased risk. At what point is that increased risk no longer acceptable? In addition, the multiple loyalties of the practicing engineer also contribute to ethical dilemmas.

Certainly, engineers have a loyalty to their employer, but engineering practice typically also involves a client or contractor, creating a second level of loyalty. Then there is the public, where the "safety of the public" as declared by Cicero has become accepted as the responsibility of the engineer. Every engineering code of ethics places the safety of the public in a prominent position. Finally, the engineer has a loyalty to the profession and to him or herself. The need to incorporate some form of ethics instruction into the engineering curriculum is no longer debated, largely because of the new ABET engineering criteria. A number of educators have noted the important relationship between ethics and engineering design and the value of integrating the two within the curriculum.

However, this is only a recent happening. Over the past fifty years, engineering educators have focused on providing students with tools and technical skills, but providing the education and skills for social decision making was not a priority. Consequently, until recently, little had been done to make students aware of the social dimensions of engineering. Stephan found that only 27 per cent of ABET-accredited institutions listed an ethicsrelated course requirement, even though an increasing number of philos-ophers, engineers, and ethicists focus their research and teaching on engineering ethics. The interest of practitioners and professional enginee-ring societies in engineering ethics has also increased. The Institute of Electrical and Electronics Engineers (IEEE) has been especially active. However, if the vision for understanding ethical and professional responsibilities as articulated in ABET is to become reality, educators must now answer a number of questions: What is the appropriate content?

What teaching methods and curriculum models are preferable? Which works best-required course, ethics across-thc-curriculum, integration of ethics and science, technology and society, or integration of the liberal arts into the engineering curriculum? Which outcome assessment methods are most suitable? Pinkus has provided an overview of these issues with emphasis on biomedical engineering. Pfatteichcr proposes that a current engineering ethics educational 'dilemma' is how to provide meaningful ethics instruction to all students without overburdening faculty, increasing graduation requirements, or removing essential technical material from the curriculum. She notes that the ABET engineering criteria call for ensuring understanding rather than demonstrating that graduates arc ethical. Hence, students should be evaluated on knowledge and skills, not values and beliefs.

Pfatteicher proposes providing students with an understanding of the nature of engineering ethics, the value of engineering ethics as opposed to the values of an ethical engineer, and the resolution of ethical dilemmas. At the University of Virginia, Richards and Gorman have effectively used case studies to teach not only design, but ethics.

They have developed (researched and written) a set of case studies for teaching engineering ethics, engineering design, and environmental issues. These cases have been used in a course on invention and design and in other courses offered by the Division of Science, Technology, and Society, which Gorman chaired. They emphasize that cases promote active learning, team-based activities, and the ability to deal with open-ended problems. With cases, students can be exposed to realistic situations involving unstructured problems with multiple possible answers, key decision points, and trade-offs. The case method, which also fosters the development of higher-level cognitive skills, enables students to address problems that require analysis, judgement, decisions, perspective taking, role playing, independent thought, and critical thinking.

AWARENESS SKILLS

Broad education to understand the impact of engineering solutions in a global and societal context and knowledge of contemporary issues: A growing number of engineering programmes recognize that these two areas can be combined with issues related to globalization, sustainability, and development, especially in lesser developed countries, and are designing highly innovative educational programmes to meet this need. By introducing design projects into the mix, often as part of a service learning experience, they are finding effective ways to teach the gamut of professional skills while reinforcing the "harder" technical skills.

We highlight some of these exemplary programmes in this section, with a particular emphasis on those with a global orientation. While traditionally few engineering students study abroad or co-op/intern abroad-the most recent data indicate that only 4,670 students (2.9 per cent) participated in a study abroad programme in as noted here, this should change as innovative programmes are designed to provide engineering students with needed global and social experiences. Lucena, one of the first academics to study globalization from an engineering perspective, notes that corporations, governments, and the engineers they hire face increasing challenges, such as mobility of capital and labour, organizational restructuring across national boundaries, and the development and implementation of more efficient production and manufacturing practices, among others.

Globalization depends on the availability of flexible workers to produce "just-in-time" products according to consumer demands and on the rapid dispersal of those products around the globe. This flexibility, demanded by globalization, presents special difficulties for engineering education and practice. Most engineers have no choice but to learn to cope with the practices changes that globalization is creating. Lucena (who holds a B.S. and M.S. in engineering and a Ph.D. in anthropology) suggests that a more appropriate education to prepare engineers to deal with the challenges brought by globalization might be a liberal-arts-based education that teaches them first to recognize and deal with the political dimensions of their work and second to deal with the ambiguity that results from working, sharing, and even valuing perspectives other than their own.

Swearengen et al., concerned with outsourcing capturing an increasing percentage of engineering work, suggest that engineers will become "free agents" in a professional services market. To thrive, future engineers will have to be able to work productively with radically different cultures, educational backgrounds, technical standards, quality standards, professional registration requirements, and time zones. The manufacturing engineer must not only master the elements of global design, manufacture, marketing, and distribution, but also prepare to participate as a contractor in a "twenty-four-hour virtual enterprise". Engineers must understand that in a global context, engineering solutions, whether consumer products or unintended consequences such as resource exhaustion and environmental pollution, increasingly cross or transcend international boundaries. Global sustainability, for example, may eventually outweigh technical and other aspects of manufacturing.

Engineering faculty are beginning to recognize that students who have participated in study abroad programmes are better problem solvers, have strong communication and cross-cultural communication skills, and arc able to work well in groups of diverse populations and understand diverse perspectives. Living overseas creates graduates who are more adaptable to new environments and have a greater under-standing of contemporary issues as well as engineering solutions in a global and social context. However, further research is required to fully support these findings.

Perhaps the prototype model for integrating international experience into an engineering education is the University of Rhode Island's (URI) International Engineering Programme. Founded in 1987 by John Grandin, professor of German, and Herman Viets, then dean of engineering, this innovative programme combines an undergraduate engineering degree with a degree in languages (initially German, but now expanded to French and Spanish). In addition, students do an internship in a country where they must use their language skills, and many also do at least one term of study in that country. This five-year programme, which has been replicated by both the University of Connecticut and Rice University, has served to increase both the quality and quantity of URI engineering students; currently 20 per cent of incoming students participate.

Worchester Polytechnic Institute (WPI) is one of the leaders in enabling its students to study engineering within a global and social context. WPI's programme is centered on the Major Qualifying Project-the equivalent of a nine-credit capstone design experience-and provides a professional-level application of the students' knowledge in their major fields. It typically involves the design, synthesis, and realization of a solution to a real-world technical problem. WPI has established project centers, including ones in Ireland, Denmark, Hong Kong, Australia, Namibia, and Costa Rica. By 2002, 35 per cent of the electrical and computer engineering students were completing their senior design project in a project centre (10 weeks).

In total, more than half of the WPI students complete at least one degree requirement internationally. To make the programmes more affordable, WPI provides free passports and financial aid incentives. The University of Michigan has created a global concentration in engineering with an initial focus on China, the United Kingdom, and Mexico. The flexible framework enables all disciplines to participate. It requires international experience, global engineering course content, and a required cross-cultural course for engineers on global understanding. A motivation to establish the programme was to better prepare engineers to deal with the global supply chain by training engineers who possess not only the appropriate technical skills but also the cross-cultural skills based on knowledge of "other" cultures and their own cultural biases.

Michigan faculty have also created an Engineering Global Leadership Honours Programme, where students select a regional focus and concentrate their humanities/social science electives in that area. Students also must complete two years of advanced language study. Teams of business and engineering students consult for a major corporation. Muzumdar and Bean feel that even though almost all business is conducted in English and students may not even work in a location where their second language is spoken, having a second language makes the student more likely to work well in any other culture.

Melsa, Holger, and Zachary have described Iowa State's Global Academic Industrial Network (GAIN), which provides U.S. students with international experiences in Germany to better prepare them for future job requirements. They note that the critical element in all international exchange programmes is the faculty; institutions must find ways to engage their faculty in international experiences, including extended stays at a foreign institution. Programmes built around a single faculty member and his or her international connections are fragile and typically fail when that individual loses interest or moves. Further, funding cannot become the limiting factor with such programmes. Institutional support at the highest levels is essential. A promising, comprehensive programme is Purdue's Global Engineering Alliance for Research and Education (GEARE). This unique eighteen-month progra-mme, developed in partnership with Karlsruhe (Germany) and Shanghai Jiao Tong (China) Universities, integrates language education, cultural orientation, three-month domestic and three-month international internships at the same partner firm, study abroad, and a two semester face-to-face multinational design team project, with one semester abroad and one at home. The bilateral programme involves equal numbers of students from each university participating in the paired exchanges.

Another model programme for providing international experience is Old Dominion University's cluster concept. Here, students take a three-course cluster with an inter-national perspective, including two required courses-"Global Engineering and Project Management" and "Commu-nications Across Cultures"-and select one other from among "World Resources," "International Business Operations," or "Sustainable Development". The cluster concept attempts to provide students with a basic understanding of the integrative nature of successful engineering practices that involve not only technical but international, cultural, communication, and busincss factors. It also attempts to provide students with the knowledge to work productively in an environment that encompasses difierent cultures, business practices, resources, communication, and engineering practices.

The University of Kentucky has created an innovative combined B.S. Engineering-M.B.A. programme with a strong international component directed at producing manufactu-ring engineers and engineering managers. The engineering undergraduate degree, coupled with the M.B.A., allows students to explore immediate interests while building a solid, long-term career foundation.

This integration of business and economics courses with a traditional engineering programme over a five-year period results in students developing a broader, more holistic view of management principles and their application to an engineering environment. The students' senior year marks the beginning of the graduate M.B.A. courses and interaction with non-engineering M.B.A. students. During the summer prior to the fifth year, students participate in a study abroad programme designed expressly for the programme, thereby enhancing and broadening their cross-cultural experiences. For the summer of 2004, the Kentucky students participated in a second innovative initiative-the University of Pittsburgh's Manufacturing and the Global Supply Chain in the Pacific Rim as part of the Semester at Sea Programme.

That programme, a joint effort between the University of Pittsburgh's School of Engineering and the International Business Centre, offered three manufacturing courses with a global perspective as students visited China, Hong Kong, Japan, Korea, Russia, Taiwan, and Vietnam. Visits to in-country manufacturing sites complemented the class activities.

Amadei at Colorado has become a leader among the engineering educators now looking at sustainability issues in the less developed world. He suggests that most past engineering achievements have been developed with little consideration of their social, economic, and environmental impact on natural systems. In many instances, engineering projects have contributed to the degradation of the Earth's natural systems. Amadei is concerned with the education of engineers interested in addressing the problems that are most specific to developing communities-water provision and purification, sanitation, power production, shelter, site planning, infrastructure, food production and distribution, and communication.

These problems arc not usually addressed in U.S. engineering curricula, despite the fact that 20 per cent of the world's population lacks clean water, 40 per cent lacks adequate sanitation, 20 per cent lacks adequate housing, and 30 per cent live in conflict zones, transition, or situations of permanent instability. As a result Amadei is helping to create a programme in Engineering for Developing Communities that will view the developing world as the classroom of the twenty-first century. This interdisciplinary effort will bring together engineering and non-engineering disciplines, thus supporting the learning of multiple professional skills. It will address a wide range of issues-water provision and purification, sanitation, health, power production, shelter, site planning, infrastru-cture, food production and distribution, communi-cation, and jobs and capital for various developing communities. The first phase involves an undergraduate certificate programme that should be in place by the time this chapter is published.

As part of this initiative, Amadei and his colleagues have formed Engineers without Borders-USA (EWB) at Colorado, which is dedicated to helping disadvantaged communities improve their quality of life by implementing environ-mentally and economically sustainablc engineering projects while developing internationally responsible engineering students. Student projects that involve the design and construction of water, sanitation, and energy systems are ongoing in Belize, Mali, Mauritania, Nicaragua, Peru, Haiti, and Thailand. Rowan University faculty are incorporating EWB projects into their junior and senior clinics as a means of introducing open-ended problem solving in conjunction with developing synthesis, analysis, teamwork, communica-tion, business, and entrepreneurial skills.

A somewhat similar programme is being developed at Colorado School of Mines (CSM), with a focus on "humanitarian engineering." With support from the William and Flora Hewlett Foundation, the goal is to nurture a cadre of engineers that is sensitive to social contexts and committed and qualified to serve humanity by contributing to the solution of complex problems at regional, national, and international levels and locations around the world. This goal is to be achieved through the development of a humanitarian component for the CSM engineering curriculum that will teach engineering students how to bring technical knowledge and skill, as well as cultural sensitivity, to bear on the real-world problems of the less materially advantaged. A complement of Engineers without Borders-U.S.A. is Engineers for a Sustainable World (ESW) (previo-usly known as Engineers without Frontiers-USA).

ESW originated in the College of Engineering at Cornell University in 2001 as a result of the efforts of Dr. Krishna S. Athreya, director of Minority and Women's Programmes in Engineering, and Regina R. L. Clewlow, a Cornell University graduate. ESW is based on the belief that engineers and community members can work together to identify and solve technology-based problems, employing solutions that can be locally sustained, leading to an improved quality of life. ESW believes that locally sustainablc engineering solutions are fundamental to the needs of communities in which issues such as lack of clean water, poor housing, and limited energy are barriers to adequate living conditions. By establishing a national network in the United States for engineers to be of service to developing communities, ESW contributes to a better world and enriches the lives of engineering professionals who seek to participate in socially responsible endeavors. ESW has almost twenty chapters, with another thirty in the formation stage. Iowa State University and the Universities of Dayton and Seattle have joined together to form Engineers in Technical, Humanitarian Opportunities of Service Learning (ETHOS).

Its purpose is to help students gain an awareness of the social and cultural fabric of the poorest of the world and perform design research focused on improving the ability of these individuals to meet their basic needs. Engineering activities are being implemented in a number of formats, ranging from classroom activities to multi-semester research studies. Both on-campus curricular and immersion service experiences arc included in its mission. Initial projects have focused on two non-governmental organizations' efforts to develop more efficient and more durable wood-burning stoves used for cooking by the world's poor.

Another example of service learning incorporated as part of undergraduate engineering education is the building of low-cost, energy-efficient houses in South Africa by students from Tuskegee University and the University of Fort Hare (South Africa). The idea behind this project is to develop a way for some of the economic benefit to stay in the local community. A number of faith-based institutions, notably Calvin, Drodt, Grove City, and Messiah Colleges, have combined engineering, service learning, and globally based humanitarian projects, thus meeting both social and student needs. However, Riley and Miller (Smith College) have raised concerns about involvement with faith-based projects, feeling that certain projects may be inappropriate if the development aid is tied to religious conversion and destroying indigenous cultures without regard for the community's traditions.

Smith College has developed an interdisciplinary project-based course that seeks to initiate critical study of the technological, cultural, and policy aspects of international development. This course requires students from different majors to share sophisticated disciplinary knowledge. Students address the promises and limitations of technology for development; the meanings of capitalism, colonialism, and globalization; and the implications of engaging in development work from places of privilege.

In developing a service component for the course, they seek to avoid sending students for only a few weeks to a country with which they have had no prior cultural experience-a situation that would make it difficult for students to acquire an adequate knowledge or sense of the community in which they are working. Since the mid-1990s, an increasing number of programmes have incorporated international design team experiences, involving students from a U.S. and one or more partner international institutions. The original concept involved using the Internet and e-mail for communication, with the team coming together at the end of the project for a final meeting and presentation. Now, with the introduction of virtual design and virtual teaming concepts, the potential exists to do these types of programmes without having students leave home.

The need to train engineers to be well prepared to collaborate with their colleagues around the world and to work effectively in geographically distributed, multicultural teams was a motivation for Union College's creation of an International Virtual Design Studio (IVDS) in 1996. The IVDS initially brought together the mechanical engineering departments at Union College and Mideast Technical University (METU) in Ankara, Turkey, in response to the need to develop skills among students to better function in the emerging global environment in today's workplace. In 1997, Queen's University (Kingston, Ontario) joined the partnership. Such projects provide international culture interaction, team building, communication, creative thinking, and project management experience. Each IVDS team has four to six members, two or three from each institution-METU and either Queens or Union. At Union, students select their project in spring term of the junior year.

Students must analyse, design, and build an autonomous robot for a given task and application. Since 1999, METU students have visited in November to compile and finish design reports. Final reports are presented before they leave. In January, after a prototype has been built, they go to Turkey for a competition at METU. Sheppard et al. propose that virtual reality (VR) has the potential to have a major impact on engineering education by permitting students to explore environments that would be otherwise inaccessible. Specifically, VR will better facilitate teaming on an international and therefore multicultural level. Hence, faculty now must address educational collaboration in the virtual environment, testing and refining it at the institutional level, between institutions and across national boundaries.

A pilot implementation at Stevens Institute of Technology involves undergraduate student teams from three universities in three countries: Stevens is providing overall design and project coordination, the University of the Philippines (Quezon City, Philippines) is the manufacturing lead, and the National Institute of Technology (Warangal, India) is the simulation lead. The project, "MEMS across the Globe" forms part of a larger pilot in virtual student design undertaken by a consortium of schools in collaboration with PTC Inc., a producer of industry standard design and collaboration tools. At Northern Arizona, language and engineering faculty are combining to utilize virtual reality to develop a pilot "Global Engineering College." When successfully implemented, it will inject international perspectives throughout the curriculum by leveraging technological, developments to create a "virtual" engineering college.

A recognition of the need for and the ability to engage in lifelong learning: Although the new ABET engineering criteria have brought lifelong learning to the forefront of engineering education, as Litzinger and his colleagues have pointed out, lifelong learning in engineering has been recognized as critical for decades. They note that the Final Report of the Goals Committee on Engineering Education contained a discussion of the importance of lifelong learning, and the theme of the 1978 ASEE Annual Meeting was "Career Management-Lifelong Learning." A number of earlier studies that investigated the types of activities involved in lifelong learning, their frequency of use, the support systems required, the barriers, and impact of lifelong learning for individual engineers are summarized in a 1985 report by a National Research Council panel. Litzinger and his colleagues, who are at the frontier of studying lifelong learning relative to engineering education, note that a major issue is how to assess the extent to which students are prepared to engage in it and also their willingness to do so. With funding from the National Science Foundation, they have been investigating how best to assess lifelong learning.

Various engineering education researchers have defined elements of lifelong learning, including Henry and Rogers, whose RIRI model consists of four components: receiving, enquiring, reflecting, and integrating. Miller, Olds, and Pavelich purport that their Cogito system for measuring intellectual development (based on assessing reflective judgement) will, when fully validated, also assess lifelong learning.

When we specified the attributes of lifelong learning as part of our NSF-funded Action Agenda study, we proposed that these include the ability to:

- Demonstrate reading, writing, listening, and speaking skills;
- Demonstrate an awareness of what needs to be learned;
- Follow a learning plan;
- Identify, retrieve, and organize information;
- Understand and remember new information;
- Demonstrate critical thinking skills; and
- Reflect on one's own understanding.

We propose that as students acquire the other professional skills, especially the other two awareness skills, as well as the process skills, that they will, in fact, acquire the ability to do lifelong learning. Hence, one will become a proficient lifelong learner as one becomes proficient in the broad spectrum of professional skills.

7

An Organization and its Advisors Development in Leadership

It is important to take time and be considerate when developing your organization. This chapter has tools to help define your organization, give direction and avoid chaos. It includes tips for goal setting, orienting new members, managing conflict, maintaining balance and much more.

AN ORGANIZATION AND ITS ADVISORS

As a student organization with competent and capable leadership, you might wonder why student organizations would want or need a faculty or staff advisor.

Consider the following:

- Do you sometimes wish your group had more support from related academic or service departments?
- Could your organization benefit from some "connections" with university policy-makers?
- And even though you are doing a super job now, will your group have to start again from scratch next year?

A faculty or staff adviser could help alleviate these and other problems WITHOUT TAKING OVER the leadership of your organization. Advisers play an important role in the development of the student organization by providing support and guidance.

The Role of an Advisor:

- Serve as a "sounding board" off which you can bounce off new ideas
- Support your group
- Intervene in conflicts between group members and/or officers
- Be knowledgeable of policies that may impact on your organization's decisions, programmes, etc.
- Provide continuity and stability as student leadership changes
- Provide your group with connections
- Serve as mediator during an organizational crisis
- Give honest feedback to group members

- Point out new perspectives and directions to the group and introduce new programme

IDEAS

The organization/adviser relationship benefits the adviser too.

Being involved with a student organization offers the faculty or staff member unique opportunities to:

- Get to know and work with students outside the classroom or office
- Informally share knowledge and expertise on relevant topics
- An opportunity to feel satisfaction and accomplishment through making a special contribution to a particular group of students
- Inform the transfer of knowledge and skills learned from the co-curricular experience
- Serves as a resource and support person as well as facilitator of creativity and innovation for the group

THE RESPONSIBILITIES OF GROUP MEMBERS TO THEIR ADVISOR

Discuss your expectations of the adviser's role with your adviser from the beginning. This information should be from all of the students with whom the adviser will work - officers, chairs, etc.

- Notify the adviser of all meetings.
- Send the adviser a copy of all minutes and other information. Too much information is probably better than too little!
- The President/Committee Chair/Executive Board should meet regularly with the adviser to discuss organizational matters and to relay and update information.
- Consult with the adviser before any changes in the structure or policies of the organization (committee) are made and before major projects are undertaken.
- Remember that the responsibility for the success or failure of a group project rests ultimately with the group, not the adviser.
- Conduct annual adviser and organization evaluations, this allows for developing an ongoing and effective adviser relationship.

Do you know how much your organization and potential adviser can benefit from one another? You probably want to know how to find this adviser? There are at least two things your organization should do. First, develop a clear statement of group goals and a clear statement of expectations of the adviser, both in terms of role and time commitment. It would also be helpful to outline what the adviser could fairly expect of the group. With this information in hand, you will be ready to approach potential advisers and discuss with them their interest and ability for advising your group. The most suitable adviser is one who shares a common interest with your organization.

Poll your group members for the names of professors or staff members who they have found helpful and interested in student life. Approach potential advisers with confidence and a positive attitude. Remember to be clear about the purpose and activities of your organization, your expectations of the adviser and all benefits the adviser will enjoy. Once your adviser begins to serve, keep him/her well-informed, clarify expectations and roles when needed and draw on his/her expertise. Occasionally, thank you notes and acknowledgments are a good idea - if you have organization t-shirts, for example, make sure your adviser has one too! Enjoy what can be an extremely rewarding and mutually beneficial relationship.

BRAINSTORMING

Is your group stumped for new ideas? Do you do the same activities the same old way, year after year? Do the leaders and just a few others seem to do all the talking?

Brainstorming may be just the technique to rejuvenate your organization and get everyone excited and involved. The purpose of this method is to get out as many ideas as possible, the more you have to choose from, the better your final choice will be! You can use brainstorming for almost anything: programme ideas, themes, slogans, publicity, group goals and problem solving.

The rules for brainstorming are deceptively simple, be sure the group understands them and someone has the job of making sure they are followed.

Set The Stage:

1. Set a time limit, 10 to 20 minutes, depending upon the size of your group and the complexity of the issue.
2. The best group size is 3-15 people. If you have more, break into two or more groups and brainstorm simultaneously.
3. Focus on one issue at a time. The question or issue must be one about which all participants can speak.
4. Record all responses on a blackboard or big sheets of newsprint so everyone can see them; don't record the name of the person suggesting. Record only key words and phrases, not word for word.

Explain (and Possibly Post) The Following Rules:

1. Do not discuss ideas until the end
2. Do not criticize, praise or judge
3. Be spontaneous—no hand-raising, just call out
4. Repetitions are OK
5. Quantity counts
6. Build on each other's ideas—"hitch-hiking" or "piggy-backing" is encouraged
7. Enjoy the silences-often the best ideas come out of them
8. It is ok to be outrageous, even silly

Make Good Use of the Members' Creativity:

1. If several groups brainstormed the same idea, put the lists on the wall and let everyone read each other's work.
2. Group ideas into related categories for review.
3. Decide which ideas are most promising and which can be eliminated; this can be done by putting pluses and minuses by items.
4. Rank the most promising.
5. Select those with greatest potential and high-ranking priority for either implementation or refinement by committee or the group.
6. Follow-up. If the ideas are to be implemented successfully by the group or by committee, ask for updates on a regular basis.
7. Review and evaluate your ideas as they are being implemented. Make any changes deemed necessary by the group.
8. Be sure to utilize the ideas generated. It is extremely demoralizing for a group to invest its time, energy and creativity and have the idea disappear. Seeing your ideas come to fruition however, is extremely rewarding.

BREAKING THE ICE

Ice breakers and acquaintanceship exercises are important when groups come together each year and when bringing in new members. They can be excellent devices to help people feel more comfortable with themselves, with others and feel more "at home" in a group. They also break up the "cliques" by inviting people to form random groupings and helping individuals meet others in a non-threatening and fun way. There are different levels of icebreakers based on the kind of group and the closeness of the group. When used to set a tone for the time a group will be together, members are encouraged to feel comfortable and this can relieve tension.

Icebreakers, figuratively, break the ice when a group newly forms or reforms after a break. Icebreakers are an effective method to initiate a new member orientation. A few examples are:

1. *Human scavenger hunt, or Human Bingo:* (Have each square in a bingo card be a characteristic of someone. As you meet someone, have them mark off a square if they match the characteristic). Find someone who:
   a. Is a graduate student
   b. Owns cross country skis
   c. Has been to Europe
   d. Wears contacts
   e. Make up your own...be creative!
2. *Hometown:* Members tell where they are from and information about their hometown. (Be careful for groups that do not know each other

very well, this could be a touchy situation based on socio-economic status).

3. *Name Game:* Why or how the member received his/her name. Share their name and hobby; members try to memorize the information.
4. *Knots:* Form a circle by placing hands in the middle of the circle. Grab someone else's hands (not on either side of you), and without letting go, try to untangle the "knot."
5. *Coat of Arms:* Have participants trace their hands, and in each finger write down a characteristic from the coat of arms exercise.

EXAMPLES OF GETTING ACQUAINTED EXERCISES:

The following exercise will encourage stronger ties, which are important when working together.

1. *Dyads:* Members form groups of two and find out information about each other. Possible questions to use:
   - Who do you think is the most important person who has lived in the past 100 years?
   - What is the best movie that you have seen recently?
   - What is the title of the last book that you have read?
   - If you could be any animal other than human, what would you be?
   - If you could travel to any place in the world, where would you go?
   - What is your favorite sport?
   - One adjective to describe me is....
   - The emotion I find most difficult to control is....
2. *Crest or Coat of Arms:* Members create their own "Coat of Arms" by filling in information about themselves using words or drawings. Information can include:
   - Significant Life Events
   - Hobbies
   - Favorite Heroes
   - Family Members
   - Five or Ten Year Goals
   - What they can bring to the organization
   - What they want to receive from the organization
3. *Forced Choice:* Ask members to stand in the middle of the room and have them move to either side to indicate their choice. Have them find a partner on the side they have chosen and discuss reasons for their choice. Are you:
   - More like a Cadillac than a Volkswagen?
   - More of a saver than a spender?

- More like New York than Colorado?
- More yes than no?
- More like a student than a teacher?
- More here than there?
- More religious than non-religious?
- More like the present than the future?
- More like a file cabinet than a liquor chest?
- More intuitive than rational?
- More like a tortoise than a hare?
- More like an electric typewriter than a quill pen?
- More like a roller skate than a pogo stick?
- More like a bubbling brook than a placid lake?
- More like a gourmet restaurant than a McDonald's?

CONSTITUTION + BYLAWS

The Constitution of an organization contains the fundamental principles which govern its operation. The bylaws establish the specific rules of guidance by which the group is to function. All but the most informal groups should have their basic structure and methods of operation in writing.

WHY HAVE A CONSTITUTION?

By definition, an organization is a "body of persons organized for some specific purpose, as a club, union or society." The process of writing a constitution will serve to clarify your purpose, delineate your basic structure and provide the cornerstone for building an effective group. It will also allow members and potential members to have a better understanding of what the organization is all about and how it functions. If you keep in mind the value of having a written document that clearly describes the basic framework of your organization, the drafting of the Constitution will be a much easier and more rewarding experience.

WHAT SHOULD BE COVERED BY A CONSTITUTION?

The following is an outline of the standard information to be included in a Constitution. The objective is to draft a document that covers these topics in a simple, clear and concise manner.

Article I - The name of the organization
Article II - Affiliation with other groups (local, state, national, etc.)
Article III - Purpose, aims, functions of the organization
Article IV - Membership requirements and limitations
Article V - Officers (titles, term of office, how and when elected)
Article VI - Advisor (term of service, how selected)
Article VII - Meetings (frequency, special meetings and who calls them)

Article VIII - Quorum (number of members required to transact business)

Article IX - Referendum and Recall (procedures and handling)

Article X - Amendments (means of proposal, notice required, voting requirements)

Article XI - Ratification (requirements for adopting this constitution)

Why Have Bylaws?

The Constitution covers the fundamental principles, but does not prescribe specific procedures for operating your organization. Bylaws detail the procedures your group must follow to conduct business in an orderly manner. They provide further definition to the Articles of the Constitution and can be changed more easily as the needs of the organization change.

What Should be Included in the Bylaws?

Bylaws must not contradict provisions in the Constitution.

They generally contain specific information on the following topics:

- Membership (selection requirements, resignations, expulsion, rights and duties)
- Dues (amount and collection procedures, any special fees, when payable)
- Duties of Officers (powers, responsibilities, specific job descriptions, procedures for filling unexpired terms of office, removal from office)
- Executive Board (structure, composition, powers)
- Committees (standing, special, how formed, chairpersons, meetings, powers, duties)
- Order of Business (standard agenda for conducting meetings)
- Parliamentary Authority (provisions for rules of order, generally Roberts Rules of Order - Newly Revised)
- Amendment Procedures (means of proposals, notice required, voting requirements)
- Other specific policies and procedures unique to your organization necessary for its operation

Once we've got them - what do we do with them?

- Remember the reasons for having a Constitution and Bylaws. They articulate the purpose of your organization and spell out the procedures to be followed for its orderly functioning. Constitutions usually require a 2/3 vote of the membership for adoption. Bylaws only require a simple majority for passage. Once you have developed your Constitution and Bylaws review them often. The needs of your group will change over time and it's important that the Constitution and bylaws are kept up to date to reflect the current state of affairs.
- Make sure every new member of the organization has a copy of them.

This will help to unify your members by informing them about the opportunities that exist for participation and the procedures they should follow to be an active, contributing member. A thorough study of the Constitution and Bylaws should be a part of officer training and transition.

GROUP DECISION MAKING

Student organization members and leaders make decisions in the group all the time. The decision making process can be stressful because people view it differently. For example, some people see it as a form of power struggle, some people cannot bear the idea of losing an argument and others simply do not like to make decisions. Decisions are an important part of group life and you may wonder how your group can improve in this area. This information is designed to help you.

There are several types of group decisions:

1. *Unilateral* - A decision made by one person, often the nominal leader, without consultation with other group members. At times, it can be appropriate. For example, a minor decision that needs to be made right away. If it is repeated and inappropriate, this type of decision can carry a very low group commitment.
2. *Handclasp* - Decisions made by two members. One suggests, the other endorses and carries it through without adequate discussion or group consideration. This type has high commitment for the two who made it, but generally not for the others.
3. *Clique* - Similar to the Handclasp but with more people involved. This type usually occurs when a close sub-group decides what is good for the rest of the group. Repeated clique decisions cause splintering of the group and low commitment.
4. *Baiting* A technique that reduces discussions around decisions. A person will say, "Now we are all agreed, right?!" and only the very brave will speak up. This usually supresses obvious dissention and lowers group commitment.
5. *Majority Rule* - A popular way of making decisions. However, if the outcome of a secret ballot vote would produce any surprises, it is not a good time to make majority rule decisions. What happens is that a sizeable segment of the group may feel devalued and decrease their commitment to the decisions in which they "lose" to the majority vote.
6. *Consensus* - Similar to Majority Rule, but everyone knows that what they think and value is being considered by all, and there will be no surprises if you vote. Each person will agree that, under the circumstances, which may not be ideal, the decision made is a fair and workable one that they can live with and support.

You may be able to think of and classify other types of decisions. Any type may prove effective under a given set of circumstances. However, it is obvious that the first five approaches are likely to reinforce the powerful people in the group and create tension. Morale and membership commitment can be lowered if these are the usual methods of making organizational decisions. Since members possess the essential ingredients for the solutions to all problems, group decisions should be based on all members' input. Certainly, if there are decisions that only take a few people to make, it may not be necessary to involve an entire group. We recommend that you consider the following points about the assets and liabilities of consensus decisions.

Assets of Group Consensus Approach:

- Greater sum total of knowledge and information.
- Greater number of approaches to a problem.
- Participation in problem solving increases acceptance — A lower-quality solution that has wide acceptance can be more effective than a higher quality solution that lacks acceptance.
- Better comprehension of the decision - The chances for communication failures are greatly reduced when the individuals who must work together in executing the decision have participated in making it.
- Greater commitment of the members to the decision.

Liabilities of Group Consensus Approach:

- Social Pressure - Minority opinions in groups can have little influence on the solution reached, even when these opinions are correct ones. Reaching agreement in a group often is confused with finding the "right answer".
- Individual Domination - Skilled manipulators or dominant individuals can emerge and capture more than their share of influence on the outcome.
- Conflicting Secondary Goal - People may aim at winning the argument at the cost of finding the best answer.
- Risk Taking - The risk of not getting their own way can prevent people from fully participating in the discussion.
- Time - Listening and considering all points of view in order to arrive at the best solution takes time.

Factors that serve as liabilities or assets depending largely upon the skills of the Discussion Leader

- Disagreement - Can serve either to create hard feelings among members or lead to a resolution of conflict and hence to an innovative solution.
- Conflicting individual interests vs. mutual interests.
- More time may be needed to reach consensus.

- Who has the greatest influence and who willingly changes their opinions can reinforce the existing power structure and stifle future member input and cooperation?

Having understood the advantages and possible problems of the consensus approach, you are encouraged to use this method to make decisions whenever possible. An operational way of defining a consensus decision is where every member of the group can say, "Well, that may not be exactly how I would have done it, but I can live with it and support it."

GROUP CONSENSUS GUIDELINES:

Effectiveness in communication is of paramount importance in the consensus decision making process. You can enhance your group communication by paying attention to the following "DO's and DON'Ts."

DO:

- Listen, not only to the words but to the rationale being offered.
- Pursue your point and be persistent if you have good information.
- Manage your time effectively, relative to the number of decisions that are being made.
- Involve all team members to ensure use of their knowledge and experience.
- Strive for the best answer. Thinking in cause-and-effect terms avoids dealing only with symptoms.

DON'T:

- Argue for the sake of winning your point. You may learn something by remaining open-minded.
- Give up on your conclusion simply to avoid conflict. Let objective reasons or sound information prevail.
- Allow the group to get hung up on a specific item. Move on and comc back latcr.
- Compete by assuming that someone must win and someone must lose. Look for the best alternative.
- Resort to voting. This tends to split the group into winners and losers.

THE LEADER'S ROLE:

This approach to group decision making places the leader in a particular role in which he/she must cease to contribute, avoid evaluation and refrain from thinking about solutions or group products. Instead he/she must concentrate on the group process by assuming responsibility for accurate communication between members.

The ways decisions are made testify to the degree of effectiveness of a group. Here is a list of characteristics of effective and ineffective groups and members:

Effective Groups:

- Generate more ideas than individuals generate independently
- Have a high level of participation
- Develop a climate where members can be relaxed, open and direct
- Are task-oriented

Ineffective Groups:

- Pool ignorance and misinformation
- Eject non-conforming members
- Force members to comply or compromise
- Engage in "groupthink" (premature acceptance of an alternative to preserve good feelings within the group)
- Take action because they can't think of any reason not to

Effective Group Members:

- Defer to members who are certain have the facts
- Form loyalties to their own group
- Encourage and support other group members
- Mediate differences in the group

Ineffective Group Members:

- Give in on items they are sure of
- Oppose or block decisions without cause
- Dominate discussions

JUMP STARTING YOUR ORGANIZATION

Whether your organization began working together winter or fall term, the beginning of your second semester is a new start. Many successful organizations are characterized by the leadership and members learning from their past mistakes and their willingness to make a new start. A "jump start" retreat might be just what the organization doctor ordered for your group! Jumpstart retreats offer an opportunity for everyone to share activities over break and visit with one another before classes really begin.3

The meeting should be a cause for celebration and a time to evaluate and revise how your organization has been working. Retreats do not mean that you necessarily have to leave the campus. The location can be anywhere!

CELEBRATE

Celebrate your successes. You wouldn't have made it to this term if you weren't successful last term. Recognize the leadership and membership who assisted the organization. Recognize the barriers you had to overcome and the resources you utilized. Many Oregon students wish to only receive constructive criticism which they use as a means to learn. Although it is imperative to continue improving, you must celebrate what you have done well.

EVALUATE

Take the opportunity to evaluate how both you and the group are doing and what areas need improvement. This will also provide you with an ideal opportunity to garner group support for new projects or resolve sticky situations.

Many groups discuss the following at retreats:

- Goals—where are we? What needs to be revised? What has been accomplished?
- How do we work together?
- How do we resolve conflict?
- Recurring or current conflicts
- Organizational meetings
- Time frame and responsibilities for term
- Election/selection of officers

You Can Also

- Plan motivators or end of year celebration
- Orient new members to the group
- Continue training on any issues
- Start on transition notebooks (if you haven't yet, start by distributing an outline of what is needed and giving members 30 minutes or so to start writing down their thoughts)
- Continue team building

A Sample Retreat Design:

1. Revisit a teambuilding activity that the majority of group members enjoyed from last term.
2. Continue teambuilding—visit the Holden Leadership Center Resource Library for many teambuilding and trust-building activities.
3. Evaluate and determine what areas need to be discussed and revisited. A successful method to gather information is to form small groups. Ask each group to discuss the issue at hand (giving specific questions is helpful) and make recommendations for improvement. For example, if you wish to generally evaluate the organization, the questions each group would discuss might be: What have we done well so far? What can we improve on? What would you like for us to continue doing? What would you like for us to do differently? Be specific about your ideas!
4. Motivate! By now, most of your members have been involved in an activity and have had many of their questions answered by experience. This term, they will probably be motivated by an intrinsic need to succeed and improve on their responsibilities. However, it is your responsibility to motivate them to continue. Occasionally pass out candy at a meeting, give members an opportunity to stand up and

thank someone in the group, celebrate everyone's birthday in one evening.

5. Celebrate. A retreat is not meant to disparage the organization of certain members. It is meant to be an opportunity to identify and solve problems. Be sure to leave on a productive and positive note.

KEEPING MINUTES + RECORDS

Being a secretary for your organization is not a job to take lightly.

The following criteria are important when considering who will best fulfill this role:

- Is this person reliable? Does he/she keep appointments?
- Is this person well organized? Does he/she complete tasks in a timely manner?
- Is this person a good listener? Is he/she able to be objective, not to make his/her own interpretations, and hear both sides of an issue
- Is this person on top of what is going on? Is he/she able to appropriately weed out the trivial information and record the important facts for the record?

As you can see, the role of a secretary is more than "just taking minutes". The secretary is in effect, the historian. What he/she records will be referred to by current members as a reminder of finished and unfinished business, what needs follow-up and what actions were taken. It will also be kept for future members to read to gain an understanding of where the organization has been and why. Many organizations make it the secretary's responsibility to notify the membership about upcoming meetings-time, date, location-as well as any important items to be discussed.

The secretary should be present at all meetings. If he/she is unable to attend, a substitute person, preferably with the characteristics defined earlier, needs to be appointed. It is also helpful for the secretary to prepare him or herself before each meeting. A secretary should be sure to read the minutes of previous meetings, paying attention to style and format and review the agenda and any attached documents. If the organization has agreed upon a standard format for minutes, a standardized form can be used and fill in discussions, etc. as they occur.

If your organization has a structure that includes committees, be they ad hoc or standing, there always needs to be a secretary present to accurately record what transpired. It is not necessary to take down everything unless someone requests that their remarks be entered for the record. It is necessary, however, to take complete notes. Motions and resolutions do need to be taken verbatim and should be read back during the meeting to make sure they have been accurately recorded. There are several ways to take meeting minutes and each organization needs to choose the most appropriate method for them.

A practical option is to record a summary of debates, agreements and disagreements with a succinct explanation of the character of each. The second method is to take action minutes when decisions are reached and responsibilities are assigned.

In either of these cases make note of the following:

- The names of the people proposing any action or stating an option of a motion.
- Take down word-for-word any motions, resolutions, amendments, decisions or conclusions.
- Who seconded the motion?
- Whether or not a motion was withdrawn and what assignments were made and to whom.

It is often helpful for both minute taking and for those attending the meeting if the chair or the secretary summarizes decisions that are reached. The summarizer should be most careful in clarifying those points of greatest controversy. It is the secretary's responsibility to signal the president or chairperson and ask questions regarding the subject being discussed if unsure. A secretary should not wait until the meeting has been adjourned to get clarification; individuals can lose their perspective, issues can become less important and one's memory can alter what actually occurred.

Immediately after the meeting, the secretary must go over the notes while everything is still fresh, checking their notes for the following information:

- Type of meeting (executive, standing committee, etc.)
- Date, time and place
- List of attendees and those absent
- Time of call to order
- Approval and/or amendments to previous meeting minutes
- Record of reports from standing and special committees
- General matters
- Record of proposals, resolutions, motions, seconding, any final disposition and a summary of the discussion; also record of vote
- Time of adjournment
- Nomination of submission and transcriber's name

Once the minutes have been transcribed into draft form, they should be submitted to the chair for review and/or correction. Once they are returned, they need to be prepared in a formal form, preferably agreed upon beforehand, for final approval at the next meeting.

These minutes should be sent out to all members within 3 or 4 days of the meeting. This allows members time to read the minutes for accuracy before the next meeting and while the previous meeting is still fresh in their minds.

LEADERSHIP TRANSITION

Your year as an officer is coming to an end and new officers are being selected. How do you leave your position gracefully? How do you ensure that the new officers are ready to continue to provide your organization with strong leadership?

A thorough leadership transition plan has several benefits:

- Provides for transfer of significant organizational knowledge.
- Minimizes the confusion of leadership changeover.
- Gives outgoing leaders a sense of closure.
- Utilizes the valuable contributions of experienced leaders, usually the most neglected members in your group.
- Helps incoming leadership absorb the special expertise of the outgoing leadership.
- Increases the knowledge and confidence of the new leadership.
- Minimizes the loss of momentum and accomplishments for the group.

When Do You Start? Early!

- Begin early in the year to identify emerging leaders.
- Encourage these potential leaders through personal contact by helping others ddevelop new leadership skills, delegating responsibility to them and clarifying job responsibility.
- When new officers have been elected, orient them together as a group with all of the outgoing officers. This process provides the new leaders with an opportunity to understand each other's roles and to start building their leadership team.
- Be sure to transfer the knowledge and information necessary for them to function well. An organization history and flow-chart might be helpful. Take time to organize any files or notebooks so they may quickly access information.
- Have individual meeting with old and new officer position. Make sure they know what they're getting into.

What Do You Need To Transfer?

Think back to your first weeks. What could you have used to do your job better?

Some suggestions are:

- Effective leadership qualities and skills.
- Problems and helpful ideas, procedures and recommendations.
- Written reports:
  - Containing traditions, ideas or completed projects; continuing projects and concerns; or ideas never carried out.
  - Personal and organizational files.
  - Acquaintance with physical environment, supplies, equipment and any office procedures.

- Introduction to personnel (advisors, administrators, contacts, etc.).
- Share what you would have done differently. Or how you could improve upon the previous year. But remember, part of the learning for the new members is figuring it out on their own.

- A complete record of the organization's structure, goals and accomplishments (through complete and organized files):
  - Constitution and By-laws
  - Organizational goals and objectives for previous year(s)
  - Job descriptions/role clarification's
  - Status reports on ongoing projects
  - Evaluations of previous projects and programmes
  - Previous minutes and reports
  - Resources/contact lists with addresses and phone numbers
  - The Leadership Resource Office Handouts
  - Financial books and the ASUO Documents/Policies
  - Mailing lists

Be a good, conscientious leader by providing your successor with these things, but at the same time, encouraging them to grow as their own leader.

OFFICER RESPONSIBILITIES

While no handout, person or any other source of information can tell you exactly what the officers of your organizations should be doing, we can give you an idea of typical responsibilities for officers. Use these generalizations as guidelines and adapt them to fit your organization.

President:

- The person "in charge," responsible for supervising/overseeing the work of the other officers and ensuring that they function together as an effective team
- Provides the overall vision and sense of direction for the organization
- Spokesperson/representative/external liaison for the organization
- Schedules and runs officer and organization meetings
- Serves as a role model for other officers and members

Vice President:

- Specific roles and responsibilities for this position need to be clearly identified to ensure effectiveness
- Supervises/oversees chair people and the work of all committees
- Selects committee chairs
- Delegates appropriate responsibilities to committee chairs
- Actively keeps up-to-date on work of committees with committee chairs
- Chairs occasional special committees or projects
- "Assumes responsibility" during absence of president

Secretary:

- Records and distributes all pertinent information to members, including meeting minutes, upcoming events and opportunities
- Handles all organizational correspondence
- Keeps accurate membership lists with names, addresses and phone numbers (including summer addresses)
- Maintains thorough organizational files and records
- Keeps office organized and stocked with supplies.

Treasurer:

- Establishes annual budget for organization and ensures that it's followed
- Reports regularly to organization officers and members the group's financial status
- Manages day-to-day financial transactions
- Records and pays bills/reimbursements
- Deposits/withdraws funds
- Records accrued interest
- Works closely with Student Organization Accounts Service (SOAS)

Historian:

- Keeps account of organizational records and documents. (Charter, awards, newspaper clippings, etc.)
- Thoroughly documents all events through photographs, video or written descriptions.

Committee Chairs:

- Manage work of committees, with appropriate direction and delegation.
- Reports to vice president and reports at organization meetings.
- Each committee will have specific responsibilities and goals.

Examples:

- *Membership:* Recruit, select, orient new members.
- *Social/programming:* Organize events, including reserving rooms, renting buses, obtaining refreshments, arranging for entertainment.
- *Publicity:* Promote a positive image of the organization by creating and designing, producing and distributing all publicity materials.

Each officer is equally important to the smooth and effective functioning of an organization. Successful officers function as a team, helping each other and contributing to the overall accomplishments and climate of the organization. Don't forget the importance of each of the members, "A chain is only as strong as its weakest link."

PARLIAMENTARY PROCEDURES

Five Basic Principles of Parliamentary Procedure

1. Only one subject may claim the attention of the assembly at one time.

2. Each proposition presented for consideration is entitled to full and free debate.
3. Every member has rights equal to every other member.
4. The will of the majority must be carried out and the rights of the minority must be preserved.
5. The personality and desires of each member should be merged into the larger unit of the organization.

DEVELOPING AN AGENDA OR ORDER OF BUSINESS

It is customary for every group to adopt a standard order of business for meetings.

The following template may be used to create your agenda:

- Call to order
- Reading and approval of minutes
- Reports from officers and standing committees
- Reports from special committees
- Unfinished business
- New business
- Programme
- Adjournment

Motions

The proper way for an individual to propose that the group take a certain action is by "making a motion." The following is the process for handling a motion.

1. A member addresses the presiding officer for recognition.
2. The member is recognized.
3. The member proposes a motion.
4. Another member must second the motion.
5. The presiding officer states the motion to the assembly.
6. The assembly can now discuss or debate the motion. Only one person at a time may speak and must first be recognized by the presiding officer. The presiding officer should try to alternate between those favoring and those opposing the motion.

Preference should be given to:

1. The person who proposed the motion
2. A member who has not spoken yet to the motion
3. A member who seldom speaks to one who frequently addresses the assembly
4. Discussion must be confined to the question that is "before the house".

7. The presiding officer takes the vote on the motion. Voting can be done by voice, show of hands or balloting.

8. The presiding officer announces the result of the vote.
9. The floor is now open and another motion can be proposed.

Amending a Motion

The purpose of the "motion to amend" is to modify a motion that has already been presented in such a manner that it will be more satisfactory to the members.

1. *Methods of amending:* By addition or insertion—to add something to the motion which it did not contain.
2. By elimination or by striking out—to subtract or eliminate something from a motion that was originally part of it.
3. By substitution—this method is a combination of the first two methods, since in amending by substitution something is stricken and something is inserted in its place. The substitution portion may consist of a word, a phrase, a clause or an entirely new motion.

An important principle to understand in connection with any form of the motion to amend is that an amendment "MAY BE HOSTILE, BUT IT MUST BE GERMANE."

- Hostile is meant opposed to the spirit and aim of the motion to which it is applied.
- Germane is meant having direct bearing upon the subject of the motion, that is, relevant or relating to it.

An amendment may be opposed to the actual intent of the original motion and in fact, nullify it. But if it relates to the same subject matter, it is germane.

Types of Amendment

1. Amendment of the First Rank: an amendment to a motion.
2. Amendment of the Second Rank: an amendment to the amendment. (The amendment to the amendment must modify and relate directly to the amendment and NOT to the main motion, otherwise it is OUT OF ORDER).

NO AMENDMENT BEYOND THAT OF SECOND RANK IS POSSIBLE.

It is never in order to propose more than one amendment of each rank at one time. If one desires to amend two separate and unrelated parts of a motion, this must be done by two amendments of the first rank and one must be voted upon before the other is proposed. It is possible, however, to have a motion, one amendment to the motion (amendment of the first rank), and one amendment to the amendment (amendment of the second rank) before the assembly at once. Until the amendment of the second rank has been voted upon, no other amendment of the second rank is in order. Until the amendment of the first rank has been voted upon, no other amendment of the first rank can be proposed.

ORDER OF VOTING UPON AMENDMENTS

Amendments are voted upon in inverse order; that is, the one of second rank is disposed of first:

1. Discussion is held and the vote taken upon the amendment to the amendment (amendment of second rank).
2. Discussion is called for and the vote is taken upon the amendment to the motion (amendment of first rank).
3. When the vote on this has been taken, discussion upon the original or main motion as amended is opened and when completed a vote is taken upon it.

PREPARING A TRANSITION NOTEBOOK

Think back to your first few days on your new job working on your first project. You probably had many, many questions and no one or nothing to turn to. Take the responsibility now to make sure this does not happen to the person who takes your place next year. Prepare a transition notebook.

Evaluation

- Completed evaluation with detailed recommendations
- Two blank evaluations (one for each term which can be written during the term)

Progress Reports:

- Completed progress reports
- Blank progress reports (to be completed throughout the year) with guidelines. A progress report provides the "working draft" for most of the transition notebook. It should provide the member with a opportunity to write down what is new or different, what has been improved upon, what is in progress, accomplishments, etc.

Officer Positions:

- Demographics from current year (number of men/women, classifications, etc.)
- Letter from former to new coordinator or officer (should include advice, what was experienced, what was improved upon this year, things to know when getting started, prioritizing the tasks for the position and anything else not mentioned; usually written very informally
- Blank "Bright Ideas" sheet (to be used throughout the year; ideas that can help move the organization)
- Current goals
- Blank goals sheet
- Detailed timeline
- Any other information pertinent to position

Training Information:

- Agendas and handouts from past training retreats or meetings

- Information on the "how to's" of the organization (such as publicity, financial matters, etc.)

Organizational Information:

- Calendar of events
- Meeting agendas and minutes
- Resources, both electronic and hard copies
- Instructions on how to sign on to your organization's electronic mail message group or conference

A transition notebook can be shared during the meetings with your replacement. It should cover all aspects of your responsibilities and how those tasks fit into the organization's big picture. We recommend that your replacement file "historical" documents in the notebook such as meetings minutes when he/she has become comfortable with the information. This way, the notebook can be used as a working tool rather than something to be completed at the end of the year (usually during finals).

Each organization is different so feel free to add and delete topics. Your replacement will thank you throughout the year!

RECRUITING NEW MEMBERS

People join organizations for many reasons: they want to get involved, meet people, make new friends, explore interests, develop leadership skills and have fun. Groups need new members because they bring new ideas and talents, in addition to replacing old members. With the vast number of existing groups on campus, as well as new organizations, it is vital that an organization has a well conceived and executed recruitment and retention plan. This information is designed to assist you in the development of such a plan.

First, it is important that both the leadership and membership know and understand the organization. Have a meeting to review and discuss your organizational goals and objectives. Are they still accurate? Is it time to update them? Where would the group like to be in six months? A year? During this "organizational housekeeping" process, a certain theme or direction should become clear. What types of people do you need to help the group succeed? Who would complement your current membership? Try to develop a member profile.

Now that you know the types of people you are interested in, your next step is to set some recruitment goals. How many new members can your organization reasonably assimilate into the group? Will you allow people to join at any time or only during a designated recruitment period? Will you hold a mass meeting or is membership by invitation only? When designing your recruitment strategy, keep in mind your member profile. What places do these prospective members most likely frequent? Do they have special interests? What kind of publicity would attract their attention? But most of all, try to think back to when you first became involved. What attracted you? How were you recruited? If you weren't, how did you hear about the group? Why have you stayed involved?

Get everyone involved. Be Honest! Have your current members identify people they know who may want to get involved and personally invite them to attend a meeting. Word-of-mouth is the best and least expensive type of publicity that you can use. Talk about your group. Tell people what you have to offer them. Ask them about themselves and really listen. Tell them how the organization can benefit from someone like them. Let them know how their talents, skills and interests would help the organization. Sending special invitations is another nice, but more expensive way to invite new members.

Recruitment campaigns need to have a visual element as well. Have those members with "artistic talents" work on your posters, flyers, banners, etc. Be creative. Your publicity can be effective only if it's noticed. Many groups find it beneficial to have a special welcoming meeting or ceremony for their new members. Group participation, in some form of official initiation process is one way to make your members feel wanted, needed and appreciated. It helps to form a unique and memorable bond between old and new members and will help increase your retention rate. However you choose to welcome your new members, it is important to include some form of group orientation programme. Many groups skip this and begin by getting new members immediately involved in group projects. Although new member involvement is essential, it is equally important to orient them to your group's goals and objectives, organizational structure, rules and norms. This demystifies the group and helps the members feel more comfortable with the group and understand its processes. Proper orientation leads to better understanding, more commitment and less frustration.

After you've successfully completed your recruitment and orientation, spend time getting to know your membership and let them get to know you too. Don't forget your old members since, without them, you wouldn't have had a group for your new members to join. Talk to all new members about their skills, interests and previous experiences. Once you have this information, it will be easy to get them involved in your group's projects. To be sure that their first organizational experience is a positive one, assign new members tasks that are well within their skill level and that they can successfully accomplish.

Finally, allow your new members time to get involved and feel comfortable with the group. After a semester, have them participate in a group evaluation process. Go over your organizational goals and objectives and look at your plans for the future. Ask for their feedback and input. It is a known fact that people are more committed and motivated if they feel that they have a stake in what's going on. Have them help to shape the organization's future. Above all, have fun together. Make time to socialize and celebrate your achievements. If all you do as a group is work, it will become a burden to participate and your members will quickly lose interest. After all, what is an organization without members? What good is a recruitment campaign if no one stays?

SETTING GOALS

Goals help define your organization, give direction and avoid chaos. Goals can help motivate members by communicating what the organization is striving for as well as providing a basis of recognizing accomplishments and successes. Organizations that set goals are more effective in recruiting members.

There are three levels of defining your organization's priorities:

1. Purpose or Mission is a broad, general statement that tells why your organization exists: usually doesn't change from year to year and is often the first statement in your constitution.
2. Goals are statements describing what your organization wishes to accomplish, stemming from your purpose or mission. Goals are the ends towards which your efforts will be directed and often change from term to term or year to year, depending on the nature of the group.
3. Objectives are descriptions of exactly what is to be done, derived from the goals; clear specific statements of measurable tasks that will be accomplished as steps towards reaching your goals. They are short term and have deadlines. Be realistic! Shoot high, but realize the implications.

SETTING GOALS TOGETHER

Set your goals as a group. Make sure you set aside enough time. Make sure everyone's ideas are represented. This creates many positive results because people will support and be responsible for what they help create. *You can expect:*

1. Greater commitment and motivation among officers and members to help achieve goals.
2. Clearer understanding of the goals and the rationale for selecting them.
3. With everyone's ideas and opinions considered, your goals will represent a group consensus rather than one person's opinion.

Steps for Setting Goals and Objectives:

1. Brainstorm a list of potential goals as a group.
2. Choose from the brainstorm list those you want to work on.
3. Prioritize.
4. Determine objectives for each goal and plans of action for each objective. (Remember there can be several objectives for each goal).

5. Move into action, follow through. (Many groups fail to evaluate and revise; thus their goals are never achieved).
6. Include a closing statement.

Developing an Action Plan:

- What is to be done?
- How will it be accomplished?
- What are your resources in terms of people, money and materials?
- Who is responsible for completing each task?
- What is the deadline?
- How will you know when it is accomplished? How will you measure the results?

STARTING A NEW ORGANIZATION

The Associated Students of the University of Oregon provide space and facilitation for student involvement. The atmosphere is one that encourages the expansion of student life on cultural, social and academic levels. As a student leader, one may need assistance in discovering and utilizing the resources available on both the individual and group levels. Both the Holden Leadership Center and the ASUO offer readily available tools for the development of essential leadership skills. While these tools are available to all students, some forms of involvement require additional administrative procedures. The following information has been made available by the ASUO in the group registration packet, available in the ASUO Executive Office.

RECOGNITION OF STUDENT ORGANIZATIONS

In order to achieve valid student group affiliation at the University of Oregon, all student organizations are required to register with the ASUO. Groups are classified as either non-fee funded, or fee-funded.

The following benefits of registration are available to all ASUO-affiliated student organizations:

- Listed in UO Telephone Directory with other ASUO groups
- Included in annual ASUO Programme Guide publication
- Included in ASUO Web site linked to UO Home Page
- Eligibility to schedule meeting rooms in the EMU for free and larger EMU event spaces at a discounted rate
- Visibility through ASUO letterhead
- Ability to advertise as an ASUO group
- Ability to establish web site, e-mail, mailbox

Groups receiving funding from the ASUO are eligible for the following additional benefits:

- Training through monthly ASUO Programmes Council Meetings
- Eligibility to check out motor vehicles from State Motor Pool

- Potential office space within the EMU
- Grant Funding assistance from the EMU grant writer
- Assistance with the management of funds

Groups that do not receive funds from the ASUO are eligible to open trust fund accounts to facilitate payment processes.

Steps to Creating an ASUO programme:

1. Fill out an ASUO Student Organization Recognition Application
2. Complete Bylaws (template provided in application packet)
3. Hold three meetings and take detailed minutes

Important information requested in the application:

- "Statement of Purpose" emphasizing how the group will promote the cultural and/or physical development of the student body
- Attached copies of the constitution or bylaws
- Explanation of group plan to provide services differing from those already provided by other university and/or ASUO programmes
- Indication of group financial sources
- Information regarding additional group affiliation (UO department, local, national, international, non-profit, etc.)
- Explanation of group project/service history; example of previous group project (details, organizational procedure, evaluation, etc.)
- References (excludes family members and students affiliated with the group)

THE REGISTRATION APPLICATION

Once the initial three steps of the application process are completed, the application will be processed as follows: Application review by the ASUO Recognition Review Committee (RRC) concerning completeness and accuracy

1. Recommendation from University President or designee regarding:
   - Relevance and compatibility of group mission statement and goals with the broader educational mission of the University
   - Compatibility with non-ASUO University programmes and services
2. Approval by ASUO Executive President
3. Introduction of group's mission and goals to ASUO Senate
4. For groups seeking funding, annual review by ASUO Programmes Finance Committee of group's mission statement and bylaws
5. For groups not seeking funding, the Programmes and Finance Committee will conduct reviews every three years during budget season

EFFECTS OF CHANGE ON ORGANIZATIONS

To effectively adapt to change, most established organizations have a daunting task ahead of them in a variety of operational and procedural areas.

Business processes must be redefined and redesigned and adapted to specific geographical and cultural settings. The workforce needs to be retrained to be ready for changes in how work is done, what skills and knowledge is needed, and how to relate to global collaborators and customers. The very culture of an organization needs to be reshaped to properly support the new processes introduced. Structures, reward systems, appraisal measurements and roles need redefinition. Leadership styles and management procedures must shift and adapt, and ways of relating with customers, suppliers, and other stakeholders need refining. Technological advances and capabilities must be introduced, and preparation of the workforce to work with the new IT structures is needed. Successful adaptation to change necessitates "an understanding about how to convert and rebuild from the complexities and legacies of the old, as well as generate designs about the new". Change necessitates that organizations realistically move beyond antiquated processes, empower and retrain employees, and incorporate advances in IT into the everyday work setting. No longer are organizations reacting to sequential or occasional change. New changes now occur as organizations are in the throes of initiating the change process. Change has become perpetual. In order to cope, organizations need a design process with strategies and guidelines for thriving amongst a multitude of changes. "Real change is an integrated process that unfolds over time and touches every aspect of an organization,".

THE ROLE AND ISSUES OF LEADERS IN GUIDING CHANGE

The creation and design of change processes within an organization is most often a role of the leaders within it. Change processes which encompass human resources, IT adoption and upgrades, tools and techniques, as well as the basic rules and controls within the organization are the mandate of leaders engaged in the management of change. It is up to the leaders to make these change initiatives tangible rather than abstract and to awaken enthusiasm and ownership of the proposed changes within the corporate milieu. Leaders are responsible for bridging the gap between strategy decisions and the reality of implementing the changes within the structure and workforce of the organization. A myriad of details and effects must be acknowledged and addressed for successful adaptation to change in all sectors of a firm. "Underlying this principle is the fact that almost everything in an organization's infrastructure has an influence on some other part of it. Management style affects culture, technology affects the way staff interact with customers, internal communication methods affect how people work together,".

A holistic approach to change management encourages the redesign and adaptation to change at all organizational levels. In essence, process itself can become the platform for change to occur, as well as the protector of the existent daily operations. A clear picture of how the business operates currently is afforded, as well as a picture of how the business must plan, schedule, and undergo the change process. Nadler and Nadler emphasized the importance of leaders in organizing and maintaining a climate for change within organizations. Although participation of all players is necessary, the role of the leader in the change process is crucial. Dubbed the "champions of change" it is the leaders, - the top management players who keep the change process moving while maintaining the operational integrity of the organization. Adaptive leaders provide direction, protection, orientation, conflict control, and the shaping of norms while overseeing the change process within the corporate structure. Priorities need to be set which encourage disciplined attention, while keeping a keen eye focused for signs of distress within the company members. Steps to transform an organization were identified by Conger et al.

The steps included:

- Establishing a sense of urgency;
- Forming a powerful guiding coalition;
- Creating a vision;
- Communicating the vision;
- Empowering others to act on the vision;
- Planning for and creating short-term wins;
- Consolidating improvements and producing still more change and
- Institutionalizing new approaches.

A new model of organizational learning is important for survival and adaptation in the new century. Learning is a key requirement for both leaders and followers for any effective and lasting change to occur. "Without learning, the attitudes, skills and behaviours needed to formulate and implement a new strategic task will not develop, nor will a new frame by which selection and promotion decisions are made". The authors proposed an action learning process, called Organizational Fitness Profiling to help leaders to learn how to skillfully transform the particular business they are managing. Scheduled dialogues with followers provide information on how leadership style and behaviours impact on values, organizational design, strategies, and follower perceptions. Organizational success is a process of mutual adaptation between leader values and behaviours, existing people, culture, and organizational design amidst an environment of continual and prolific change. This profiling process requires that leaders are courageous enough to learn about their own assumptions and values about change, leadership and management roles and tasks. In essence, "...a paradigm shift in management thinking about leadership and organization development is needed".

TYPES AND COMPLEXITIES OF CHANGE

According to Wilson technology has become the engine of change for many organizations. Nadler and Nadler credited increased competition and globalization as the most sweeping factors in the new global change environment. Eccles outlined six contexts of change common to the corporate world. Takeover change, injection change, succession change, renovation change, partnership change, and catalytic change were all identified as inherent and challenging for most modern organizations. Takeover change primarily entails a change in management players. Injection change purports a change in CEO or the top senior manager. Succession change is felt when the top management layer is succeeded by current members who move up the ladder as the existent management retires or moves on. Renovation change entails the planned change process set by management, while partnership change occurs when the decisions for change is shared across the spectrum of organizational players. "Finally, and in a different style to the other five contexts, there is catalytic change in which an agency, typically a set of consultants or advisors, intervenes on behalf of one or more stakeholders, usually the management,". Lasting change must occur on many levels within an organization. The people, the work, and the formal as well as the informal organization are all key factions to be considered and worked on. Nadler and Nadler identified four different types of organizational change. Incremental or continuous change is the orderly sequence of change that is expected as time and growth progress. Step by step continuous improvement is the most logical reaction to incremental change. Discontinuous or radical change is another matter. "Complex, wide-ranging changes brought on by fundamental shifts in the external environment are radical, or discontinuous, changes". Discontinuous change requires radical departures in approach and strategy, often leading to a complete overhaul of the organization. Anticipatory change is done in the absence of threat, and in preparation for anticipated environmental changes. Reactive changes represent the opposite of anticipatory change, and are responses to threats and competition in the environment. Nadler, Shaw and Walton warned that the present era is swiftly becoming one of discontinuous change.

"The core competency for business leaders in the twenty-first century will be change management". Leaders will need both skill and the motivation to become constant visionary change agents. Discontinuous change profoundly affects three key areas of any organization: leadership capability, organizational architecture, and corporate identity. Improvisation, innovation and visionary awareness will be the name of the game for successful firms. Planned spontaneity and deliberate opportunism will be the key to survival in a turbulent global environment. Changes may occur in several different sectors of an organization simultaneously. Strategic, structural, cultural, technological, merger and acquisition, breakup and spin-off, downsizing, and expansive changes are all common, complex, and challenging to incorporate into the organizational milieu.

LEADERSHIP CHANGE TOOLS AND STRATEGIES

Bainbridge outlined a five step process of redesign for organizations undergoing planned change.

The five steps included:

- The design stage to determine overall requirements;
- The definition stage where the design is specified and documentation of the design stage requirements occurs;
- The development stage, where new capabilities are cultivated through training, education and restructuring;
- The dismantling stage, where redundant parts of the organization are removed or converted into new capabilities; and
- The deployment stage, where new capabilities are introduced into the new organizational environment, both internally and externally.

This design process is accomplished within a carefully arranged change process architecture. "This includes the link to strategic objectives, the definition of measures and the production of the high-level design itself". The vision of change must be expressed as clearly as possible and used consistently to spearhead every step of the change design process, including the specification of design principles. Design principles reflect the context and also the content of both internal and external desired change outcomes. Specification and communication of these principles by leaders are necessary to facilitate adoption and adaptation within the organizational culture. Pettigrew pointed out the wisdom of considering the content, the context (inner and outer) and the process of change within organizations.

There is a need to "explore content, context and process linkages through time". Strategies of organizational change have become a viable vehicle for business success and the creation of competitive performance. The ability to handle strategic change is now a defining characteristic of successful post-industrial organizations. "The leitmotiv of modern management theory is that of understanding, creating and coping with change. The essence of the managerial task thus becomes one of establishing some rationality, or some predictability, out of the seeming chaos that characterizes change processes". An open systems approach can facilitate emergent change processes within an organization. The linkages and interdependencies between the organization and the external environment can be used to create a pattern for emergent change adaptation. Galpin described a process for implementing planned change at a grassroots level, using the strengths and capabilities of the human resources within an organization as the central hub for change.

This process included stages of:

- Setting goals;
- Measuring performance;
- Providing feedback and coaching and

- Instigating generous rewards and recognition.

Galpin also outlined the strategic steps leaders needed to employ in order to initiate the change process.

These steps were:

- Defining the need to change;
- Developing a vision of the result of change;
- Leveraging teams to design, test, and implement changes;
- Addressing the cultural aspects of the organization that will help and sustain change; and
- Developing the essential attributes and skills needed to lead the change effort."

Cognitive mapping and computer assistance for group decision support are alternative change strategies that can help to cultivate group support for the planned initiatives. The cognitive maps or strategic belief systems of managers and employees can have a profound effect on how change is planned and implemented. Cognitive maps become a practical tool "by acting as a device for representing that part of a person's construct system they are able and willing to make explicit,". However, the cognitive map is "significantly biased by the necessary social interaction, or social gaze, that is the basis of elicitation through interview". Still, cognitive maps can be a strategic tool for negotiation and decision making in the change planning and implementation process.

Flamholtz and Randle identified strategic transformational planning as a key tool for change in an organization. This process describes the planning necessary to transform an organization into what it needs to become to maximize the fit and reduce the gaps between corporate size, environment, business concept and organizational design. Flamholtz and Randle labeled these transformations as First, Second, and Third kinds. A First kind transformation related to professional management transformation. Planning revitalization or second kind transformation related to all layers of the corporate pyramid, while business vision transformations focused on changes needed to address new markets and the firm's role in the existing markets. *All three of these transformations were addressed by using the transformational planning process:*

- Assessing the environment;
- Reviewing the existing business;
- Resolving core transformational issues and
- Developing the written strategic transformational plan.

Organizational managers at the top must exhibit leadership, commitment, and conviction to the change and transformation process. Incremental change, often the result of a carefully thought out analysis and planning process, has been the most common form of planned change within organizations. A feeling of control is afforded, enough time and commitment are present, and each step of the process can be trialed and adapted to. However, with the advent of technology and globalization, a deep change is necessary. "Deep change differs from incremental change in that it requires new ways of thinking and behaving. It is change that is major in scope, discontinuous with the past and generally irreversible. Deep change means surrendering control". Deep change on any level entails inherent risk. To adapt to the profound changes of our times, leaders must be willing to go out on a limb, to take some big risks by stepping outside of well-established boundaries.

8

Theory of Organizational Processes in Leadership Development

Leadership development underpins all of our work. We believe that most organisational processes - change, talent, teams, engagement, innovation, collaboration – stand or fall on the quality of leadership. Leadership proves, over and over again, to be the critical enabling factor. We aim all of our energy and resources at that point of maximum leverage, helping our clients develop their leadership capacity and leadership capital, helping people define themselves as leaders and supplying the practical skills and knowledge that supports them in their journey to leadership.

We understand that there is a limit to what we can do to re-engineer personality. We reject the idea that there is an ideal character for leadership. We work instead from the principle that just about any configuration of human traits and capabilities can be deployed as leadership when a person learns to monitor, manage and master the processes of awareness, decision-making and action.

We develop leadership capacity at entry level, building self-awareness, confidence and initiative; we work with the talent that is an organisation's future leadership and we support the development of a leadership culture. We enable established role-holders and managers to find their natural authority, broaden horizons and develop skills for collaboration, dialogue and innovation. For the most senior managers, we support the development of political awareness, increase skills for scanning and critical thinking and deepen understanding of governance and of the widest social, environmental and economic context of leadership.

The best future leaders are probably already in your organisation. There is no better way to make sure your organisation stays competitive and effective than by challenging, nurturing and enabling your most talented people – and earning the loyalty that is the reward for considered, extended and judicious investment.

HOW COMPANIES DEVELOP GREAT LEADERS

At first glance, Zappos.com, the online retailer, appears to have little in common with General Electric (GE), the multinational conglomerate. Hit hard by the recession, GE is in the throes of scaling down its financial services subsidiary, GE Capital, by an estimated 40 per cent. Zappos, on the other hand, is tapping into changing consumer habits and ramping up for 30 per cent growth over the next 12 months.

Yet surprisingly, these two organizations with their rapidly shifting environments face similar challenges in motivating and engaging their employees. For Zappos, it's about creating and maintaining passion in a call-center culture. For GE, it's about keeping people engaged in a changing climate. Named among the 20 Best Companies for Leadership in a recent BusinessWeek.com/Hay Group survey, both GE and Zappos put a premium on selecting, developing, and retaining strong leaders at every level. What sets them and the other companies on the list apart, however, is not just their emphasis on good leadership, but also how they approach it. They carefully tailor their developing leaders to fit their unique business strategies and organizational cultures.

IN BAD TIMES AS WELL AS GOOD

While the data suggest there is no one best way to grow leaders, the companies that do it best share certain key characteristics. The top 20 companies address leadership development on multiple fronts, from articulating how leadership behaviour needs to change to meet the challenges of the future to managing their pools of successors for mission-critical roles. And, despite the chaotic, crisis-strewn atmosphere of the past year, they've continued to make leadership a top priority.

"The best companies for developing leaders recognize the value of strong leadership in both the good times and the bad," says John Larrere, who heads Hay Group's leadership and talent practice in the U.S. "Culturally they just cannot do away with leadership development, even in a recession. They don't see it as a perk but as a necessity." People at the Best Companies for Leadership sense the urgency to develop leaders more than their industry peers. In fact, while 94 per cent of respondents among the Best Companies for Leaders say their organization actively manages a pool of successors for mission-critical roles, only 68.6 per cent of the other organizations surveyed report the same.

"POSITIONING FOR THE FUTURE"

Indeed, leadership feels different at the Best Companies. In the survey, more than 64 per cent of respondents from the top 20 say people in their companies are expected to lead even when they are not in a formal position of authority. At other companies, that figure hovers around 35 per cent. And respondents from the Best Companies for Leadership are significantly more likely than those from other companies to believe they will emerge stronger from tough times. They say their leaders are more likely to be involved in leadership development. And they are twice as likely to say that everyone at every level of their organization has the opportunity to develop and practice capabilities needed to lead others.

In the survey, respondents were asked about their companies' current focus. Among all the respondents, 65.1 per cent said, "positioning for the future." Among the Best Companies for Leadership, the figure was 81.9 per cent. Executives at the Best Companies for Leadership confirmed this in follow-up interviews. "Our culture is committed to leadership development," says Jayne Johnson, GE's director of leadership education. "Crotonville [the site of GE's corporate university] opened in 1956. Today more than ever, we need our leaders going to Crotonville. It's these very leaders who will make us successful today and in the future."

According to PandG's (PG) Chief Human Resources Officer Moheet Nagrath, the primary way of developing future leaders it to offer "Accelerator Experiences," a programme that provides developing leaders the experience of running a small business with huge strategic potential. "We continually move people across regions and countries," says Nagrath. "The more discontinuous the experience, the more you accelerate growth. We have to move people around businesses for them to become well-groomed." One benefit of this experience, he says, is that it helps people manage in the organization's matrixed environment.

MAPPING BACKWARDS

Nagrath notes that at P&G, "We start with the destination role and then help future leaders acquire a deep understanding of the role. It's about understanding the individual from a deep perspective. We look at the timing for when a leader should go into the destination role, and we map backwards from the destination role to where they are currently." GE takes a different approach, identifying talented leaders early on, and placing them in stretch assignments, often before they think they're ready, according to Johnson. "And we support them, with over $1 billion a year in structured training. But today, change is such a continual force that even we at GE are taking a fresh look at how to develop talent."

At Zappos, a challenge is developing leaders at a pace that will accommodate the company's growth. "We are projecting 30 per cent growth in 2010," says Rebecca Ratner, the online retailer's director of human resources. "We will need more supervisors. How can we best integrate them into the company in terms of how they treat employees?" Noting that Zappos managers spend "10 per cent to 20 per cent of their time doing team building outside the office, our challenge is figuring out how to assimilate people into what we do."

EVENTS OUTSIDE THE OFFICE

For anyone coming in from the outside, she says, it's not a typical recruitment process, where they meet with three or four people before either being hired or rejected. "What we do instead is spend seven to 10 hours over four occasions at happy hours, team building events, or other things outside the office. We can see them and they can see us." The process seems to be good for retention. "In 2009, we will have a 20 per cent turnover rate," says Ratner. That's impressive for call-center employees. What keeps people at Zappos? "We pay 100 per cent of employee benefits," says Ratner. But there's something more, something Zappos calls its "wow factor."

Says Ratner: "We can't ask someone to wow a customer if they haven't been wowed by us." In fact, Zappos is so eager to wow employees and make sure who they hire is really committed that the company offers people $3,000 after they've been trained to walk away if they feel they and Zappos aren't a good fit. Ratner is quick to point out that almost no one takes the $3,000 walk-away money. But many trainees return for more Zappos training to become managers and supervisors. Ratner admits that one of her big concerns is how to keep the wow factor alive as the company adds more people and ramps up its leadership development.

ABB, a leading provider of power and automation technologies, is also facing challenges posed by a double-digit growth trajectory, according to Julia Blake, vice-president for human resources at the company's Power Products Division in North America. "We were growing our business and rapidly filling positions. Our challenge now is the rapid development of the organization's bench strength," says Blake. "We recognize that we need to accelerate development to get people ready to fill key positions. We want to get back into a growth surge and use development as a tool to retain talent as the business picks up." Survey respondents from the Best Companies for Leadership are 20 per cent more likely than respondents from other organizations to say that people stay at their companies primarily for growth opportunities.

THREE TYPES OF CORPORATE CULTURE

Not only are the best-in-breed companies more urgent about leadership development; they also spend more time on it—and more money, too. In the survey, respondents from the Best Companies for Leadership were more likely to say that they invest in the development of even their mid- and low-performing employees. And when asked about time spent developing leaders, once again, the Best Companies for Leadership report investing more time than peer organizations in developing future leaders. While 16.4 per cent of all respondents report spending 25 or more days per year developing senior leaders, 22 per cent of the Best Companies for Leadership spend 25-plus days developing their top talent.

In an analysis of how survey respondents described their companies' cultures, three categories of organizations emerged. Some, such as Zappos.com and Southwest Airlines, are modern, learning-oriented, fun workplaces. Other large, global giants, such as P&G and GE, are complex companies with cultures that are more traditional. And some, including ABB, are known as "collaboration for innovation" companies that accomplish work though self-organizing project teams and encourage employees to seek new approaches to solving problems. According to Elizabeth Bryant, senior director of talent management at Southwest Airlines, the leadership-development process reflects the company culture. "It goes beyond formal training and is part of everyday life at Southwest, where employees at every level are exposed to leaders so they get to see how the leaders think," she says. "Even informal mentoring and exposure to company executives helps to broaden people's perspectives and stimulate their passion about the job."

A HUNGER TO LEARN

According to Jeff Lamb, Southwest's chief people officer, the culture in which Southwest's employees work every day is no different from the culture in which the airline develops its future leaders. "This kind of thing happens organically. There's no course on how to get so engaged that you volunteer to come in on a weekend." Lamb insists that what makes the airline a great place for leaders is the same thing that makes it a great place for employees: "the freedom to be yourself ... a lack of pretense; the hunger to learn." He says it's not about any kind of programme or leadership training, or how well the company develops talent, but in "allowing people to enjoy their work."

Concludes Hay Group's Mary Fontaine: "The real thing leaders do is create environments that drive performance. Leaders engage and enable people. It's that simple, but it requires a shift of focus from solely outcomes, production numbers, and revenues to motivating people so they're passionate about helping the company achieve its goals." Another key aspect of leadership, she says, is removing the obstacles that hinder them. She likes to quote a senior client at IBM, who says, "My job is to take the rocks out of the campers' knapsacks so that they can run faster and further."

METHODOLOGY

To conduct the 2009 Best Companies for Leadership study, Hay Group and Bloomberg BusinessWeek.com invited organizations from around the globe to participate. The survey was open to all employees of any organization and asked respondents to rate the leadership-development practices at their own organization. Separately, respondents were asked to nominate three organizations, regardless of size and industry, that thcy believed are the best at developing leadership at all levels.

A total of 1,869 individuals from 1,109 organizations completed the survey. Only responses on behalf of a parent organization were considered in the ranking process, resulting in a total of 740 organizations considered in the final ranking. In the case of multiple respondents on behalf of a parent organization, responses from those self-identified as "leaders" were combined, and responses from those self-identified as "employees" were combined, to allow comparative perspectives on the same organizations. For an organization's final score, we calculated an average of the two group scores. Respondents that completed the survey were from 98 countries, with 45 per cent from North America, 27 per cent from Europe/Middle East, 16 per cent from Asia, 6 per cent from South America, 3 per cent from the Pacific, and 2 per cent from Africa.

ABOUT HAY GROUP

Hay Group is a global strategic-consulting firm that works with leaders in the private, public, and not-for-profit sectors to transform strategy into reality. With 85 offices in 47 countries, we work with more than 7,000 clients across the world.

BEST-PRACTICE LEADERSHIP

Virtually every corporate and academic leadership development programme is founded on the same model—we can call it the formulaic model. It tries to collect all the various approaches to leadership, shaves off the weird outliers, and packages the rest into a formula. To those of us who toil in the field of leadership development, the model works like this: We convene top performers, pick their brains for their best techniques and practices, and codify those techniques into a leadership competency formula. We then use 360-degree surveys to assess other managers' grasp of the competencies. We bake the formula into our performance appraisals and use it to mark the rungs on our succession-planning ladders. It gets coded into our talent management software and provides the building blocks of our online learning content and the titles of our corporate university handouts.

The notion behind all this is simple: The right way to lead is out there. A best-practice model exists. Once we discover it and turn it into a formula, development is just a matter of bringing you in line with that formula. But could it be otherwise? Should leadership development instead be tailored to individuals? The answer is yes, as long as two things are true—if leadership is not generic, meaning that there's no best practice, even for the majority; and if it's feasible to build a system that delivers appropriately different training content to different types of leaders. Perhaps the first of these concepts, that leadership might be idiosyncratic, seems obvious to you. You may have been assessed as a leader, found to have certain strengths, and been encouraged to run with them. Or it may be that you have seen enough successful leaders to know that they are not all from the same mold. If you haven't realized this, meet Ralph Gonzalez.

A few years ago, while conducting a study of top-performing managers for the electronics retailer Best Buy, I interviewed Ralph. He was a star, having transformed one of Best Buy's lowest-performing stores into a repeat award winner. On virtually every metric, from revenues to profitability to employee engagement, he had taken his team from the bottom 10 per cent to the leading 10 per cent. What had he done, I asked, to effect such dramatic change? Ralph said that he had played on his likeness to the young Fidel Castro. He had called his store "La Revolución," posted a "Declaración de Revolución" in the break room, and made supervisors wear army fatigues. As I was scribbling all this down, he told me about the whistle.

Because his team was at the bottom of every district performance table, he wanted to give people a way to celebrate the fact that good behaviours were actually happening in the store, and to make them aware that they were happening all the time. So he issued a whistle to all employees and told them to blow it whenever they saw someone do something good. It didn't matter if the person they observed was their superior or worked in another department; if they saw anyone go above and beyond, they were to blow the whistle.

"Didn't it make the store incredibly loud?" I asked.

"Sure," he replied, with a wide Castro grin. "But it energized the place. It energized me. Heck, it even energized the customers. They loved it."

SCALE CONCEPTS, NOT TECHNIQUES

Clearly, Ralph Gonzalez is one of a kind. Not everyone leads like him, or could. However, the typical leadership development paradigm would not make that assumption. It would try to incorporate Ralph's standout behaviour into a competency model and spread it throughout the leadership ranks. Sure enough, the whistle technique started down that path. Having been shared at a number of company gatherings, Ralph's story began to take on a life of its own. All of a sudden it was cropping up in districts and regions around the country. "Whistles for everyone!" There was talk of a whistle hierarchy: green whistles for store managers, white ones for supervisors, regular silver ones for frontline blue-shirts. There was talk of checklists: the 12 conditions when whistles may be blown, and the 20 conditions when they must never be.

What had begun as a vibrant expression of a particular leader's personality was fast mutating into a standard operating procedure. Fortunately, some wise Best Buy executives, realizing that the technique was almost entirely dependent on the presence of Ralph himself, killed the mutation before it could spread. If this application of the formulaic model felt misguided to the executives, think about how it would have felt to Ralph's peers and Best Buy's aspiring leaders. Many of us go through the motions of creating a formulaic model, but on some level we know the model is askew. It might work in the theoretical world of leadership formulae, but in the real world it's very rare to discover an excellent technique that can be effectively transferred to all leaders.

The problem has to do with authenticity. A technique that's perfectly natural when used by one leader may look forced, fake, and foolish when used by another. Richard Branson standing on the steps of a Virgin America jet brandishing a champagne bottle and surrounded by a coterie of comely flight attendants makes a bold, dashing image. Warren Buffett striking the same pose on one of his NetJets would not. The story of Ralph's whistle reveals a fundamental organizational reality: Leadership excellence doesn't scale easily. Leadership conceptsare scalable, because a concept is easily transferable from person to person. In Ralph's case, the concept is that the best leaders capture moments of excellence and reflect them back to the team. You can teach this concept to anyone who wants to grow as a leader, and she will benefit—just as you can usefully teach all aspiring leaders the concept that employee engagement drives customer loyalty, or the concept that your existing customers are your best prospects.

But in the hands of an individual leader, a concept turns into a practice, a sequence of behaviours, a set of techniques. There is a person involved, someone actually applying the concept—in other words, a Ralph. And a technique that works for Ralph won't work for people who lead differently from him. Again, by "won't work" I mean "won't look authentic." The borrowed technique will appear stilted and uncomfortable; the person trying to adopt it will find that his movements are disjointed and his instincts are off—he's a Franken-leader. If you're a leader, authenticity is your most precious commodity, and you'll lose it if you attempt techniques that don't fit your strengths.

No one wants to follow a Franken-leader. He's slow, he's dangerous, and—worst of all—he's not predictable. Predictability is a characteristic of people who operate according to their own internal compass; even when they venture into new territory, what they do is somehow consistent with what they have done. You know where they stand, and you know where you stand with them. A leader trying on behaviours that don't align with his compass displays no such consistency. One borrowed technique-of-the-day clashes with the next.

Nothing scares an employee more than a leader who lurches unpredictably from one technique to the next, sending unclear, inconsistent signals. We know this from research on groups of many kinds; we also know that the inverse is true. In 2002, when Jim Harter and colleagues at Gallup published a meta-analysis of employee engagement studies—covering the experiences of 310,000 employees on 10,885 teams, it was the largest such analysis to date—they found that the second most powerful driver of both engagement and turnover was an employee's answer to the question "Do I know what is expected of me?" If you're a leader, authenticity is your most precious commodity, and you'll lose it if you attempt techniques that don't fit your strengths. This doesn't mean you can't learn from other leaders. It simply means you'll learn best from leaders whose strengths match yours.

THE ALGORITHM OF YOU

This brings us to the second question I raised earlier, when I suggested that leadership development should be personalized if two conditions could be met. The first condition involved whether leadership is truly idiosyncratic; I hope I've reassured you that it is. What about the second condition: Is it feasible for an enterprise training many leaders to accommodate all the variations in style?

Over the past couple of years, many organizations have begun doing just that. The effort at Hilton Worldwide's focused-service brands—Hampton, Homewood Suites, Hilton Garden Inn, and Home2 Suites—is a good example. Like many top leaders, Phil Cordell, the head of these brands, had noted the inconvenient truth that his best leaders didn't all resemble one another. However, he and his leadership team also saw that their population contained several birds of a feather—leaders with similar styles, who might profitably learn from the same kind of training and from one another's practices. In partnership with my company, Phil's team used a five-step process to capitalize on that realization. The sequence, detailed below, will be helpful to any organization interested in creating an algorithmic model of leadership development.

Choose an Algorithmic Assessment.

Netflix has its movie quiz; the New York Timeshas its recommendation engine. Before implementing an individualized leadership development programme, a firm needs a tool for identifying each person's leadership type. That type will then become the filter through which some, though not all, leadership development content will be delivered. Organizations can use an existing personality metric, such as Myers-Briggs, DISC, or the Herrmann Brain Dominance Instrument, or they can create their own. For our work, we designed an algorithm within StandOut, our online strengths-assessment tool. StandOut is a situational judgement test, meaning that people indicate their likeliest response to a series of situations. By focusing on behaviours, this type of test captures how people come across to others better than assessments that ask respondents to rate themselves on a variety of traits. We built StandOut by surveying more than 430,000 individuals whose subsequent performance could be tracked.

Our analysis showed that the range of behaviours seen across those thousands of people could be divided into nine categories, which we call strength roles. These represent the most common ways specific strengths cluster and combine in individual leaders.

Give the Assessment to the Company's Best Leaders.

We administered StandOut to 150 people selected from among the top 10 per cent of general managers in the Hilton focused-service brands. Contrary to the formulaic model of leadership development, we did not find that all leaders had one or two top strength roles in common; we discovered a broad distribution across all nine roles. This pattern is not an anomaly: We found a similar range among leaders at Microsoft, Kohl's, and Habitat for Humanity and among principals belonging to the National Association of Independent Schools. At Hilton, we identified a number of exceptional leaders in each category and set out to learn what fueled their success.

Interview a Cross Section of Leaders to Discover their Techniques.

Even though they had attained similar levels of success, leaders with different strength roles had very different approaches. Diana, who runs a Hampton Inn and Suites in Pennsylvania, says that the key is using a mascot to symbolize the behaviour and attitudes she wants employees to exhibit and to get people to rally around. The mascot she's chosen is a turtle—"because you won't make any progress unless you stick your neck out," as she puts it. It's vital, she says, to imbue the workplace with "a personality, a purpose." It makes sense that she would say that: Her StandOut results reveal that she's a Stimulator, prone to creating energy, excitement, and drama.

Tim, the general manager of the Hilton Garden Inn in Times Square, is predominantly a Teacher. One of his techniques is to run a lending library for employees at the hotel. He asks every worker to contribute a book, fiction or nonfiction, each month. Like other teachers, Tim recognizes the value of constant learning. In a dynamic service-oriented business such as hospitality, employees encounter new kinds of problems every day. Through the lending library, Tim is sending a symbolic message that workers are empowered—indeed, expected—to share their knowledge of the hotel's operations with one another.

Melanie (lead strength role: Provider) believes in a bimonthly "paycheck lunch" for employees at her hotel in Wilmington, North Carolina. Its purpose is to allow team members to share stories and details of what they appreciate about one another, and Melanie leads by example. At the end of the lunch she distributes paychecks, which feel less like contractual compensation and more like a tangible expression of her gratitude.

Then there's Steve, who's the general manager of the Hilton Garden Inn at the Toronto airport. It's unlikely that he could successfully implement Diana's, Tim's, or Melanie's techniques even if you begged him to try. For

Steve, the approach to live by is "the law of three and two": Check guest feedback three times a day and respond to all comments, whether good or bad, within two hours. Steve is an Equalizer. His most effective techniques will always revolve around structure, rules, fairness, and making things right. None of the techniques I've just described can be found in any manual of standard operating procedures. And telling everybody to employ them would be a mistake. But there are somemanagers who could benefit from using someof them or who might be sparked to create effective variations of their own. The challenge is to convey successful leaders' practices to the developing leaders who have similar strength roles.

Use the Algorithm to Target Techniques to the Right People.

Companies should assess all developing leaders and feed each one practices derived from excellent leaders who have the same top two strength roles. Our algorithm draws on a constantly growing database of concepts, innovations, and practices and pushes them out to leaders as a series of techniques they might try. Because the suggestions reflect only what has worked for others who "look like" the recipients, they accelerate creativity without eroding authenticity.

Results may show up quickly. Kevin, a Hampton general manager in Atlanta, found that this was the case for one of the hotel's key metrics, a measure of guest satisfaction known as SALT (Service and Loyalty Tracking). Soon after assessing individual strengths on the management and front-desk teams and targeting suggested techniques accordingly, the hotel saw the SALT score for front-desk helpfulness rise by 4.8 per cent, while the overall service score rose by 3.7 per cent. New knowledge evaporates if it isn't reinforced. Realizing this, Phil Cordell charged us and the Hampton brand team with sustaining the learning at Hampton's 1,850 hotels by developing a web application for laptops, tablets, and smartphones (it's little surprise that Phil's lead strength role is Pioneer). Twice a week the app feeds new techniques, in video and text format, from top-performing general managers to other leaders. When devising the app, we relied on certain principles.

We wanted every communication to be:

- Short.Each technique is delivered as a staccato burst. Some commentators believe that society's fascination with alerts, updates, and tweets is harmful, raising levels of distraction and shortening attention spans. We think the causal arrow points the other way: People like alerts, updates, and tweets precisely because the brain is built to pay more attention to short, frequent stimuli than to sustained input.
- Personalized.Although the algorithm ensures that most of the techniques someone receives come from leaders whose strengths

match his, occasionally the app delivers techniques from leaders with different sorts of strengths, both to add surprise and to avoid the echo-chamber effect.

- Interactive.After receiving a technique, an employee can either "ditch" it or "bank" it. Those that are ditched disappear, and those that are banked are stored in an ever-growing idea vault of the leader's own making, where they can be organized and "favorited" for later use.

If you're a Hampton team member, every Tuesday and Thursday the app delivers a new tip to your inbox, and you decide how to react. You might put it into practice right away. David (lead strength role: Adviser) recently received this tip: "Cultural differences are never an excuse for not getting along. People will default to culture to explain rocky exchanges. More often than not, the issue is tied to something far simpler and more pragmatic. Get people back to the table to work it out. You will excel at this kind of pragmatism." As it happened, David had been avoiding a sensitive issue within his team. The tip jolted him to step up as a leader and give the team suggestions about how to come together and move forward.

The tip might even resonate so strongly that you'd wish to have it tattooed on your forehead. Jean (lead strength role: Stimulator) received this tip: "Your presence fills a room. If you're having a good day, everyone feels it and is buoyed by it. If not, the opposite happens—you drag your people down. On those days, don't fake it—they won't buy it. Instead, take a break and get out of the office, or stay in your office and shut the door until you've rekindled your energy." Jean's reaction? "I banked it and keep watching it," she says. "First thing in the morning, I flip it on. I need constant reminding of the emotional impact I have on my people."

Make the System Dynamically Intelligent.

Intrinsic to the notion of a personalization algorithm is that it must get to know you better over time. With every interaction, the app adds detail to your leadership profile. As you rate the effectiveness of the techniques you receive, the system tracks your reactions and becomes smarter about which techniques to feed you. As the sample size of leaders, techniques, and reactions grows, this two-way communication channel should become as good as the very best consumer recommendation engine at offering content that is relevant to you. The system should also become smarter about itself. As usage data accumulate, it should be able to answer a host of important questions: Do the most effective leaders bank more tips than others, or fewer? Which sorts of tips tend to be favorited—video, audio, or text? Do the answers vary by strength role—for example, do Pioneers love video, while Equalizers respond better to text? As we write this, the StandOut web application has delivered more than 12,000 personalized tips. From the responses, we know that the Teachers in the group bank the most tips, the Influencers the fewest. Such data points are invaluable to ongoing research.

We've described how the steps work at Hilton. We're now applying the model at other organizations, where we move quickly to step five. At this stage, interviews with the very best leaders add raw material for the ongoing tip feed, and each leader's reactions to the tips continually refine her leadership algorithm. We're finding, as you will if your organization adopts this model, that step five feels like a start of its own. The power of a dynamically intelligent system that draws on peer-to-peer sharing wholly overturns the prevailing model of leadership development.

UNBOUNDED LEADERSHIP

That old model of leadership development, the formulaic model, has an appealing simplicity, but it runs afoul of two realities: Each leader leads differently, and the techniques used by one don't necessarily translate to another. The old model also ignores the extra engagement that we know results when people feel recognized and valued for what they bring to the table. In the Gallup meta-analysis we described earlier, employees whose strengths were called on every day were 38 per cent more likely to be on high-performing teams, 44 per cent more likely to have top customer satisfaction scores, and 50 per cent more likely to be in the low-turnover category of employees. And when leaders are taught how to apply their strengths, their level of engagement increases. In a recent study of senior district managers and district managers in a retail company, average scores on an engagement index jumped 25 points in the nine months after the firm adopted a strengths-based leadership development model. At Hampton, an analysis of recent performance showed that the revenue per available room generated by the most-engaged general managers was six and a half points higher than that of less engaged managers. The potential difference in revenue from the two groups is hundreds of thousands of dollars per hotel.

Companies should assess all developing leaders and feed each one customized tips—tips drawn only from outstanding leaders who have similar strengths.

We need a new model—one that is scalable but accommodates the uniqueness of each leader's techniques; one that is stable enough to permit the training of hundreds of leaders at once but dynamic enough to incorporate and distribute new practices and other innovations in real time. Happily, prototypes of that model are all around us. Content creators of every type have realized that they must make their content relevant, and the most effective route to relevance is to filter content through the Algorithm of You.

Of course, it's inevitable—and desirable—that the new model will quickly break through organizational boundaries. Soon there will be a place, somewhere in the cloud, that continually gathers the best techniques, tips, and practical innovations from high-performing leaders around the world; sorts them according to each individual's unique leadership algorithm; feeds you the techniques that fit you best; and refines its filtering as it learns how you react to those techniques. It will be your own personal leadership coach, powered by the top leaders who are most like you.

THE ROLE OF ORGANISATIONAL LEADERSHIP IN TRANSFORMATIONS

ISSUES TO MANAGE

The issues leaders need to manage during an organisational transformation can be broadly categorised as the instrumental/technical aspect and the people/emotional aspect. Leaders tend to focus their efforts on the instrumental/technical aspect of transformations. This is about having the proper systems, structures, technologies, processes and rewards in place, such that the work setting supports, motivates and sustains people in their transformation efforts. The issues here can typically be addressed through a rational and technical approach.

Dealing with the instrumental/technical aspect alone is not sufficient; this must be complemented by a consideration of the people/emotional aspect of change. In reality, the people aspect is often less well thought through. Yet, organisations are made up of people and so, Branson (2008) argued that the consideration of people should precede the non-human parts of the organisation in any change effort. Different leaders have different beliefs and values about leadership, change, and people in general. These lead them to adopt different roles to manage the instrumental/technical aspect and the people/emotional aspect of change.

LEADERS AS SHAPERS

Within the traditional management and leadership paradigm, it is thought that the leader should control everything, so that everything turns out according to plan and there are no unwanted outcomes. Moreover, the assumption that everything can be controlled leads to the thinking that change is a predictable process and leaders can choose how a transformation effort will turn out (Higgs and Rowland, 2005), and this premise underlies much of the organisational change literature emphasising the steps that leaders should take or the behaviours they should display to drive transformations (Herold et al., 2008). Within this paradigm, in a transformation context, the leader plays the role described by Higgs and Rowland (2005) as "shaper", one who personally controls what gets done, sets the pace for others, and expects others to follow their example.

The leader is expected to be responsible for shaping a transformation through a top-down process and managing it according to a detailed step-by-step plan. The leader is thought to know what is right and necessary for the organisation, and it is thought that people will embrace the change agenda if they are similarly informed. Thus, resistance of the people to making the changes they are told to, is interpreted as the need for stronger leadership in the form of more guidance and education (Diefenbach, 2007). This is largely in line with the view of leadership that the leader plays a directive role and holds much influence over his followers.

Essentially, for a shaper, change leadership is equated with pushing through the leader's change agenda and overcoming resistance from the people in order to make them think and act differently. The people are considered to be the targets or recipients of change initiatives. Research has found that the shaper role tends not to be effective in a transformation. Even though the leader may have set up the right processes and structure to support the transformation, and have provided direction and a clear strategy for the way forward, the transformation is likely to fail because the people are not emotionally invested in the change.

There may be compliance at best, but not emotional alignment. Furthermore, when a leader tries to shape change, he may end up taking on too much personally, and thus prevent people from growing and transforming (Higgs and Rowland, 2010). Add to this the fact that transformations are complex and chaotic and cannot be dictated to meet predetermined outcomes, it is not surprising that empirical evidence shows that leader-centric behaviours are associated with less successful changes.

LEADERS AS ENABLERS

Higgs and Rowland (2011) noted that the focus of change efforts needs to be more on "doing change with people rather than doing change to them" (p.331, italics added). This alternative paradigm is where leaders play an enabling role in a transformation, creating the conditions that encourage and energise people to contribute to and grow from the transformation process. Such leaders provide the instrumental/technical framework for change, and seek to engage people, facilitating sense-making and bringing about emotional alignment. Given the complex and emergent nature of change, some conclude that it may "elude or defy managerial and organisational control" (Kuepers, 2011, p.22). However, this does not mean there is no need for leadership. It means that there is no need for strictly planned and controlled management interventions and that it is all the more important for leaders to play an enabling role. In such a context, it is still possible for leaders to influence the direction and development of the change, and this is by focusing on key issues the people are facing (Karp and Helgo, 2008).

Specifically, Karp and Helgo (2008) emphasised the need for change leaders to facilitate the formation of identity and relationships in the organisation, as these sense-making processes are at the heart of why people change. Leaders can do this through various methods, such as role-modelling the necessary behaviours, communicating the values and purpose of the organisation, paying attention to relationships and the communication of stories and symbols that are important for the organisation.

Within this environment, people have the opportunity to experience the uncertainty and conflict in a transformation process, and through this, create meaning for themselves.

Essentially, the crux of the people aspect of transformations is emotional alignment. Gioia and Thomas (1996) described change as "primarily not a technical but a political issue" (p.378), as it is largely about personal interests and agendas. When people perceive that there is alignment between themselves and the organisation's agenda, and there is a new identity for them that they are willing to accept, they become emotionally invested in the change (Dehler and Welsh, 1994). They then slowly begin to modify their behaviours and how they relate with themselves and others, and collaborate in determining how the transformation will proceed (Dehler and Welsh, 1994; Kuepers, 2011). Collectively, when there is a critical mass of people who are prepared to change, transformation will occur at the organisational level. Such organisational energy, where everybody in the organisation is motivated and enthusiastic and committed to the shared goals, is important for successful transformations (Aiken and Keller, 2007). Summing up the various sources in the literature, we conclude that leaders can create emotional alignment by providing:

A Shared Vision of the Future

A compelling vision provides direction and a sense of purpose and inspiration. When leaders frame the vision in a way that appeals to people's need for meaning and achievement, people understand the need for change and will be aligned with the organisational purpose, and hence, intrinsically motivated to change their behaviours (Dehler and Welsh, 1994). Importantly, this is not a vision that is thrust upon people, but one which they jointly create (McNaughton, 2003).

Clarity About and Ownership of the Strategies

Leaders need to ensure there is clarity about the strategies to bring the organisation's vision into reality, so people know what is to be done and how they contribute to the whole. Crucially, people should be involved in the development of the strategy and be empowered with the necessary skills and resources to carry out the strategy.

A Supportive Culture and Shared Values

An organisation's culture strongly influences how people behave, from the way they interact with each other, to how they work and how they think. Only when the organisational culture supports the new vision can there be sustainable changes (McNaughton, 2003). Values underlie an organisation's culture. During a transformation, it is important that leaders provide the opportunity for the organisation to clarify its values and encourage people to embrace them in their everyday organisational behaviours. Leaders also need to be aware of negative group norms which can undermine the transformation effort (Higgs and Rowland, 2010).

Motivation and Inspiration

A compelling vision, empowerment in the change process, and a supportive culture and alignment with the organisational values all serve to motivate and inspire people. Beyond that, leaders can find other means of inspiring people, such as planning for and creating positive outcomes that people can attain and celebrate in the near term while working towards the longer term goals of the transformation, so that people can continue to feel a sense of movement and progress in the transformation. While the above efforts all contribute towards aligning people emotionally with the organisation's transformation agenda, leaders need to remember that people cannot develop emotional alignment on demand and in accordance to a rigid schedule. This means that leaders have to decide how best to balance the need for people to be given enough time and space to discover their emotional alignment against the competing need to meet organisational timelines and milestones for their transformation journey. As a final point to note, while enabling leaders may provide the direction and approximate definition of the destination for the transformation, the transformation process may take a different route from what they had in mind and achieve unexpected outcomes. This is especially likely when leaders nurture conflict, making use of the diverse points of view raised by different people to improve decisions made for the organisation (McNaughton, 2003). Karp and Helgo (2008) expressed this well when they wrote that, "leaders may find that they have to live with the paradox of being in control and not being in control simultaneously" (p.91). But for these leaders who display more facilitating behaviours that frame the change and create capacity in people and the organisation, they are likely to be rewarded with greater change success (Higgs and Rowland, 2011).

WHO IS THE LEADER OF ORGANISATIONAL TRANSFORMATIONS?

POSITIONAL LEADERS AT DIFFERENT LEVELS OF THE ORGANISATION

Even though the word "leader" has been used in a fairly generic manner in this paper, in an organisation where there is a hierarchy of leaders from top leaders to line managers, the role played by leaders at each level might have a somewhat different emphasis. In general, top leaders are expected to play a more significant role in creating the vision and driving the change agenda, while middle level and line managers play a more significant role in operationalising and implementing the change initiative (Caldwell, 2003; Gilley et al., 2009). These are complementary roles, working together to help bring about the organisational transformation.

NON-POSITIONAL LEADERS

Another consideration is that the leadership role may be played by positional leaders as well as other members of the organisation. According to Pye and Pettigrew (2006), the power to influence others is at the heart of leading transformations. The leader needs to acquire sources of power and be able to use his power skilfully, in order to get people to change their behaviours. Typically, organisational transformations are led by positional leaders, especially top management. These are the people with ready access to many sources of power, including positional power, control over resources, as well as networks of relationships both inside and outside the organisation (Pye and Pettigrew, 2006). Power may also be derived from control over information flow, one's expertise, and other social, human and intellectual capital such as one's track record, credibility, personality, and relational abilities. As positional authority is not necessarily needed to influence others, it is possible that non-positional leaders could possess the power to lead transformations. These may be people who are highly influential in the organisation's informal network. Positional leaders could find ways to tap on these informal leaders to guide or catalyse organisational transformations. For instance, these informal leaders could help to explain management's ideologies to the people and garner their support for new initiatives, and at the same time, they could get a good feel of ground sentiments and provide relevant input to management to guide decision-making.

In addition, bottom-up efforts in driving the change can make a difference, as change may sometimes be so rapid that it is impossible for senior management to know and plan everything. It may even be possible that an organisational transformation is initiated through bottom-up efforts rather than a top-down direction, in which case the experience and role of the positional leader will be somewhat different from what is typically presented in the literature. Importantly, regardless of who the leader is, it is important that the power is exercised in an empowering manner. As Rooke and Torbert (1998) contend, it is only such power that can generate whole-hearted transformation.

COLLECTIVE LEADERSHIP

Much of the literature on leading transformations (and leadership in general) tends to adopt the perspective of the positional leader as an unusually talented hero, with a strong emphasis on individual behaviour in initiating and leading organisational changes. However, "the most successful organisations are not those led by a single powerful, charismatic leader, but are the product of distributive, collective, and complementary leadership" (Kets de Vries, 2007). Similarly, the significance of distributed leadership in bringing about organisational transformation cannot be underestimated. Organisational transformation could possibly be brought about more effectively by a leading coalition with complementary skills. Thus, even if a single positional leader is put in charge of a transformation effort, it may be worthwhile for him to consider bringing on board other people to collectively lead the changes.

CRITICAL FACTORS FOR LEADING TRANSFORMATIONS

LEADERS' PERSONAL QUALITIES

The question of what factors are critical for leading transformations has been approached from different angles. One perspective is offered by change-oriented models of leadership. These explore what types of leaders are effective in bringing about change in their people and organisation. The focus is more general and longer term, and is not specific to any change initiative. Some of these models of leadership refer to the leader as a transformational leader who raises "followers' aspirations and activate their higher-order values (*e.g.*, altruism) such that followers identify with the leader and his or her mission/ vision, feel better about their work, and then work to perform beyond simple transactions and base expectations" (Avolio et al., 2009). These leaders inspire their followers by providing a desirable vision, articulating how it can be reached, acting as a role model, setting high standards of performance, and showing determination and confidence. They also pay individual attention to the development of their followers, and stimulate them intellectually, helping them become more innovative and creative. There is some evidence that transformational leaders have greater success with change initiatives (*e.g.*, Herold et al., 2008).

Another perspective of factors critical for leading transformations is offered by the change leadership literature, which has explored the leadership characteristics and behaviours that are associated with the successful implementation of a change initiative. These studies tend to view the change initiative as a specific event requiring particular behaviours from the leader. The focus is on the here-and-now and the leader's behaviours are tactical (Herold et al., 2008). Some of these studies propose a comprehensive list of competencies covering all aspects of a change process (*e.g.*, Higgs and Rowland, 2000), while some focus on a few critical competencies (*e.g.*, Graetz, 2000). In summary, the qualities that are identified to be important can be broadly clustered as follows:

Interpersonal Skills

Interpersonal skills frequently emerge as an essential quality for leaders to possess (*e.g.*, Graetz, 2000), which is not surprising considering that people issues are at the heart of leading transformations. This is supported by empirical evidence—for instance, a study by Gilley et al, (2009) largely corroborated previous studies when it found that leaders who effectively implemented change possessed a set of multidimensional interpersonal skills, including the abilities to motivate, communicate, build teams, coach, involve others, and reward them appropriately.

Beyond these, leaders need to be astute about others' interests and resources, as this will help them tap more effectively on the different strategic actors in the transformation process and consider how best to strategise an intervention (Pye and Pettigrew, 2006). Astuteness about the organisation dynamics is also important, as that will help leaders have a clear understanding of the underlying systems that are influencing people's behaviours and decision whether to change (Higgs and Rowland, 2005).

Cognitive Skills

Cognitive skills are important too, as a certain degree of intelligence is needed to understand issues, make judgements, solve problems, make decisions, and come up with a vision. Leaders' judgement about the change approach to be adopted is particularly important when the change is more complex (Higgs and Rowland, 2011). In sum, cognitive skills are essential for strategising and planning the change.

Self-Awareness

Leaders who are self-aware are more likely to be aware of their own needs, biases and agendas, and the impact of their own behaviours on the transformation process. This helps them to raise difficult issues clearly (Higgs and Rowland, 2010) and to make more considered decisions (McNaughton, 2003). This is because such leaders tend to be more aware of their impulses and struggles and to reflect on what they could have done differently. They also seek feedback regularly and consider how their leadership is experienced by others, and this helps them learn how they can improve (Higgs and Rowland, 2010).

If we examine this list of qualities, we find that they are not very different from generic competencies for effective leadership; the only difference is that they are applied to the transformation context. Some researchers contend that managing change is a core role of leadership, and this is not limited to leadership from the transformational leadership point of view. Furthermore, it takes time for a leader to build a trusting relationship with his followers. Thus, transformations should not be regarded as an isolated event where the leader demonstrates a particular kind of leadership behaviour only in this instance and expects to be effective. As Herold et al., (2008) found, change-specific leadership practices were less strongly related to followers' commitment to a change initiative, compared to general perceptions of the leader's leadership. Moreover, as change is becoming a more frequent aspect of organisational life and change takes time to unfold, it is difficult to make the distinction between effective change leadership and effective leadership. Colville and Murphy (2006) even equated effective leadership with change leadership, as they contended that "leadership has no meaning in a steady-state environment. Only when we enter a new territory, when we don't know the way, do we need people to step forward and lead."

LEADERS' WORLD VIEWS

Possessing certain skills and competence is essential for effective leadership and effective change leadership. No less important are the set of beliefs, mindsets and values that underlie a leader's behaviours. Our world view, or mental model, shapes how we perceive, interpret, and respond to the world around us (Argyris and Schön, 1977). Some of these that are particularly relevant to leading transformations are examined in the following paragraphs.

World Views that are More Complex

Whether leaders adopt an enabling, facilitative role or a shaper role in the transformational process depends in part on the complexity of their world views. In their review of different models of adult constructive development, McCauley, Drath et al., (2006) noted that people who have developed world views that are more complex perceive: the world more in terms of dynamic, mutually-transforming systems rather than in terms of dichotomies; the self as revisable as a result of interaction with others and self-assertion.

Torbert and his colleagues proposed that leaders with these perspectives are more effective in leading organisational transformations because they are open to thinking about their assumptions and purposes. They also have a broader, more flexible and imaginative perspective, and like to cultivate relationships with many stakeholders. All these help them handle people's instinctive resistance to change better as they are genuinely open to engaging in mutual exploration of differences with other organisational members in order to discover new shared understandings, which is an important part of the transformation process.

In their review, McCauley et al., (2006) noted that there is some empirical support for this proposition, with·such leaders putting more emphasis on their role as an agent of cultural change. This suggests that leaders operating from this frame of mind are arguably more likely to adopt an enabling, facilitative role in the transformation process, which makes them a change catalyst. In contrast, leaders who rely primarily on their self-generated values and standards when acting, and who examine the opinions of others with the intent to help clarify and improve their own ideologies, are more likely to adopt a command-and-control perspective of leadership, which means that they are more likely to play the, ineffective, role of shaper when leading an organisational transformation.

Some studies have linked complexity of world view with authentic leadership (*e.g.*, Eigel and Kuhnert, 2005), in which the leader shows balanced processing of relevant information before making a decision, has an internalised moral perspective for self-regulation, demonstrates relational transparency through openly sharing information and feelings as appropriate for the situation, and possesses self-awareness (Avolio et al., 2009). Similarly, McNaughton (2003) noted that leaders who have a transformational influence on their followers have undergone self-transformation themselves. Having gained self-mastery, they are authentic, and behave according to the highest principles of moral reasoning and integrity. They are able to deal with others openly and with compassion, and sincerely want to help develop others. People trust them, and this helps to generate whole-hearted transformation.

Perspective of Change as a Complex Event

At a more micro level, a leader's handling of an organisational transformation is also influenced by his mental model of change. Some people view change as a complex event while others view change as a linear and predictable event, and this has implications for how they understand the situation and what strategy they formulate to deal with it (Higgs and Rowland, 2005). As discussed above, transformation is a complex event, and those leaders who recognise this tend to adopt a change approach that leads to greater success (Higgs and Rowland, 2005). Conversely, when leaders underestimate the complexity of change, they adopt an ineffective approach, focusing on the technical aspect rather than the issues that their followers are experiencing (Karp and Helgo, 2008).

Situational Factors

Leaders do not act in a vacuum and the situational context should be considered as another factor that influences the success of an organisational transformation. A social environment where followers are hostile or an incompatible organisational system could render the leader powerless (Bolden and Gosling, 2006). For instance, while a leader might be willing to play an enabling role in an organisational transformation and is open to the possibility that the transformation could follow a different route from planned, such unpredictable outcomes might not be wholly acceptable to the management and/or executive board—the more fluid transformation process might conflict with the more traditional ideology of management and leadership adopted by some people, who expect a predictable and controlled transformation process, and expect certain broad goals and objectives to be achieved by the transformation. The temporal context is important too as notions of what constitutes an effective leader are tied to the prevailing social norms and expectations. Thus, while an engaging, empowering leader tends to be more acceptable to followers in this day and age and would thus bring about greater organisational success, such ideas may evolve over time as society changes.

IMPLICATIONS FOR LEADERSHIP SELECTION AND DEVELOPMENT

As effective change leaders are essentially effective leaders, the considerations when selecting and developing a leader to lead an organisational transformation are not that different from the considerations for the selection and development of effective leaders. A few points do warrant further emphasis though.

PAY ATTENTION TO LEADERS' WORLD VIEWS

Fundamentally, in selecting and developing leaders who can facilitate transformations, it is important to pay attention to their mindsets as values and attitudes drive behaviours. Sustainable changes in behaviour only come about when there is a shift in values and mindsets (Charan et al., 2001). In development, the emphasis is generally on lateral development, which is about learning new skills, behaviours and knowledge, and how to apply these to widening circles of influence (Cook-Greuter, 2004), and there is certainly a place for such learning. However, more emphasis needs to be placed on vertical development, which is about helping people to interpret their experiences through an expanded and more integrated perspective (and thus develop more complex world views). Cook-Greuter (2004) pointed out that development occurs through the interplay between the individual and his environment, and this can be facilitated by providing the appropriate challenge and support. Self-reflection, action enquiry, and learning from others who show a greater degree of development, have all been shown to be effective, and such interventions to support leaders' vertical development could viably be part of a leadership development path.

At a change-specific level, it is important to encourage leaders to adopt the perspective of change as a complex process and to accept the need for a more enabling and facilitative style of leadership, as both these world views are associated with greater success in organisational transformation.

HELP LEADERS GAIN THE NECESSARY SKILLS AND KNOWLEDGE

It would also be important to help leaders to understand how the transformation is experienced by the members of the organisation and to clarify leaders' role in an organisational transformation, and to help them acquire the skills necessary for them to be effective in this role. In particular, people-related skills, such as the ability to communicate, facilitate, and involve others, are important as a large part of leaders' role is about dealing with people and helping them find alignment with the organisational agenda.

CONSIDER COLLECTIVE CAPACITY

Beyond focusing on positional leaders, it is important to explore how the organisation as a whole can work together to bring about transformations. Bottom-up efforts, for instance, could be tapped on for new ideas and to drive certain initiatives, and leadership for the organisational transformation could appear anywhere in the organisation. Tapping on these different resources may provide better ideas for and generate greater emotional alignment with the transformation efforts.

CHALLENGES AND LIMITATIONS

A limitation of the literature on leading organisational transformations is that it is mostly theoretical and conceptual, with few empirical studies. Furthermore, the empirical research that has been done is largely descriptive and based on observations of a leader's competencies and effectiveness by his managers, peers, or subordinates (Gilley et al., 2009). The studies conducted on constructive-developmental theory have similarly been criticised for using restricted samples and research designs that are limited (McCauley et al., 2006). Thus, more robust research is needed. Nonetheless, the findings that are currently available do suggest important areas of focus for leadership development that may lead to greater success in implementing organisational transformations.

LEADERSHIP DEVELOPMENT: STRATEGIC POWERHOUSE

The moment a CEO starts a job, the clock starts ticking. With SandP 500 CEOs seeing an average tenure of nine years, senior leaders must hit the ground running—formulating and executing transformational strategies and, ultimately, creating a better organization. Korn Ferry research has identified the alignment of business and talent strategies as a critical task for directors, CEOs, and chief human resources officers. And some of the notable strengths of the top 20 per cent of CEOs, based on Korn Ferry's comprehensive leadership performance simulation, include developing strategies and driving growth. But even these outliers among CEO talent don't do it alone. Success requires the hard work of leaders at all levels, who must make countless decisions and behave in ways that support the strategic direction and overarching purpose of the organization.

Unfortunately, many organizations lack the leadership capabilities they need. In a recent survey by Korn Ferry with almost 7,500 respondents, more than 80 per cent of whom said they were at the C-suite or director level or above, 62 per cent have examined their organization's leadership capabilities and see gaps that need filling. Further, only 17 per cent of survey respondents said they were confident they have the talent needed to deliver on strategic priorities.

Developing leaders from within the organization is a priority for driving change. As Korn Ferry has found through its work with clients across all industries, leadership development can and should be a powerful tool at the CEO's disposal to advance strategic growth and change. CEOs have relatively few strategic levers to drive real strategic change. The predictable levers include compensation, budgeting, process improvement, increased measurement and accountability, new technologies, reorganization, and revitalized communications. That should make leadership development even more alluring. But to be effective, leadership development needs to be more than aligned with the business strategy—it needs to be part of the strategy.

Effective leadership development is a CEO's most underutilized tool to advance the execution of an ambitious strategic agenda. The Korn Ferry survey revealed that nearly 40 per cent of respondents said they don't regularly review leadership needs against their business strategy. This is clearly a missed opportunity. Organizations invest heavily in leadership development, even as they know it must change. US companies have been estimated to spend about $14 billion a year on leadership development training. Overall corporate training expenditures, which are considerably larger, have been growing by 10 per cent to 15 per cent per year as the economy recovers. Given the size of this resource commitment, leadership development should be expected to contribute to performance improvement and deep competitive advantage. In some instances, however, leadership development proves less than effective— even to the point of having a weak or negative return on investment (ROI). In the Korn Ferry survey, more than half of the executives rated the ROI of their leadership development efforts as "fair to very poor."

This paper will show that, more than ever, focused leadership development programmes are needed to help drive an organization's strategic agenda. By developing current and future leaders, these programmes can promote and create culture change to support a more purpose-driven, sustainable, and socially conscious organization that commits to people so its talent can execute the business strategy and achieve desired results. With effective leadership development programmes, CEOs can build high-performing organizations as their legacy.

TALENT TO DRIVE THE STRATEGIC AGENDA.

Many organizations commit massive amounts of resources to create new business strategies they hope will take them from where they are to where they want to be. The result is often a very convincing slide deck stipulating the "what" and "why" of the new strategy. Some strategies are replete with technical details, financial projections, forecasts of future market share, a roadmap for product and service development, and so forth. But, as Korn Ferry's experience with clients has shown, many organizations have a blind spot on the human side of things. At best they have a headcount or workforce projection, but few have a development plan for their people, let alone a leadership strategy.

Recognizing the strategic importance of leadership and leadership development places a higher priority on the talent pipeline. As the Korn Ferry survey showed, less than 20 per cent of respondents were confident they have the leaders they need to deliver on strategic priorities. A lack of talent to fulfill mission-critical roles (as and when needed) can put a business at risk competitively, and may force external recruitment for crucial skill sets that could be developed internally. All organizations must retain their relevance to individual customers and broad markets, and they cannot do so unless they also keep pace with societal change. This means that organizations must work even harder to develop many more leaders who are female and who are from underrepresented communities and points of view. These individuals must be valued and welcomed into leadership development programmes, especially with the full support of top executives. Further, participants in leadership development programmes must learn how to change existing cultures to be as inclusive as possible. They need to see the advantages of broadening points of view to benefit their organizations, clients, and communities. Further, as they participate with colleagues, all the future leaders in development programmes need to see that they all have roles in including others and ensuring that the broadest points of view benefit their organizations.

Leadership development is the tangible manifestation of the organization's point of view on leadership. How at all levels it invests in, supports, and sponsors the strategic development of leaders is a direct reflection of how aggressively it is working to close its own strategy-execution gap.

Leadership development can drive organizational change and progress:

- It can and should drive the organization's strategy and advance the corporate agenda.
- It can and should help build a strong and differentiated bench and talent pipeline—the leaders who will execute the strategy of both today and the future.
- It can be used to promote and create culture change that is aligned to the strategy.
- It can help promote a more purpose-focused, sustainable, and socially conscious organization.

However, even committed and well-intentioned organizations sometimes fall short—because they fail to see that leadership development needs to be part of the strategy—not just aligned with the strategy.

THE FOUR PILLARS OF LEADERSHIP DEVELOPMENT.

Leadership development falls short all too often because it lacks relevance. The key to making it more effective is rooting it more deeply in the real world to produce real outcomes. To illustrate, we turn to Korn Ferry's Four Pillars of Leadership Development: context, whole person, development as a journey, and purpose.

Context is Critical.

To accelerate leadership development and close critical gaps, real context and practical application are essential. An organization's leaders should grow into future challenges by being exposed to current and impending obstacles, problems, and opportunities. These real experiences accelerate development in conjunction with formal structured learning programmes and are far more effective than hypotheticals or semi-relevant case studies. Leaders developed in context produce real outcomes and solve real problems as they grow and develop. This approach also aligns with the experiences of most senior leaders. When asked what shaped them, most executives cite real-world, on-the-job experiences.

Develop the Whole Person.

For an organization to change, individual leaders need to change and grow. Simply stated, the organization gets better as each individual also gets better. By putting the individual at the center of organizational learning—while acknowledging their individuality and unique experiences, motivators, values, vitality, and traits—organizations increase the chances of realizing value-added changes from leadership development in support of strategic direction.

Korn Ferry promotes a whole-person approach by tapping prior experiences and the lessons gained from them, which are instrumental to readiness for new challenges and roles. Experiences are considered one of four dimensions of leadership, along with traits (personality characteristics that exert a strong influence on behaviour), competencies (leadership skills that matter most for success), and drivers (the preferences, values, and motivations that influence a person's career).

Development is a Journey

Leadership development is not an event. Rather, it is a process that occurs over time with a pace and intensity that match the scope and ambition of the business strategy and desired change. Leaders should never stop or postpone development. Leaders should have a clear and coherent, multi-level development plan that puts them on a personal journey of growth.

Creating learning journeys requires a new approach to the programme design, using the current context of the organization as a starting point. In this way, leadership development becomes more effective in activating the organization's strategy at all levels.

Service Promotes Purpose

To create a sustainable impact, leaders need to embrace a purpose beyond themselves. A sense of purpose motivates leaders to create, serve, build, and improve in the service of a broader and longer-term goal. To unleash the potential within, an organization must help its people experience the power of service. One way to make leadership development more purposeful is to embed broader meaning into the leadership journey.

The Risks of Failing to Transform Leadership Development

As Korn Ferry's survey indicates, dissatisfaction can run high with leadership development programmes as they currently exist. Why does leadership development fail to deliver the expected benefits? Why does it fail to deliver on its promise? There is no single or simple answer to this difficult question.

Based on our work with clients over the years (and listening to their past experiences to better meet their needs), we have identified these key root-cause reasons:

- Lack of alignment between the leadership development strategy and the business strategy.
- Disconnected and sometimes contradictory programmes at different levels of the organization.
- Visible behaviours at the top that do not reflect messaging and priorities conveyed to levels deeper in the organization.
- Programmes that benefit either the individual or the organization, but not both.
- A theoretical approach to leadership development that does not bring the concepts into practical reality.
- Outdated delivery models that don't put the learner at the center of the process.
- Neglect of cultural aspects in an organization that allow leadership to thrive.
- Lack of qualitative and quantitative analyses to document impact and outcomes.
- Prevailing and overriding assumptions that time spent in leadership development is "time offline."

- Lack of strong governance models to guide effective and strategic investment in leadership development.

Overcoming these potential pitfalls requires a deliberate and focused approach to drive measurable and meaningful organization change and help narrow the strategy execution gap.

CONCLUSION

Leadership development can and should be one of the most powerful strategic tools in the CEO's arsenal. With measurement lacking and adding to skepticism about the programs' impact and ROI, leadership development too often has been considered a cost, not an investment. The solution is to devise and implement leadership development that is tailored to the organization and the talent needs of its current and future leaders. Leadership development then becomes an organizational priority because it is embedded in business strategies, in recognition that it is not enough to know what must be done—but who is needed to accomplish it.

THE CHANGE PROCESS

THE CHANGE PROCESS AS "UNFREEZING, CHANGING AND REFREEZING"

The process of change has been characterized as having three basic stages: unfreezing, changing, and re-freezing. This view draws heavily on Kurt Lewin's adoption of the systems concept of homeostasis or dynamic stability. What is useful about this framework is that it gives rise to thinking about a staged approach to changing things. Looking before you leap is usually sound practice. What is not useful about this framework is that it does not allow for change efforts that begin with the organization in extremis nor does it allow for organizations faced with the prospect of having to "hang loose for extended periods of time. In other words, the beginning and ending point of the unfreeze-change-refreeze model is stability – which, for some people and some organizations, is a luxury. For others, internal stability spells disaster. A tortoise on the move can overtake even the fastest hare if that hare stands still.

THE CHANGE PROCESS AS PROBLEM SOLVING AND PROBLEM FINDING

A very useful framework for thinking about the change process is problem solving. Managing change is seen as a matter of moving from one state to another, specifically, from the problem state to the solved state. Diagnosis or problem analysis is generally acknowledged as essential. Goals are set and achieved at various levels and in various areas or functions. Ends and means are discussed and related to one another. Careful planning is accompanied by efforts to obtain buy-in, support and commitment. The net effect is a transition from one state to another in a planned, orderly fashion. This is the planned change model. The word ¯problem carries with it connotations that some people prefer to avoid. They choose instead to use the word ¯opportunity. For such people, a problem is seen as a bad situation, one that shouldn't have been allowed to happen in the first place, and for which someone is likely to be punished – if the guilty party can be identified. We will set aside any cultural or personal preferences regarding the use of ¯problem or ¯opportunity. From a rational, analytical perspective, a problem is nothing more than a situation requiring action but in which the required action is not known. Hence, there is a requirement to search for a solution, a course of action that will lead to the solved state. This search activity is known as ¯problem solving. From the preceding discussion, it follows that ¯problem finding is the search for situations requiring action. Whether we choose to call these situations ¯problems or whether we choose to call them ¯opportunities is immaterial. In both cases, the practical matter is one of identifying and settling on a course of action that will bring about some desired and predetermined change in the situation.

THE CHANGE PROBLEM

At the heart of change management lies the change problem, that is, some future state to be realized, some current state to be left behind, and some structured, organized process for getting from the one to the other. The change problem might be large or small in scope and scale, and it might focus on individuals or groups, on one or more divisions or departments, the entire organization, or one or on more aspects of the organization's environment. At a conceptual level, the change problem is a matter of moving from one state to another state.

Moving from A to A' is typically accomplished as a result of setting up and achieving three types of goals: transform, reduce, and apply. Transform goals are concerned with identifying differences between the two states. Reduce goals are concerned with determining ways of eliminating these differences. Apply goals are concerned with putting into play operators that actually effect the elimination of these differences. As the preceding goal types suggest, the analysis of a change problem will at various times focus on defining the outcomes of the change effort, on identifying the changes necessary to produce these outcomes, and on finding and implementing ways and means of making the required changes. In simpler terms, the change problem can be treated as smaller problems having to do with the how, what, and why of change.

CHANGE AS A "HOW" PROBLEM

The change problem is often expressed, at least initially, in the form of a ¯how question. How do we get people to be more open, to assume more responsibility, to be more creative? How do we introduce self-managed teams in Department W? How do we change over from System X to System Y in Division Z? How do we move from a mainframe-centered computing environment to one that accommodates and integrates PCs? How do we get this organization to be more innovative, competitive, or productive? How do we raise more effective barriers to market entry by our competitors? How might we more tightly bind our suppliers to us? How do we reduce cycle times? In short, the initial formulation of a change problem is means-centered, with the goal state more or less implied. There is a reason why the initial statement of a problem is so often means-centered and we will touch on it later. For now, let's examine the other two ways in which the problem might be formulated – what or as –why questions.

CHANGE AS A "WHAT" PROBLEM

To frame the change effort in the form of ¯how questions is to focus the effort on means. Diagnosis is assumed or not performed at all. Consequently, the ends sought are not discussed. This might or might not be problematic. To focus on ends requires the posing of ¯what questions. What are we trying to accomplish? What changes are necessary? What indicators will signal success? What standards apply? What measures of performance are we trying to affect?

CHANGE AS A "WHY" PROBLEM

Ends and means are relative notions, not absolutes; that is, something is an end or a means only in relation to something else. Thus, chains and networks of ends-means relationships often have to be traced out before one finds the ¯true ends of a change effort. In this regard, ¯why questions prove extremely useful. Consider the following hypothetical dialogue with yourself as an illustration of tracing out ends-means relationships.

- Why do people need to be more creative?
- I'll tell you why! Because we have to change the way we do things and we need ideas about how to do that.
- Why do we have to change the way we do things?
- Because they cost too much and take too long.
- Why do they cost too much?
- Because we pay higher wages than any of our competitors.
- Why do we pay higher wages than our competitors?
- Because our productivity used to be higher, too, but now it's not.
- Eureka! The true aim is to improve productivity!
- No it isn't; keep going.
- Why does productivity need to be improved?
- To increase profits.
- Why do profits need to be increased?

- To improve earnings per share.
- Why do earnings per share need to be improved?
- To attract additional capital.
- Why is additional capital needed?
- We need to fund research aimed at developing the next generation of products.
- Why do we need a new generation of products?
- Because our competitors are rolling them out faster than we are and gobbling up market share.
- Oh, so that's why we need to reduce cycle times.
- Hmm. Why do things take so long?

ask –why questions is to get at the ultimate purposes of functions and to open the door to finding new and better ways of performing them. Why do we do what we do? Why do we do it the way we do it? Asking ¯why questions also gets at the ultimate purposes of people, but that's a different matter altogether.

THE APPROACH TAKEN TO CHANGE MANAGEMENT MIRRORS MANAGEMENT'S MINDSET

The emphasis placed on the three types of questions just mentioned reflects the management mindset, that is, the tendency to think along certain lines depending on where one is situated in the organization. A person's placement in the organization typically defines the scope and scale of the kinds of changes with which he or she will become involved, and the nature of the changes with which he or she will be concerned. Thus, the systems people tend to be concerned with technology and technological developments, the marketing people with customer needs and competitive activity, the legal people with legislative and other regulatory actions, and so on. Also, the higher up a person is in the hierarchy, the longer the time perspective and the wider the range of issues with which he or she must be concerned.

For the most part, changes and the change problems they present are problems of adaptation, that is, they require of the organization only that it adjust to an ever-changing set of circumstances. But, either as a result of continued, cumulative compounding of adaptive maneuvers that were nothing more than band-aids, or as the result of sudden changes so significant as to call for a redefinition of the organization, there are times when the changes that must be made are deep and far-reaching. At such times, the design of the organization itself is called into question. Organizations frequently survive the people who establish them. AT&T and IBM are two ready examples. At some point it becomes the case that such organizations have been designed by one group of people but are being operated or run by another. Successful organizations resolve early on the issue of structure, that is, the definition, placement and coordination of functions and people.

Other people then have to live with this design and, because the ends have already been established, these other people are chiefly concerned with means. This is why so many problem-solving efforts start out focused on means. Some organizations are designed to buffer their core operations from turbulence in the environment. In such organizations all units fit into one of three categories: core, buffer, and perimeter. In core units, coordination is achieved through standardization, that is, adherence to routine. In buffer units, coordination is achieved through planning. In perimeter units, coordination is achieved through mutual adjustment. People in core units, buffered as they are from environmental turbulence and with a history of relying on adherence to standardized procedures, typically focus on ¯how questions. People in buffer units, responsible for performance through planning, often ask ¯what questions. People in the perimeter units are as accountable as anyone else for performance and frequently for performance of a financial nature. They can be heard asking ¯what and ¯how questions. ¯Why questions are generally asked by people with no direct responsibility for day-to-day operations or results.

The group most able to take this long-term or strategic view is that cadre of senior executives responsible for the continued well being of the firm: top management. If the design of the firm is to be called into question or, more significantly, if it is actually to be altered, these are the people who must make the decision to do so. Finally, when organizational redefinition and redesign prove necessary, all people in all units must concern themselves with all three sets of questions or the changes made will not stand the test of time. To summarize: Problems may be formulated in terms of ¯how, ¯what and ¯why questions. Which formulation is used depends on where in the organization the person posing the question or formulating the problem is situated, and where the organization is situated in its own life cycle.

- How questions tend to cluster in core units.
- What questions tend to cluster in buffer units.
- People in perimeter units tend to ask ¯what and ¯how questions.
- Why questions are typically the responsibility of top management.

In turbulent times, everyone must be concerned with everything.

LEADERSHIP THEORIES AND STYLES

Leadership style is the combination of traits, skills, and behaviours leaders use as they interact with employees (Lussier and Achua, 2004). In order for one to favour a leadership style, one must understand where the leadership styles originated. Throughout the years, the topic of leadership has been debated. However, research indicates that certain characteristics or traits are inherent in leaders.

According to research, the 1940's proffered leaders as maintaining certain traits. These traits were based on physical and personality characteristics as well as intelligence and interpersonal skills. Marquis and Huston (2000) associated the Great Man Trait Theory with that of the Aristotelian philosophy, which indicated that leaders were born and not made and depending on the need a leader would surface. The limitations of trait theory are that leaders can not be developed through their skills and education (as cited in Murphy, 2005).

In contrast with trait theories, the behavioural methodology centered on the recognizable actions that made a person an effective leader. Personal Behaviour Theories discussed in the University of Michigan and Ohio State University studies identified two more Styles of Leadership: job-centered (task) and employee-centered (people). The job-centered (task-initiating structure) behaviour focuses on the leader taking control in order to get the job done and the employee-centered (people-consideration) behaviour focuses on the leader meeting the needs of employees and developing relationships (Lussier and Achua, 2004). The findings in the Michigan study indicated that leaders who were highly employee oriented and allowed participation fostered more productive teams. On the other hand, leaders who were more concerned about accomplishing tasks cultivated lower producing teams. The findings from the Ohio State University study emphasized the consideration and initiating structure as the two underlying structures found in the University of Michigan study.

The Ohio State University study concluded that both structures were separate components, but if a leader were dedicated in both they could achieve higher results. Research at the University of Iowa expounded on the studies above and identified two basic leadership styles: Autocratic and Democratic. These and other research studies asserted four (4) main leadership styles: concern for task, concern for people, Directive Leadership and Participative Leadership.

Fiedler (1967) explored the idea that there was not just one ultimate style of leadership for a given circumstance, but leaders would be more effective by varying their leadership style depending on the situations that faced them. Fiedler's Model based leadership styles on either being task or relationship oriented and the style use depended on whether the situation was one of leader-member relations, task structure or position power (as cited in Murphy, 2005).

Hersey and Blanchard theorized that the style of leadership was determined by the employee's perceptions. Hersey and Blanchard's theory expounded on Fiedler's model by creating four (4) leadership styles: Directing, Coaching, Supporting and Delegating. Building on the same principles of the contingency theories above, House (1971) suggested that the path- goal theory influences and motivates employee's views and opportunities. Employee contentment, accomplishment of goals and improved functioning would be derived from the leader's direction, training, guidance and support. Despite the findings of this research, Marquis and Huston (2000) disagreed and noted that situational theory focused on the situation rather than the interpersonal and intrapersonal factors. The following leadership styles are derivatives of the ones discussed above.

AUTOCRATIC LEADERSHIP

Merriam-Webster's Online Dictionary defines an autocrat as "a person (as a monarch) ruling with unlimited authority or one who has undisputed influence or power". This style of leadership is considered job-centered as identified by the University of Michigan and Ohio State University studies.

The job-centered (task-initiating structure) behaviour focuses on the leader taking control in order to get the job done quickly. It relies heavily on employees taking orders from the leader instead of the leader offering much clarification or dialogue (Professional Organizations, n.d.). According to a (University of Central Florida [UCF], (n.d.) study, employees are inspired through threat of correction and reprimand. The autocratic leadership style offers several advantages: swiftness of project completion keeps group members from producing alternatives that influence the minority negatively, guarantees the leader is heard and informs members when their conduct is undesirable. The disadvantages of the autocratic leadership style are: dissociates group members, non-development of employees and convenience of use instead of round tabling quandaries (Professional Organizations, n.d.). One might use this style of leadership when the group is in danger of not accomplishing a task in a timely manner or in a crisis situation.

LAISSEZ-FAIRE LEADERSHIP

The Laissez-Faire leadership style frequently has a negative connotation. This style of leadership depicts an inert leader who is averse to stimulating subordinates or giving focus.

The Laissezz Faire leadership style places an emphasis on the employee centered attribute that was discussed in the University of Michigan and Ohio State University studies (Professional Organizations, n.d.). Leaders who use this style fail their employees because they offer no positive or negative direction nor do they interfere at any time. According to Deluga (1990), Laissezz-Faire leaders renounce their leadership thus giving employees a wide spectrum of decision-making which could lead to amplifying their power and influence.

Another assessment of research reported these leaders shun goal-setting, opportunities to succeed, fail to coordinate organizational objectives, ignore responsibilities, and routinely avoid making decisions on important matters (van Eeden, Cilliers, and van Deventer, 2008). Leaders assume the employees will make decisions in a timely manner and handle whatever problems that arise (Professional Organizations, n.d.).

There are some advantages and disadvantages of using this style of leadership. It allows team members to develop a working relationship in an informal setting and generates an opportunity to be successful by making their own decisions. On the other hand, a team member can dominate and take control which could lead the team to make incorrect decisions and possibly have the team reprimanded which would lead to negativity within the group; affecting the process and their motivation (Professional Organizations, n.d.). This absence of leadership leads to nothing happening which promotes ineffective leadership.

PARTICIPATIVE (DEMOCRATIC) LEADERSHIP

A participative leader must have a pioneering, imaginative and adventuresome mindset in order to empower employees to make decisions involving the organization. Participative leaders empower their employees in the decision-making process by meeting with them periodically and listening and trusting them (UCF, n.d.). Wolf, Boland and Aukerman (1994b) defined empowerment as "the awareness of a person's potential talents, gifts, and power and how a person can contribute to the organization's goals (as cited in Thyer, 2003). Participative leadership requires and encourages participation from everyone and shares decision-making for the betterment of the organization. Employee motivation is derived through obtaining financial and self-image awards. Leaders reward employees through financial gains and positive evaluations which in turn increases motivation and morale.

The research contends there are some advantages and disadvantages to using this style of leadership. Skogan (2006) noted that leaders who allowed employees to participate in decision-making showed improvement in labour-management relations, encouraged employee commitment, enhanced community service, and diminished employee rejections of police restructuring (as cited in Steinheider and Wuestewald, 2008). Research provides a plethora of findings for implementing participative leadership such as: increased occupational contentment, organizational allegiance, an organizational ownership behaviour, apparent support, labour-management collaboration and employee performance (Steinheider and Wuestewald). Smith (2008) suggested that the police rank structure impeded this style of leadership. Furthermore, the police organizational system has embedded a culture of risk aversion by continuing in a hierarchical structure.

The researcher suggested that since the hierarchical system promoted employees to rank that it actually blocked participation at different levels within the organization due to a lack of trust or experience. Other researchers suggest that some have been left out of the decision-making process by allowing employees to participate at a suggestion level or their discretionary decision-making on the street. Labour unions have increased their control within the police organization, but have not been included in the decision-making process.

Flynn (2004) and Skogan (2004) contend these labour unions are not being asked to help in the decision-making process because of the hierarchical ethos of the police organization and the selfishness of the labour unions (as cited in Steinheider and Wuestewald, 2008). Ospina and Yaroni (2003) suggested that labour union representatives and police leaders only cooperate with each other when there is a critical situation (as cited in Steinheider and Wuestewald, 2008).

TRANSACTIONAL LEADERSHIP

Burns (1978) and Bass (1985) portrayed a transactional leader as one whom:

(1) recognizes what it is one wants to get from his/her work and tries to see that one gets what his/her wants if performance warrants it; (2) exchanges rewards and promises of reward for effort; and (3) is responsive to one's immediate self-interests if they can be met by getting the work done.

Bolden, Gosling, Marturano, and Dennison, (2003) presented that employees are inspired through the use of recompense and chastisement (as cited in Taylor, 2009). Taylor (2009) asserts that employees are held accountable regardless of competency or resource availability.

Transactional theories of leadership assert that people will follow leaders who are inspirational. The leader will develop a vision (possibly collaboratively), sell the vision and lead the way. van Eeden et al (2008) defined transactional leadership as a transactional process between the leader and employee. Hartog, Van Muijen and Koopman (1997) added that the leader-employee relationship not only involves exchanges, but bargaining as well. Deluga (1990) supported this by stating that leaders and/or employees can exercise a significant amount of control and influence over one another during this exchange and bargaining process.

Pettigrew (1972) and Mechanic (1962) stated "a leader's control over vital information or an employee's special skill in solving crucial organizational problems provides each participant leverage from which to negotiate" (as cited in Deluga, 1990). The overall success of the organization depends on whether the leader has the power to strengthen the process in which work is completed by staff (Jogulu and Wood, 2007). McGuire and Kennerly (2006) report that transactional leaders are only interested in maintaining the "status quo" for their organizations. Transactional leaders are known to establish performance specifications and make sure they are accomplished by a given deadline, limit the contentment of employees and create a low amount of employee commitment.

Transactional leadership is divided into three distinct processes that influence employees: active management by exception, passive management by exception and contingent reward (van Eeden et al., 2008). In the case of active management by exception, the leader looks for mistakes, indiscretions, exceptions, divergence from standards, complaints, infractions of policy and regulations, and failures and he or she takes corrective action before or when these occur.

A non-listening, reactive leader who does nothing to curb foreseeable errors or problems is considered to be leading by the passive management exception. Leaders identify the outcomes (reward or punishment) that will be bestowed based upon the employee's performance (van Eeden et al.). Leaders using contingency rewards engage the path-goal theory that was outlined by House (1971) because it rewards and motivates employees based on performance (Bass, 1997). Contingency rewards used in transactional leadership use contingency rewards for employees when they attain pre-set goals and objectives. Chan and Chan (2005) suggested employees receive rewards for accomplishments, proposals to augment pay and promotion, or praise for superior hard work. Webb (2007) contends that a leader who recognizes the attributes of their employees will assign tasks that will allow the employee to accomplish the mission and obtain their just reward which in turn will motivate them to do more. Webb (2007) indicated there was an optimistic association between contingent rewards and organizational results.

Transactional leadership has more shortcomings than merit. Rugieri (2009) contends that a transactional leader is more commanding, has high confidence and is usually more fixated on the job. Trott and Windsor (1999) stress that transactional leadership is best suited for group settings that are under crisis because it offers satisfaction through an urgent resolution. Medley and Larochelle (1995) noted the results with transactional leadership are not very valuable over time (as cited in Trott and Windsor, 1999). Although transactional leaders center on employee needs; they do not offer opportunities for obtaining motivation, job contentment or allegiance.

Generally the transactional leadership style is used mostly in organizations dominated by command and control procedures. Silvestri (2007) reported that employees in a transactional framework obtain their position within the structure through competition and conformity. Furthermore, police leaders continue to work within the transactional style and tend to be autocratic.

TRANSFORMATIONAL LEADERSHIP

According to Sullivan and Decker (1997), the transformational leader is not concerned with the status quo, rather with "effecting revolutionary change in organizations and human service" (as cited in Trott and Windsor, 1999). Bass (1996) defined transformational leadership as the ability of a leader to motivate employees to surpass their own individual aspirations for the greater good of the organization. Burns (1978) depicted the transformational leader as a morally responsible manager who focuses on developing the moral maturity, values, and standards of his or her subordinates and strengthening their devotion to serve the well-being of others, their organization, and society beyond self-interest (as cited in Olsen and Johnsen, 2006). Lowe, Kroeck, and Sivasubramaniam (1996) described the transformational leader as being pioneering and less likely to support the current situation, seeking opportunities in the face of risk, and attempting to mold and create rather than react to environmental conditions (as cited in van Eeden, et al, 2008). Van Eeden, et al (2008) added that a transformational leader is one who conveys a vision to inspire others, sets long-term goals and emphasizes social and interpersonal skills. The transforming leader looks for potential motives in employees, seeks to satisfy their needs and engages the full person of the follower.

Jogulu and Wood (2007) insinuated transformational leadership involves establishing oneself as a role model by gaining the trust and confidence of employees and to develop their staff by sanctioning and guiding them to excel beyond the organizational day-to-day obligations. A transformational leader could be categorized as a visionary, a futurist or a mechanism for change that assumes a proactive approach to management.

Bolden et al (2003) posed change as the key focus for transformational leadership (as cited in Taylor, 2009). Sofarelli and Brown (1998) suggested that a transformational leader must possess high self-esteem, self-regard and self-awareness to effectively transform organizations and employees (as cited in Murphy, 2005). Taylor (2009) described the following fundamental features of transformational leadership: build a shared vision, see the big picture and deal with convoluted issues, test thinking analytically, encourage involvement and motivation, share information and enable trust through team working, recognize contributions and celebrate accomplishments, create opportunities for incessant learning and support people's growth, including own; adaptable and able to deal with unexpected issues, role model through behaviours and goal setting, and network effectively (McNichol 2006, Shaw 2007).

Transformational leadership is based on four primary dynamics to influence the behaviours and attitudes of others: idealized influence ("charisma"), inspirational motivation, intellectual stimulation, and individualized consideration.

Bass (1985) regarded the charismatic component as idealized influence. Idealized influence implies the employees imitate their leader's behaviour and values and are committed to and make sacrifices for the leader's vision. In order for a leader to have idealized influence, an employee must be able to see that the leader is unfailing in word or deed and they actually stand for something they aspire to do and inspire their employees towards the same goal (Murphy and Drodge, 2004). Leaders with these attributes are highly admired, respected, trusted, and have a high level of self-confidence, self-esteem, and self-determination. They are usually regarded as role models and demonstrate high standards of ethical and moral conduct (Chan and Chan, 2005). Chan and Chan (2005) described inspirational motivation as the ability of leaders who can stimulate and inspire employees and colleagues by building self-assurance, filling and arousing enthusiasm and determination in the group. In general, this is the method of inspiring their vision and encouraging employees to implement it for the future growth of the organization. This type of leader provides symbols, metaphors, and simplified emotional appeals to increase awareness and understanding of mutually desired goals (Bass and Avolio, 1997). Murphy and Drodge (2003) pointed out that communicating the vision to everyone and reiterating it often was the key ingredient of inspirational motivation.

Bass et al (1987) describes intellectual stimulation as encouraging employees to think of creative ways to solve old problems, examining their own values and beliefs, and when suitable, those of their leader (as cited in Deluga, 1990). As a result, the employees can extend themselves with capabilities of discovering, examining, and resolving problems with a more liberated thought in order to survive rapidly changing organizational environments. Curtin (1995) confirmed this by suggesting that employees welcome new experiences as long as they are not intimidated. Employees want to be included in the decision-making process and know that their views are valued and desired.

Webb (2007) described individual consideration as the need employees have for personal appreciation and the need to acknowledge the unique strengths and skills of each employee in an organization. Chan and Chan (2005) agreed and believed if leaders acted as coaches or mentors, and gave particular attention to individual employees' needs for personal growth, advancement, and achievement it would foster mutual trust and effect a positive impact on satisfaction with the leaders, as well as overall productivity. Murphy and Drodge (2003) claimed a vital aspect of individual consideration is assigning jobs to employees that offer opportunities to obtain enthusiasm for what they are doing and providing the necessary tools to accomplish it.

The literature reviewed pointed out some benefits and drawbacks in using the transformational leadership style. Taylor (2009) reasoned that transformational leaders place an emphasis on team building, and empowering and developing potential in order to reach long-term goals. Thyer (2003) reported a transformational leader creates a collaborative learning environment, improves morale, embraces accountability and conflict resolution, proactive towards change management, ignites communication and supports empowerment. These leaders also facilitate employees towards motivation and being involved in the vision they produce. Webb (2007) noted an advantage of transformational leadership is having highly motivated and satisfied employees. Montana and Charnov (1993) stated these employees displayed a decrease in occurrences of absenteeism and an escalation in production while on the job (as cited in Webb, 2007). In turn, Yukl (2003) claimed employees who distinguish their leader as caring for the interests of each individual worker, are likely to exhibit increased allegiance, confidence, and to have a stronger sense of emotional well-being.

When these issues are present, leaders tend to preserve a higher level of prominence in the organization and the organization has a tendency for greater production (as cited in Webb, 2007).

Silvestri (2007) added that transformational leaders have a capability of infusing a higher degree of passion into leadership by engaging employees and making them feel appreciated. Murphy (2005) agreed and pointed out that transformational leaders could achieve this passion by motivating and energizing employees to pursue goals, visions and the empowering culture. If transformational leaders are passionate about appreciating their employees this will provide them with opportunities to grow and develop. Sheldon and Parker (1997) believe, if a leader effectively empowers employees, it develops an atmosphere of joint trust, increases job contentment, and promotes dedication to the organizational goals which culminates in the delivery of quality service (as cited in Murphy, 2005). Bass (1990) reported that transformational leaders motivated employees to perform past their expectations (as cited in Adebayo, 2004).

Silvestri (2007) insisted that since the police organization culture is rank-oriented it presents significant limitations for those employees wishing to implement alternative, transformative ways of working that require more open and participatory forms of engagement and interaction with colleagues. The ability of the police organization to integrate a transformative style of working then becomes increasingly problematic. Transformative leaders can be seen as being ineffectual and lenient. Another problem seen by many researchers is the culture of police management demands speedy judgements and good decision makers; the transformational approach takes too long and is therefore alleged to be unsuccessful (Silvestri). Sofarelli and Brown (1998) refuted the advantages of the transformational leadership style because it tends to interrupt a balanced and organized method of doing work (as cited in Murphy, 2005).

Wuestewald and Steinheider (2006) and Adebayo (2004) claimed the transformational leader can institute a vision that will move the organization towards the future and an authentic caring environment and procure employee support via idealized influence (charisma), inspirational motivation, intellectual stimulation and individualized consideration. The use of transformational leadership is gaining momentum because it is directly in contention with the outdated autocratic unilateral style of leadership that has been forced on employees for many years. Bass (1990) argued that the doctrine of transformational leadership related to all organizational levels (as cited in Kane and Tremble, 2000). Curtin (1995) stated the transformational leader:

Does not simply strike a fair bargain with people; he/she adds something more by calling them to a higher value, which in turn, increases their self-worth as they learn to value their own contributions to the accomplishment of a mission. Burns (1978) contended that transformational leaders could lead their employees to a higher level of needs that was outlined in Maslow's hierarchy of needs. This was done by increasing the employee's level of knowledge in achieving valued conclusions, a vision and the plan to accomplish these traits. It also involved employees exceeding their own concerns for the sake of the team or organization and raising their awareness to enhance themselves and what they want to achieve (as cited in Chan and Chan, 2005). This style of leadership can possibly turn employees into leaders and leaders into change agents. Transformational leadership qualities are learned from leaders accepting their own mistakes (Murphy). Silvestri (2007) suggested that leaders using the transformational style of leadership not only affected their employees, but it spilled over into the community as well.

This was accomplished by having motivated officers that related better to the community they served. Murphy and Drodge (2003) sum transformational leadership as follows: The key point here is that a police organisation's explicit values must reflect the core values of the broader society which the organisation serves, and that police leaders must demonstrate the utmost respect for those values both personally and professionally to be truly transformational.

9

Leadership and the Qualities of a Leader

WHAT IS LEADERSHIP?

Leadership can be described as the ability of an individual to influence, motivate, and enable others to contribute towards the effectiveness and success of an organization or group of which they are members. A person who can bring about change, therefore, is one who has this ability to be a leader.

WHAT QUALITIES DOES A LEADER POSSESS?

Leaders possess a number of common qualities:

- *Self-awareness:* Knowledge of your own values, passions, skills, strengths and weaknesses, an ability to admit and learn from mistakes and to seek information to fill knowledge gaps.
- *Integrity:* A strong sense of "what is right" and a demonstration of ethical practices that sets the tone for others. A commitment to teaching by example.
- *Courage:* The strength to act in accordance with your own values and the greater good despite pressures pushing you in other directions. The ability to put the cause before the desire to be popular.
- *Confidence:* A belief in your ability to meet most challenges that come your way.
- *Vision:* A strong sense of where you are going as a person and where you think society, your community and your organization should be going – and how it might get there.
- *Enthusiasm:* A lively interest in the people, issues and events around you, a feeling of excitement about the possibilities, and the energy to guide them towards fruition.
- *Innovation:* The ability to "think outside the box;" take risks and develop new and effective solutions to old and emerging problems.
- *Wisdom:* Intelligence coupled with insight and empathy, as opposed to raw intelligence.
- *Adaptability:* A willingness to be flexible and to respond quickly and

effectively to changing circumstances, along with a commitment to continual learning – formal and informal – and the ability to put that learning into practice.

- *Strong inter-personal skills:* An ability to interact and work harmoniously with others, while being prepared to take on individual responsibilities.
- *Effective communication:* A willingness and ability to listen to and understand the thoughts, ideas and concerns of others and to clearly communicate your own. A vision is nothing if it can't be sold to others.
- *Belief in others:* The desire to build the capabilities of others, praise them where appropriate, go into bat for them when appropriate, provide them with helpful feedback and motivate them to do their best.
- *Peer respect:* An ability to inspire respect, allowing a person to capably lead discussions, maintain discipline and encourage the contribution of others.
- *Insight:* The ability to see the big picture, a strong sense the stage attained by followers and intuits problems before they arise or before they become insurmountable.
- *Sense of humour:* The ability to laugh at yourself and relieve tense or stressful situations with humour
- *Competence:* Others are unlikely to follow the lead of a person who does not appear to know what s/he is doing.
- *Delegation skills:* A willingness to trust others and cede some responsibility.
- *Spiritual sensitivity:* Is the key to a better communication with others, but primarily towards a better understanding of privacy. It marks your positive attitude in life, determines you to seek and to focus on what it is right and not on what it is wrong. Also, it indicates that you are a wonderful person with a rich spiritual life.

LEADERSHIP STYLES

Here we will look at 4 styles of leadership known as democratic, autocratic, laissez-faire, and charismatic. We will consider the advantages and disadvantages or both of each style.

DEMOCRATIC

The democratic leader makes decisions by consulting a team, whilst still maintaining control of the group. The democratic leader allows the team to decide how the task will be tackled and who will perform which task. A good democratic leader encourages participation but never loses sight of the fact that they bear the responsibility of leadership. The democratic leader values group discussion and input from the team. The democratic leader motivates the team by empowering them to direct themselves. The leader and group jointly analyse the problem, and decide together on a course of action. The leader does some things, but not everything, helps the group get its way, pulls with the group and respects others.

Disadvantages:

- Slower decision making
- Less initial production
- Leader can be unsure and makes everything a matter for group discussion.

Advantages:

- More individual responsibility
- More friendliness
- Better implementation
- More personal growth
- More motivation
- Greater ultimate production

AUTOCRATIC

The autocratic leader dominates team members and makes decisions on their own without seeking or allowing input from group members. Autocrats set timelines, tasks and then asks for suggestions/ objections. They are quick to both praise and punish. This results in passive resistance from team members and requires continual pressure in order to get things done. Some instances call for urgent action and the autocratic style may be best. Most people are familiar with autocratic leadership and accept it.

Disadvantages:

- More group hostility
- More dependence on leader
- More apathy in group
- Slower execution of decisions

Advantages:

- More group productivity while leader watches
- Group makes quicker decisions
- Often does the task themselves as it is quicker
- Pushes the group.

Disadvantage/ Advantage:

- Some people are happy to be told what to do – they might say they are patricians or 'nuts and bolts' people, others like to own the task – visionaries.

LAISSEZ-FAIRE

The Laissez Fare leader performs a minimum of leadership functions and lets the group sort out their own roles and tackle their own work in their own way without his participation. The Laissez-Fare technique is usually only appropriate when leading a team of highly motivated and skilled people who have produced excellent work in the past. Once a leader has established that his team is confident, capable and motivated it is often best to step back and let them get on with the task since interfering can generate resentment and detract from their effectiveness.

Disadvantages:

- Less group satisfaction
- Less group productivity
- Poorer quality of work
- Less personal growth
- Jobs fall back on someone else or are not completed
- Who takes credit or blame?

Advantages:

- No work for the leader
- Frustration may force others into leadership roles
- Allows the visionary worker the opportunity to do what they want, free from interference
- Empowers the group

CHARISMATIC

Charismatic leaders tend to be very good listeners and great information gatherers. They like to expose themselves to a wide range of individuals in order to get new ideas. Charismatic leaders create a sense of purpose for their organisation that is motivating and inspiring. Charismatic leaders express things simply so that everyone gets it, they use positive language, often use stories, symbols, metaphors to get their point across. They walk the talk, show empathy, remain optimistic, make everyone feel important and build confidence. Charismatic leaders question the status quo, take risks and thrive on innovation and change.

Disadvantages:

- Can be spectacular failures
- Create a personality cult
- Can wear out the workers

Advantages:

- Work usually done well
- Workers inspired to perform
- Workers valued.

AUTHORITARIAN LEADERSHIP STYLE

An authoritarian leadership style is being used when a leader dictates policies and procedures, decides what goals are to be achieved, and directs and controls all activities without any meaningful participation by the subordinates.

This leader has full control of the team leaving low autonomy within the group. The leader has a vision in mind and must be able to effectively motivate their group to finish the task. The group is expected to complete the tasks under very close supervision while unlimited authority is granted to the leader. Subordinate's responses to the orders given are either punished or rewarded.

BACKGROUND

Authoritarian leaders are commonly referred to as autocratic leaders. They sometimes, but not always, provide clear expectations for what needs to be done, when it should be done, and how it should be done. There is also a clear divide between the leader and the followers. Authoritarian leaders make decisions independently with little or no input from the rest of the group. Authoritarian leaders uphold stringent control over their followers by directly regulating rules, methodologies, and actions. Authoritarian leaders construct gaps and build distance between themselves and their followers with the intention of stressing role distinctions. This type of leadership dates back to the earliest tribes and empires. It is often used in present day when there is little room for error, such as construction jobs or manufacturing jobs. Authoritarian leadership typically fosters little creativity in decision-making. Lewin also found that it is more difficult to move from an authoritarian style to a democratic style than from a democratic form to an authoritarian form of leadership. Abuse of this style is usually viewed as controlling, bossy and dictatorial. Authoritarian leadership is best applied to situations where there is little time for group discussion.

VIEWS OF AUTHORITARIAN LEADERS

A common belief of many authoritarian leaders is that followers require direct supervision at all times or else they would not operate effectively. This belief is in accordance with one of Douglas McGregor's philosophical views of humankind, Theory X. This theory proposes that it is a leaders role to coerce and control followers, because people have an inherent aversion for work and will abstain from it whenever possible. Theory X also postulates that people must be compelled through force, intimidation or authority, and controlled, directed, or threatened with punishment in order to get them to accomplish the organizational needs. In the minds of authoritarian leaders, people who are left to work autonomously will ultimately be unproductive. "Examples of authoritarian communicative behaviour include a police officer directing traffic, a teacher ordering a student to do his or her assignment, and a supervisor instructing a subordinate to clean a workstation."

Communication Patterns of Authoritarian Leadership:

- Downward, one-way communication (*i.e.* leaders to followers, or supervisors to subordinates)
- Controls discussion with followers

- Dominates interaction
- Independently/unilaterally sets policy and procedures
- Individually directs the completion of tasks
- Does not offer constant feedback
- Rewards acquiescent obedient behaviour and punishes erroneous actions
- Poor listener
- Uses conflict for individual gain

Ways to Properly Incorporate Authoritarian Leadership:

- Always explain rules- it allows your subordinates to complete the task you want done efficiently.
- Be consistent- if you are to enforce rules and regulations, make sure to do so regularly so your subordinates take you seriously. This will form a stronger level of trust.
- Respect your subordinates - always recognize your subordinates' efforts and achievements.
- Educate your subordinates before enforcing rules - do not present them with any surprises. This can lead to problems in the future due to false communication.
- Listen to suggestions from your subordinates, even if you do not incorporate them.

Effects of Authoritarian Leadership Communication Styles:

- Increase in productivity when leader is present
- Produces more accurate solutions when leader is knowledgeable
- Is more positively accepted in larger groups
- Enhances performance on simple tasks and decreases performance on complex tasks
- Increases aggression levels among followers
- Increases turnover rates
- Successful when there is a time urgency for completion of projects
- Improves the future work of those subordinates whose skills are not very applicable or helpful without the demands of another

Downfalls of Authoritarian Leadership:

- Long term use can cause resentment from subordinates. Use this form of leadership sparingly and when absolutely necessary
- It has been found by researchers that these type of leaders lack creative problem solving skills
- Without proper instruction and understanding from subordinates, confusion may arise

EXAMPLES OF AUTHORITARIAN LEADERS

Engelbert Dollfuss, chancellor of Austria from 1932 to 1934, destroyed the Austrian Republic and established an authoritarian regime based on conservative Roman Catholic and Italian Fascist principles. In May of 1932 when he became chancellor, Dollfuss headed a conservative coalition led by the Christian Social Party. When faced with a severe economic crisis caused by the Great Depression, Dollfuss decided against joining Germany in a customs union, a course advocated by many Austrians. Severely criticized by Social Democrats, Pan-German nationalists, and Austrian Nazis, he countered by drifting towards an increasingly authoritarian regime.

The Italian leader Benito Mussolini became Dollfuss' principal foreign ally. Italy guaranteed Austrian independence at Riccione, but in return Austria had to abolish all political parties and reform its constitution on the Fascist model. In March 1933, Dollfuss' attacks on Parliament culminated that September in the permanent abolition of the legislature and the formation of a corporate state based on his Vaterländische Front ("Fatherland Front"); with which he expected to replace Austria's political parties.

In foreign affairs he steered a course that converted Austria virtually into an Italian satellite state. Hoping therewith to prevent Austria's incorporation into Nazi Germany, he fought his domestic political opponents along fascist-authoritarian lines.

In February 1934 paramilitary formations loyal to the chancellor crushed Austria's Social Democrats. With a new constitution of May 1934, his regime became completely dictatorial. In June, however, Germany incited the Austrian Nazis to civil war. Dollfuss was assassinated by the Nazis in a raid on the chancellery.

Adolf Hitler was extremely authoritarian. He required the population of the Third Reich to accept everything that he said as absolute law, and was able to impose a death sentence on anyone who failed to do so. Hitler was obsessed with being in control, and with being the alpha male in a rigid male dominance hierarchy. Martha Stewart constructed her empire through her own special attention to every detail.

She was meticulous, demanding, thorough and scrupulous. She flourished in her ventures and in using her authoritarian leadership style. John F. Kennedy had a vision to change the space programme forever - by sending a man to the moon and to return safely. This type of vision and idea came to light through his constant motivation of the U.S. to see his vision. This shows he was an authoritarian leader due to his motivation and direct contribution to how it was going to be accomplished.

Autocratic leadership style works well if the leader is competent and knowledgeable enough to decide about each and everything. Authoritative is considered one of the most effective leadership styles in case there is some emergency and quick decisions need to be taken. Bill Gates adopted this style and has steered Microsoft towards great success. According to Bill Gates, he had a vision when he took reins of the company and then used all the resources available to make that vision a reality.In the personal computer workplace, many operating conditions call for urgent action, making this style of leadership effective. While Gates does not exhibit this style consistently, his success can be judged by his decision making process and the growth of the computer industry in the world.

TRAIT LEADERSHIP

Trait leadership is defined as integrated patterns of personal characteristics that reflect a range of individual differences and foster consistent leader effectiveness across a variety of group and organizational situations (Zaccaro, Kemp, and Bader, 2004). The theory of trait leadership developed from early leadership research which focused primarily on finding a group of heritable attributes that differentiated leaders from non-leaders. Leader effectiveness refers to the amount of influence a leader has on individual or group performance, followers' satisfaction, and overall effectiveness (Derue, Nahrgang, Wellman, and Humphrey, 2011).

Many scholars have argued that leadership is unique to only a select number of individuals and that these individuals possess certain immutable traits that cannot be developed. Although this perspective has been criticized immensely over the past century, scholars still continue to study the effects of personality traits on leader effectiveness. Research has demonstrated that successful leaders differ from other people and possess certain core personality traits that significantly contribute to their success. Understanding the importance of these core personality traits that predict leader effectiveness can help organizations with their leader selection, training, and development practices (Derue et al., 2011).

HISTORY OF RESEARCH ON TRAIT LEADERSHIP

The emergence of the concept of trait leadership looks back to Thomas Carlyle's "great man" theory, which stated: "The History of the World [...] was the Biography of Great Men." Subsequent commentators interpreted this view to conclude that the forces of extraordinary leadership shape history (Judge, Piccolo, and Kosalka, 2009). Influenced by Carlyle, Francis Galton in Hereditary Genius (1869) took this idea further.

Galton found that leadership was a unique property of extraordinary individuals, and suggested that the traits which leaders possessed were immutable and could not be developed. Throughout the early 1900s, the study of leadership focused on traits. Cowley (1931) commented that the approach to the research of leadership has usually been and should always be through the study of traits.

Many theorists, influenced by Carlyle and Galton, believed that trait leadership depended on the personal qualities of the leader; however, they did not assume that leadership only resides within a select number of people (Judge, Bono, Ilies, and Gerhardt, 2002). This trait perspective of leadership was widely accepted until the late 1940s and early 1950s, when researchers began to deem personality traits insufficient in predicting leader effectiveness (Stogdill, 1948; Mann, 1959).

In 1948, Stogdill stated that leadership exists between persons in a social situation, and that persons who are leaders in one situation may not necessarily be leaders in other situations. This statement has been cited ubiquitously as sounding the death knell for trait-leadership theory. Furthermore, scholars commented that any trait's effect on leadership behaviour will always depend on the situation (Huges, Ginnett, and Curphy, 1996; Yukl and Van Fleet, 1992). Subsequently, leadership stopped being characterized by individual differences, and behavioural and situational analyses of leadership took over and began to dominate the field of leadership research. During this period of widespread rejection, several dominant theories took the place of trait leadership theory, including Fiedler's (1967) contingency model, Blake and Mouton's (1964) managerial grid, Hersey and Blanchard's (1969) situational leadership model, and transformational and transactional leadership models (Avolio, Sosik, Jung, and Berson, 2003; Bass, 1985; Podsakoff, MacKenzie, Moorman, and Fetter, 1990).

Despite the growing criticisms of trait leadership, the purported basis for the rejection of trait-leadership models began to encounter strong challenges (Kenny and Zaccaro, 1983; Lord, DeVader, and Alliger, 1986) in the 1980s. Interestingly, Zaccaro (2007) pointed out that even Stogdill's (1948) review, although cited as evidence against leader traits, contained conclusions supporting that individual differences could still be predictors of leader effectiveness.3

With an increasing number of empirical studies directly supporting trait leadership (Judge et al., 2002; Judge, Colbert, and Ilies, 2004), traits have reemerged in the lexicon of the scientific research into leadership. In recent years, the research about leader traits has made some progress in identifying a list of personality traits that are highly predictive of leader effectiveness. Additionally, to account for the arguments for situational leadership, researchers have used the round-robin design methodology to test whether certain individuals emerge as leaders across multiple situations (Kenny and Zaccaro, 1983).

Scholars have also proposed new ways of studying the relationship of certain traits to leader effectiveness. For instance, many suggest the integration of trait and behavioural theories to understand how traits relate to leader effectiveness (Derue et al., 2011). Furthermore, scholars have expanded their focus and have proposed looking at more malleable traits (ones susceptible to development) in addition to the traditional dispositional traits as predictors of leader effectiveness. Context is only now beginning to be examined as a contributor to leaders' success and failure. Productive narcissistic CEOs like Steven Jobs of Apple and Jack Welch of GE have demonstrated a gift for creating innovation, whereas leaders with idealized traits prove more successful in more stable environments requiring less innovation and creativity.

LEADER TRAITS

The investigations of leader traits are always by no means exhaustive. In recent years, several studies have made comprehensive reviews about leader traits which have been historically studied (Derue et al., 2011; Hoffman et al., 2011; Judge et al., 2009; Zaccaro, 2007). There are many ways that traits related to leadership can be categorized; however, the two most recent categorizations have organized traits into (1) demographic vs. task competence vs. interpersonal and (2) distal (trait-like) vs. proximal (state-like). Both these categorizations are described below.

DEMOGRAPHIC, TASK COMPETENCE AND INTERPERSONAL LEADERSHIP

Based on a recent review of the trait leadership literature, Derue and others (2011) stated that most leader traits can be organized into three categories: demographic, task competence, and interpersonal attributes. For the demographics category, gender has by far received the most attention in terms of leadership; however, most scholars have found that male and female leaders are both equally effective. Task competence relates to how individuals approach the execution and performance of tasks. Hoffman grouped intelligence, Conscientiousness, Openness to Experience, and Emotional Stability into this category. Lastly, interpersonal attributes are related to how a leader approaches social interactions. According to Hoffman and others (2011), Extraversion and Agreeableness should be grouped into this category.

DISTAL (TRAIT-LIKE) VS. PROXIMAL (STATE-LIKE)

Recent research has shifted from focusing solely on distal (dispositional/trait-like) characteristics of leaders to more proximal (malleable/state-like) individual differences often in the form of knowledge and skills (Hoffman et al., 2011).

The hope is that emergence of proximal traits in trait leadership theory will help researchers answer the ancient question: are leaders born or made? Proximal individual differences suggest that the characteristics that distinguish effective leaders from non-effective leaders are not necessarily stable through the life-span, implying that these traits may be able to be developed. Hoffman and others (2011) examined the effects of distal vs. proximal traits on leader effectiveness.

He found that distal individual differences of achievement motivation, energy, flexibility, dominance, honesty/integrity, self-confidence, creativity, and charisma were strongly correlated with leader effectiveness. Additionally, he found that the proximal individual differences of interpersonal skills, oral communication, written communication, management skills, problem solving skills, and decision making were also strongly correlated with leader effectiveness. His results suggested that on average, distal and proximal individual differences have a similar relationship with effective leadership (Hoffman et al., 2011).

TRAIT-LEADERSHIP MODEL

Zaccaro and colleagues (2004) created a model to understand leader traits and their influence on leader effectiveness/performance. This model, shown in the figure below, is based on other models of leader traits and leader effectiveness/performance (Mumford, Zaccaro, Harding, Fleishman, and Reiter-Palmon, 1993; Mumford, Zaccaro, Harding, et al., 2000) and rests on two basic premises about leader traits. The first premise is that leadership emerges from the combined influence of multiple traits as opposed to emerging from the independent assessment of traits.

Zaccaro (2001) argued that effective leadership is derived from an integrated set of cognitive abilities, social capabilities, and dispositional tendencies, with each set of traits adding to the influence of the other. The second premise is that leader traits differ in their proximal influence on leadership.

This model is a multistage one in which certain distal attributes (*i.e.* dispositional attributes, cognitive abilities, and motives/values) serve as precursors for the development of proximal personal characteristics. Adopting this categorization approach and based on several comprehensive reviews/ meta-analysis of trait leadership in recent years, we tried to make an inclusive list of leader traits. However, the investigations of leader traits are always by no means exhaustive.

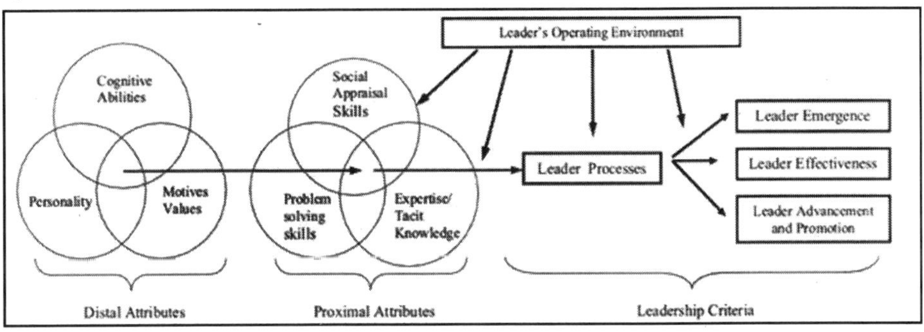

Table. Leader Traits based on Zaccaro's (2004) Model.

Extraversion (Distal - Dispositional)	One dimension of Big-Five Personality Model; represents the tendency to be sociable, assertive, active, and to experience positive affects, such as energy and zeal. In Judge and other's (2002) meta-analysis, Extraversion was significantly positively related to leadership (r = .31).
Agreeableness (Distal - Dispositional)	One dimension of Big-Five Personality Model; refers to the tendency to be trusting, compliant, caring, and gentle. The relationship between Agreeableness and leadership is still ambiguous. In Judge and other's (2002) meta-analysis, Agreeableness was not significantly related to leadership (r = .08).
Conscientiousness(Distal - Dispositional)	One dimension of Big-Five Personality Model; it comprises two related facets, namely achievement and dependability. In Judge and other's (2002) meta-analysis, Conscientiousness was significantly positively related to leadership (r = .28).
Openness (Distal - Dispositional)	One dimension of Big-Five Personality Model; the disposition to be imaginative, nonconforming, unconventional, and autonomous. In Judge and other's (2002) meta-analysis, Openness was found to be significantly positively related with leadership (r = .24).
Neuroticism (Distal - Dispositional)	One dimension of Big-Five Personality Model; represents the tendency to exhibit poor emotional adjustment and experience negative affects, such as anxiety, insecurity, and hostility. In Judge and other's (2002) meta-analysis, Neuroticism was significantly negatively correlated with (r = -.24).
Honesty/integrity (Distal - Dispositional)	Defined as the correspondence between work and deed, and as being truthful and non deceitful . In Hoffman and other's (2011) meta analysis, honesty/integrity was found to be positively related to leadership effectiveness (r = .29).
Charisma (Distal - Dispositional)	Charismatic leaders are able to influence followers by articulating a compelling vision for the future, arousing commitment to organizational objectives and inspiring commitment and a sense of self-efficacy among followers. Hoffman and others (2011) found it has a significant influence on leadership (r = .57).
Intelligence (Distal - Cognitive Abilities)	Intelligence is regarded as the most important trait in psychology. It has been identified as one of the most critical traits that must be possessed by all leaders (Judge et al., 2004).
Creativity (Distal - Cognitive Abilities)	Creativity has been proposed as an important component of effective leadership; Hoffman and others (2011) found a significant relationship between creativity and leader effectiveness (r = .31).
Achievement motivation (Distal - Motive/Value)	The motivation to achieve has been proved to have significant relationship with leader effectiveness (r = .23) (Judge et al., 2002).
Need for power(Distal - Motive/Value)	Characterized by the satisfaction leaders derive from exerting influence over the attitudes and behaviors of others. Need for power has a positive relationship with leader effectiveness (McClelland & Boyatzis, 1982).
Oral/written communication (Proximal - Social Skills)	Oral and written communication skills are found to be significantly correlated with leader effectiveness (Hoffman et al., 2011).
Interpersonal skills(Proximal - Social Skills)	Including a broad range of skills associated with un understanding of human behavior and the dynamics of groups (Locke, 1991; Yukl, 2006), interpersonal skills were found to be significantly correlated with leader effectiveness (Hoffman et al., 2011).
General problem solving(Proximal - Problem Solving)	General problem solving skills were found to be one of the factors most strongly correlated with leader effectiveness (Hoffman et al., 2011).
Decision	Decision skills were also found to be one of the factors most strongly

OTHER MODELS OF TRAIT LEADERSHIP

Multiple models have been proposed to explain the relationship of traits to leader effectiveness. Recently, integrated trait leadership models were put forward by summarizing the historical findings and reconciling the conflict between traits and other factors such as situations in determining effective leadership. In addition to Zaccaro's Model of Leader Attributes and Leader Performance described in the previous section, two other models have emerged in recent trait leadership literature. The Leader Trait Emergence Effectiveness (LTEE) Model, created by Judge and colleagues (2009), combines the behavioural genetics and evolutionary psychology theories of how personality traits are developed into a model that explains leader emergence and effectiveness.

Additionally, this model separates objective and subjective leader effectiveness into different criterion. The authors created this model to be broad and flexible as to diverge from how the relationship between traits and leadership had been studied in past research. Another model that has emerged in the trait leadership literature is the Integrated Model of Leader Traits, Behaviours, and Effectiveness (Derue et al., 2011). This model combines traits and behaviours in predicting leader effectiveness and tested the mediation effect of leader behaviours on the relationship between leader traits and effectiveness. The authors found that some types of leader behaviours mediated the effect between traits and leader effectiveness. The results of Derue and colleagues' (2011) study supported an integrated trait-behavioural model that can be used in future research.

CRITICISMS OF TRAIT LEADERSHIP

Although there has been an increased focus by researchers on trait leadership, this theory remains one of the most criticized theories of leadership. Over the years, many reviewers of trait leadership theory have commented that this approach to leadership is "too simplistic" (Conger and Kanugo, 1998), and "futile" (House and Aditya, 1997). Additionally, scholars have noted that trait leadership theory usually only focuses on how leader effectiveness is perceived by followers (Lord et al., 1986) rather than a leader's actual effectiveness (Judge et al., 2009). Because the process through which personality predicts the actual effectiveness of leaders has been relatively unexplored, these scholars have concluded that personality currently has low explanatory and predictive power over job performance and cannot help organizations select leaders who will be effective (Morgeson and Ilies, 2007). Furthermore, Derue and colleagues (2011) found that leader behaviours are more predictive of leader effectiveness than are traits.

Another criticism of trait leadership is its silence on the influence of the situational context surrounding leaders. Stogdill (1948) found that persons who are leaders in one situation may not be leaders in another situation. Complimenting this situational theory of leadership, Murphy (1941) wrote that leadership does not reside in the person, and it usually requires examining the whole situation. In addition to situational leadership theory, there has been growing support for other leadership theories such as transformational, transactional, charismatic, and authentic leadership theories. These theories have gained popularity because they are more normative than the trait and behavioural leadership theories.

Further criticisms include the failure of studies to uncover a trait or group of traits that are consistently associated with leadership emergence or help differentiate leaders from followers (Kenny and Zacarro, 1983). Additionally, trait leadership's focus on a small set of personality traits and neglect of more malleable traits such as social skills and problem solving skills has received considerable criticism. Lastly, trait leadership often fails to consider the integration of multiple traits when studying the effects of traits on leader effectiveness.

IMPLICATIONS FOR PRACTICE

Given the recent increase in evidence and support of trait leadership theory, scholars have suggested a variety of strategies for human resource departments within organizations. Companies should use personality traits as selection tools for identifying emerging leaders. These companies, however, should be aware of the individual traits that predict success in leader effectiveness as well as the traits that could be detrimental to leader effectiveness. For example, while Derue and colleagues (2011) found that individuals who are high in Conscientiousness, Extraversion, and Agreeableness are predicted to be more likely to be perceived as successful in leadership positions, Judge, Woolf, Hurst, and Livingston (2006) wrote that individuals who are high in narcissism are more likely to be a liability in certain jobs. Narcissism is just one example of a personality trait that should be explored further by HR practitioners to ensure they are not placing individuals with certain traits in the wrong positions.

Complementing the suggestion that personality traits should be used as selection tools, Judge and colleagues (2002) found that the Big Five Personality traits were more strongly related to leadership than intelligence. This finding suggests that selecting leaders based on their personality is more important than selecting them based on intelligence. If organizations select leaders based on intelligence, it is recommended by Judge and colleagues (2002) that these individuals be placed in leadership positions when the stress level is low and the individual has the ability to be directive.

Another way in which HR practitioners can use the research on trait leadership is for leadership development programmes. Although inherent personality traits (distal/trait-like) are relatively immune to leadership development, Zaccaro (2007) suggested that proximal traits (state-like) will be more malleable and susceptible to leadership development programmes. Companies should use different types of development interventions to stretch the existing capabilities of their leaders.

There is also evidence to suggest that Americans have an Extrovert Ideal, which dictates that people, most times unconsciously, favour the traits of extroverted individuals and suppress the qualities unique to introverts. Susan Cain's research points to a transition sometime around the turn of the century during which we stopped evaluating our leaders based on character and began judging them instead based on personality. While both extroverted and introverted leaders have been shown to be effective, we have a general proclivity towards extroverted traits, which when evaluating trait leadership, could skew our perception of what's important.

TASK-ORIENTED AND RELATIONSHIP- ORIENTED LEADERSHIP

Task-oriented (or task-focused) leadership is a behavioural approach in which the leader focuses on the tasks that need to be performed in order to meet certain goals, or to achieve a certain performance standard. Relationship-oriented (or relationship-focused) leadership is a behavioural approach in which the leader focuses on the satisfaction, motivation and the general well-being of the team members. Task-oriented and relationship-oriented leadership are two models that are often compared, as they are known to produce varying outcomes under different circumstances.

QUALITIES OF TASK-ORIENTED LEADERSHIP

Task-oriented leaders focus on getting the necessary task, or series of tasks, at hand in order to achieve a goal. These leaders are typically less concerned with the idea of catering to employees, and more concerned with finding the step-by-step solution required to meet specific goals. They will often actively define the work and the roles required, put structures in place, and plan, organize, and monitor progress within the team.

The advantages of task-oriented leadership is that it ensures that deadlines are met and jobs are completed, and it's especially useful for team members who don't manage their time well. Additionally, these types of leaders will tend to exemplify strong understanding of how to get the job done by focusing on the necessary workplace procedures, thus can delegate work accordingly in order to ensure that everything gets done in a timely and productive manner.

However, because task-oriented leaders don't tend to think much about their team's well-being, this approach can suffer many of the flaws of autocratic leadership, including causing motivation and retention problems.

QUALITIES OF RELATIONSHIP-ORIENTED LEADERSHIP

Relationship-oriented leaders are focused on supporting, motivating and developing the people on their teams and the relationships within. This style of leadership encourages good teamwork and collaboration, through fostering positive relationships and good communication. Relationship-oriented leaders prioritize the welfare of everyone in the group, and will place time and effort in meeting the individual needs of everyone involved. This may involve offering incentives like bonuses, providing mediation to deal with workplace or classroom conflicts, having more casual interactions with team members to learn about their strengths and weaknesses, creating a non-competitive and transparent work environment, or just leading in a personable or encouraging manner.

The benefits of relationship-oriented leadership is that team members are in a setting where the leader cares about their well-being. Relationship-oriented leaders understand that building positive productivity requires a positive environment where individuals feel driven. Personal conflicts, dissatisfaction with a job, resentment and even boredom can severely drive down productivity, so these types of leaders put people first to ensure that such problems stay at a minimum. Additionally, team members may be more willing to take risks, because they know that the leader will provide the support if needed.

The downside of relationship-oriented leadership is that, if taken too far, the development of team chemistry may detract from the actual tasks and goals at hand. The term "people-oriented" is used synonymously, whilst in a business setting, this approach may also be referred to as "employee-oriented".

TASK-ORIENTED VS. RELATIONSHIP-ORIENTED LEADERSHIP

In the 1940s, research in leadership began straying away from identifying individual leadership traits, to analyzing the effects of certain leadership behaviours - predominantly task-oriented and relationship-oriented leadership. The table below compares task-oriented and relationship-oriented leadership styles side-by-side:

Task-Oriented	Relationship-Oriented
Emphasis on work facilitation	Emphasis on interaction facilitation
Focus on structure, roles and tasks	Focus on relationships, well-being and motivation
Produce desired results is a priority	Foster positive relationships is a priority
Emphasis on goal-setting and a clear plan to achieve goals	Emphasis on team members and communication within
Strict use of schedules and step-by-step plans, and a punishment/incentive system	Communication facilitation, casual interactions and frequent team meetings

Mixed conclusions have risen from studies that try to determine the effects of task-oriented and relationship-oriented leadership: some show that relationship-oriented leadership produces greater productivity, while some show that task-oriented leaders create greater group efficacy. However, a common finding is that relationship-oriented leadership will generate greater cohesion within groups, as well as greater team learning. It is also supported that relationship-oriented leadership has stronger individual impact, and a positive effect on self-efficacy. A meta-analysis (Burke et al., 2006) conducted in 2006 integrated a wide spectrum of theoretical and empirical studies, and looked at the effects of leadership behaviours through multiple dimensions, including breaking down the specifics of task-oriented and relationship-oriented leadership into subgroups such as "initiating structure", "consideration", and "empowerment". Its main set of analyses investigated the relationship between task-oriented and relationship-oriented leadership behaviours on the following outcomes: perceived team effectiveness, team productivity, and team learning/growth. Results concluded that task-oriented leadership and relationship-oriented leadership produce a relatively similar perceived team effectiveness, however actual team productivity was higher for relationship-oriented led teams than for task-oriented teams (measured increase of 8 per cent and 4 per cent respectively).

It has also been theorized that groups who perceive their leaders as more task-oriented achieve higher levels of task accomplishment.

FIEDLER CONTINGENCY MODEL

The Fiedler Contingency Model argues that three situational components can determine whether task-oriented or relationship-oriented leadership is the better fit for the situation:

1. Leader-Member Relations, referring to the degree of mutual trust, respect and confidence between the leader and the subordinates.
2. Task Structure, referring to the extent to which group tasks are clear and structured.
3. Leader Position Power, referring to the power inherent in the leader's position itself.

When there is a good leader-member relation, a highly structured task, and high leader position power, the situation is considered a "favorable situation." Fiedler found that low-LPC leaders are more effective in extremely favourable or unfavourable situations, whereas high-LPC leaders perform best in situations with intermediate favourability.

The table below shows a breakdown of the theory:

Leader-Member Relations	Task Structure	Leader's Position Power	Most Effective Leader
Good	Structured	Strong	Task-oriented
Good	Structured	Weak	Task-oriented
Good	Unstructured	Strong	Task-oriented
Good	Unstructured	Weak	Relationship-oriented
Poor	Structured	Strong	Relationship-oriented
Poor	Structured	Weak	Relationship-oriented
Poor	Unstructured	Strong	Relationship-oriented
Poor	Unstructured	Weak	Task-oriented

RELEVANT STUDIES

An experiment was conducted in 1972 with a total of 128 United States Military cadets in 4-man groups, to test the predictive validity of Fiedler's contingency model of leadership effectiveness. The experiment, which involved strong manipulation and specification of variables affecting situational favorableness, produced strong support for the contingency model.

A study was conducted that determined if basketball athletes of different age groups (lower high school to university level) preferred training and instruction (task-oriented) behaviour or social support (relationship-oriented) behaviour. Analyses and results revealed a quadratic trend for preference in task-oriented behaviour that progressively decreased lower high school through junior to senior levels, and increased at the university level. A linear trend was seen for preference in relationship-oriented behaviour, which progressively increased as age went up.

SITUATIONAL LEADERSHIP THEORY

In the 1950s, management theorists from Ohio State University and the University of Michigan published a series of studies to determine whether leaders should be more task or relationship oriented. The research concluded that there is no single "best" style of leadership, and thus led to the creation of the Situational Leadership Theory, which essentially argues that leaders should engage in a healthy dose of both task-oriented and relationship-oriented leadership fit for the situation, and the people being led. The Blake Mouton Managerial Grid, also known as Managerial grid model, serves as a framework to determine how one can balance task-oriented and relationship-oriented leadership. It plots the degree of task-centeredness versus relationship-centeredness and identifies five combinations as distinct leadership styles.

Bibliography

A.K. Banerjee: *Art of Leadership*, Lotus Press, 2004.

Angela Wadia: *Broadcast Management in India : Major Guidelines and Policy Frameworks*, Kanishka, Publication, Delhi, 2007.

Aravind V. Karabasanagoudra and Noorjehan N. Ganihar: *Leadership Behaviour of School Heads in India*, Global Vision Publication, Delhi, 2012.

Arvind Virmani: *Accelerating Growth and Poverty Reduction: A Policy Framework for Indias Development*, Academic Foundation, 2004.

Asit K. Biswas, R. Rangachari and M.M. Sainju: *Ganges-Brahmaputra-Meghna Region : A Framework for Sustainable Development*, The University Press Limited, 2001.

Avinash D. Pathardikar: *Leadership and Occupational Stress*, Shree Publication, Delhi, 2009.

B.L. Gupta: *Competency Framework for Human Resources Management*, Concept, Publication, Delhi, 2011.

Hemlata Talesra, Indu Kothari, Rajesh Mantri, Uma Shankar Sharma and Anita Talesra: *Leadership for Global Excellence in Education, Vols. I and II*, Authorspress, Delhi, 2011.

Jeff Gold: *Gower Handbook of Leadership and Management Development*, Richard Thorpe and Alan Mumford, Gower Publishing Ltd, 2013.

Jogendra Mehta: *Art of Leadership*, Yking Books, 2011.

K. Ravichandran and S. Nakkiran: *Cooperative Entrepreneurship in Action: A Conceptual Framework*, Studera Press, 2015.

Madan Mohan Upadhyay: *Leadership in Government : The Art of Work: 100 Ways for Working Effectively in Government*, Pentagon Press, New York, 2011.

N.C. Asthana and Anjali Nirmal: *Leadership Failure in Police*, Manas Publications, Delhi, 2014.

Nihar Nayak: *Cooperative Security Framework for South Asia*, Pentagon Press, 2013.

Noorjehan N. Ganihar and B.M. Hurakadli: *Leadership Behaviour and Teacher Morale*, Discovery Publishing House, Delhi, 2005.

P B Rathod: *Framework of Public Policy : The Discipline and Its Dimensions*, Commonwealth, 2005.

Pawan Kumar Oberoi: *Business Regulatory Framework*, Global Vision, 2011.

Pradeep M Tulachan and Juhani Maki-Hokkonen: *Community Empowerment in Livestock Resource Planning : A Suggested Participatory Policy Framework*, International Centre for Integrated Mountain Development, 2002.

Pradeep S. Chauhan: *Asian Economic and Financial Integration in Global Framework*, New Century, 2009.

R.H.G. Rau: *Leadership Excellence*, Himalaya Publishing House, Delhi, 2010.

R.K. Tailor and Sunita Tailor: *Leadership in Management*, Prateeksha Publications, Delhi, 2010.

S Sundar and S K Sarkar: *Framework for Infrastructure Regulation*, TERI Press, 2000.

S.K. Chakraborty and Pradip Bhattacharya: *Leadership and Power Ethical Explorations*, Oxford University Press, Delhi, 2001.

S.K. Singh: *Leadership and Management Development*, Pearl Books, 2010.

Stefano Mostarda: *Entity Framework 4 In Action*, Marco De Sanctis and Daniele Bochicchio, Dreamtech Press, 2011.

Stephen S Kaagan: *Leadership Games : Experiential Learning for Organizational Development*, Response Books, Delhi, 1999.

Sumita Mishra: *Leadership and Politics in Rural India*, Radha Publication, Delhi, 2006.

Uday Kumar Haldar: *Leadership And Team Building*, Oxford University Press, Delhi, 2010.

V.C. Pandey: *Framework for ICTs and Teacher Education*, Isha Books, 2005.

Index